THE

Good Provider

H. J. HEINZ AND HIS 57 VARIETIES

Books by Robert C. Alberts

*The Most Extraordinary Adventures
of Major Robert Stobo*

*The Golden Voyage: The Life and Times
of William Bingham 1752–1804*

*"A Charming Field for an Encounter"
The Story of George Washington's
Fort Necessity*

*The Good Provider: H. J. Heinz and
His 57 Varieties*

"The Founder" in 1918, age seventy-four. Of the picture he wrote, "This is the one that I had made in Chicago, and when it came I objected to having all the lines removed from the face, and stated to the artist that it cost me fifty years of hard work to place them there."

THE
Good Provider

H. J. HEINZ
AND HIS
57 VARIETIES

Robert C. Alberts

Illustrated with Photographs

HOUGHTON MIFFLIN COMPANY BOSTON

1973

FIRST PRINTING   V

PRINTED IN THE UNITED STATES OF AMERICA

Library of Congress Cataloging in Publication Data

Alberts, Robert C
    The good provider.

    Bibliography: p.
    1. Heinz, Henry John, 1844–1919.   2. Heinz (H. J.)
Company.   I. Title.
HD9321.H4A65   338.7'66'40280924 [B]   73-9625
ISBN 0-395-17126-1

I dedicate this book with gratitude to *George Ketchum,* who prodded me to work in American history and biography.

The discovery of a new dish does more for the happiness of man than the discovery of a new star.

The kitchen is a country in which there are always discoveries to be made.

Anthelme Brillat-Savarin,
The Physiology of Taste,
1825

Preface

H. J. Heinz was a small man with prodigious energy and drive. His blue eyes sparkled, his reddish muttonchop whiskers bristled, and he seemed always to move along at a half trot. He carried a pocket diary, a notebook, and a steel tape measure that he whipped out on any occasion to record interesting dimensions — the width of a doorway, the thickness of a sill, the circumference of a column. He was a cheerful man who greeted you, in the words of a contemporary, "with the old-fashioned courtesy of the last generation." He had overpowering enthusiasms: for work and success, for travel, for his family, for religious pursuits and kind deeds, for good horses and bad paintings. He liked others to enjoy what he enjoyed; so far as is known, he is the only American industrial magnate who ever returned from Florida (in 1898) with an 800-pound, 14½-foot, 150-year-old live alligator and installed it in a glass tank atop one of his factory buildings so that his employees might share his pleasure in the sight.

In Edith Wharton's phrase, Heinz was one of the "Lords of Pittsburgh" — one of five Pittsburgh millionaires who were commanding figures in their own time and are legends in ours. Four of them — Carnegie, Frick, Westinghouse, and Mellon — exercised their power and made their fortunes in coal and coke, iron and steel, aluminum and oil, railroads and heavy machinery. Heinz chose in this most unlikely location — a city built among hills and based on the heaviest of heavy industry — to work at the primary business of feeding people. For half a century he was a dominant force in developments that revolutionized American agriculture, the processing of food, and the kitchen habits of the nation. He carried his company's products and his own industrial philosophy to four continents with a promotional flair and showmanship that probably have never been surpassed. In the furious battle over the 1906 Pure Food Law, he was a hero to reformers and, to many of his fellow food processors, an archtraitor. In a city torn with the worst labor strife the country had known, he built a factory complex on paternalistic principles and did it so successfully that some sociologists and at least one authentic leader of a union brotherhood declared (prematurely) that H. J. Heinz had found the solution to the conflict between capital and labor.

Heinz was one American industrialist of capitalism's Iron Age who kept a personal diary over a span of years and whose diary has survived for use in a biography. These little volumes, eighteen of them, cover the years 1875–1894. They are peopled by a cross section of the human species of that day: a numerous family, small-town neighbors, stable hands, office clerks, salesmen, executives, disgruntled creditors, competitors, the girls on the food processing lines — 1000 of them in the Pittsburgh factory in 1900. In its homespun prose, the diary gives a picture of life in that time: the way people worked, played, traveled, worshiped, and died; their illnesses and their education; the wages they got and the prices they paid; the way a company was run; the reception of such marvels as electric power, natural gas, the telephone, the automobile. It provides material for a look into a subject not often explored in American biography: the mind, character, and rise to command of an industrial pioneer.

I am beholden and extend my grateful thanks to *American Heritage* magazine, which commissioned me to write an article on H. J. Heinz and gave permission to use it, with its title, as the nucleus of this biography; to the Heinz family for making available the founder's diary and a mass of letters, documents, and scrapbooks without reserve or restriction; to the generous men and women (named on page 281) who submitted to taped interviews on their experiences of sixty and seventy years ago; to the Historical Society of Western Pennsylvania, which has sponsored this biography, published two of its chapters in its quarterly magazine, and provided a research-writing grant that made the work possible.

ROBERT C. ALBERTS

MAY 25, 1973

Contents

Illustrations

THE
Good Provider

H. J. HEINZ AND
HIS 57 VARIETIES

CHAPTER 1

Beginnings

Napoleon once said to Madame Campan, "What is wanting in order that the youth of France be well educated?" She replied, "Good mothers." To which the Emperor replied, "Here is a system in one word."

From the eulogy at the
funeral services of Anna Heinz,
January 31, 1899

HER NAME was Anna Margaretha Schmitt, and she was a daughter of Jacob Schmitt of the village of Kruspis, near the Rhine River in the province of Kurfurstentum in the grand duchy of Hesse-Darmstadt. Her father was a Councilor of the Lutheran Church and Bürgermeister of Kruspis, where his ancestors had lived for many generations. She sailed for America on March 4, 1843, traveling with relatives, a single girl twenty-one years old. She journeyed inland over the mountains to Pittsburgh, at the southwestern end of Pennsylvania, where the Monongahela and Allegheny rivers meet to form the Ohio. There she settled across from the city on the south bank of the Monongahela, in an industrial community called Birmingham, rough, brawling, smoky, home of factories that were making some of America's finest glass.

We do not know why Fraülein Schmitt left her home and parents to come to America, or with whom she lived, or for whom she worked, but if she was searching for a husband she was successful. She met John Henry Heinz, also of Birmingham, eleven years her senior, who had left Germany three years earlier. Heinz had grown up in a village fifty miles from Kruspis, in Kallstadt, province of the Rheinpfalz, in Bavaria, where his people, mostly vineyard owners, dated back to 1608 and had become prosperous, in the person of Lorenz Heinz, at the end of the seventeenth century. The Heinz farmlands had been divided and redivided many times, there being no law of primogeniture in Bavaria, and so John Heinz had left for broader opportunities in America. Anna married him on December 4, 1843, less than seven months after her arrival, and on October 11, 1844, she bore him a son, the first of nine children. She resolved that their first-born would become a Lutheran minister. He was christened Henry John and nicknamed Harry.

When Harry Heinz was seven months old he became desperately ill. In her prayers Anna made a bargain with God: if He spared her son, for the rest of her life she would fast and attend church on the anniversary of that day. Harry was spared, and for the next fifty-four years Anna fulfilled her promise, refraining on March 30 from even drinking water for twenty-four hours.

Life in Birmingham was ameliorated when a new bridge was built across the river to Pittsburgh, but when Harry was five his parents decided to remove with their three children to the village of Sharpsburg, six miles up the Allegheny Valley on the north bank of the river. Sharpsburg, incorporated in 1841 as the second oldest borough of Allegheny County, stretched in the shape of a crescent for a mile and a quarter along the river, good flat farmland extending a scant quarter mile back to a sheer wall of hills. The great Main Line Canal connecting Pittsburgh and Philadelphia, opened in 1829 (and to be ruined by the coming of the railroad in 1851), ran beside the river. Two things made this an important community in the 1850s: it was near a lock of the canal, and it had the Guyasuta Iron Works (six puddling furnaces and three trains of rolls), named after the famous Seneca warrior-chief who had lived his last years on the hillside with his two wives — "a very provident

Indian," one observer said, "having two wives, one well stricken in years who paid great attention to his food and his clothes, the other a handsome young squaw." Sharpsburg was a pleasant rural community, remote in many ways from Pittsburgh. It held fewer than 1400 inhabitants, most of them Germans of quiet, conservative, and religious character. Most of the houses were built of brick, for the borough was noted for its fine quality of brick clay and it had many brickyards.

There John Heinz bought or built a kiln and set himself up in the brickmaking business and later as a brick contractor and builder. In 1854 he constructed with his own hands and bricks a family homestead on Main Street, on four acres of land facing the canal and the river some 800 feet distant. He must have had taste, for he designed and built a nicely proportioned two-story, four-room house with thick walls, two chimneys, a Palladian doorway, and nine shuttered front windows. Harry many years later described John Heinz as "a giant in strength and endurance and a very indulgent father."

Anna Heinz was a loving but not an indulgent mother. Her discipline was firm and, with a family of four boys and four girls,* she expected immediate compliance with her requests and commands. The children were required to work in the family garden beginning at the age of eight. The child who for any reason missed church had to sit down and hear her retell at length the minister's sermon. Anna Heinz was strong on passages memorized from the Bible and on the character-building qualities of the precepts she drilled into her young. Her favorites were "Do all the good you can; do not live for yourself," "Do not aim to be rich, for riches never come that way," "Always remember to place yourself in the other person's shoes," and "Remember that the bee goes to the same

---

* Henry, John, Peter, Jacob, Elizabeth (Lizzie), Margaretta (Maggie), Mary, and Henrietta (Hettie). One other child, a girl, died at one year of age in 1858.

flower for its honey where the spider goes for its poison."

Despite the discipline, the children were normally high-spirited and mischievous. Peter J. (he had no middle name but put in a J because all his brothers had a J) was the ringleader in all pranks, but generally escaped punishment by shifting the blame to John, who was less crafty than he. When there were guests and the children could not have dinner until the elders had finished, they raided the store of dried prunes in the attic or the apples in the cellar. One of the elders was in the cellar when she saw the window open and a long pole with a nail at the end come stealthily through, spear an apple, and withdraw. On the second pass she seized the apple, pole, and culprit. After that, when the children were given permission to go to the cellar for one apple each, they would toss several more out the window.

Anna played no favorites among the children, but Harry was the eldest and they got on well together. (Son John was lazy by Heinz standards and Peter was forever getting into trouble.) Harry wrote of his mother decades later, "She could handle me because she knew how to inspire me; because she knew what to say, when and how."

Harry went to school under the pastorship of the Lutheran Church, of which his father was treasurer. It was in Etna, the neighboring community, one and a half walking miles downriver toward Pittsburgh. Before and after school hours he worked in the garden, in his father's brickyard, on the canal towpath leading horses, and, for a time, for a local farmer named Cook, who paid him twenty-five cents a day and meals for picking potatoes. Cook stimulated his workers one day by giving three prizes to those who picked the most potatoes: twenty-five cents, twelve-and-a-half cents, and six-and-one-quarter cents ("a fi-penny bit"). Competing against twenty hands, most of them adults, Harry won and carried home the third prize. That spring he spent some weeks building an embankment around the family garden to protect it against the floods of the Allegheny, using a scraper and an old horse named "Baldy" to draw and pile up great quantities of gravel from the riverbank. In later years, when asked how he found time to do so much, he replied, "We country boys work."

Almost every Sharpsburg family had a garden, but the Heinz tract — in the custom of the day, the sole responsibility of Anna Heinz — was of superior quality and appearance: neat, weed-free, with straight, orderly rows, and so bountiful that it produced a surplus even above the demands of ten at the family table. When he was eight, Harry undertook to peddle the surplus to other households in Sharpsburg, a basket in each hand, and did it so capably that at ten years he graduated from handbaskets to a wheelbarrow, and his parents gave him three quarters of an acre of his own. ("They wanted to encourage me.") At twelve he enlarged his garden to three-and-a-half acres, bought a horse and cart, and included the local merchants among his customers. He had the intuitive German feeling for soil and seed, a fine rapport with horses, and in his blood a sure sense of where and how to make money.

His mother apparently worked closely with him on these early trading ventures. The manuscript of a three-page biography, company-written around 1900, contains the sentence, "Mr. Heinz attributes his success in life largely to the moral qualities inherited from his mother." He edited the sentence in pencil to read, ". . . to the moral and business qualities inherited from his mother."

At fourteen, after his confirmation in the German Evangelical Lutheran Church in Etna — the equivalent of graduation — he went for a while to the newly opened Allegheny Seminary in Sharpsburg. He or his parents gave up the idea of a career in the ministry, however — Harry was clearly destined for the world of business and commerce. At fifteen he became his father's practical assistant in the brickyard and, following a

course at Duff's Mercantile College in Pittsburgh, his bookkeeper. One winter he and his father contracted to cut ice on
Hemlock Creek, some fourteen miles above Oil City, north of
Pittsburgh. It was a cold winter, all the streams and rivers
froze, everyone began to cut ice, and the bottom dropped out
of the ice market, the price falling from five cents to one cent a
pound. Harry had the profitless task of driving four horses and
an empty wagon some eighty miles back to Sharpsburg.
Halfway home, at Butler, he induced a produce merchant, a
stranger, to trust him with a load of butter, eggs, and oats for
sale in the Pittsburgh market. He sold the goods, left the
money with one of the merchant's friends in Etna, and cleared
$25 on the transaction.

Harry continued his produce business during these activities, helped by two of his younger brothers, two younger sisters, and after-hours schoolchildren. He made three deliveries
a week to grocers in Pittsburgh. Such deliveries were always
made between four and five o'clock in the morning, the farmers
picking and loading their produce the night before. After
some months of rising at 3:00 A.M. to start the six-mile journey
to Pittsburgh, Heinz proposed to his customers that he deliver
his goods between eight and nine o'clock of the evening before. The vegetables, he explained, would remain as fresh
overnight in the store as on a wagon, and he would be spared
the unpleasantness of waking them three or four hours before
they opened their doors. The customers agreed to this revolutionary proposal. In the year he turned seventeen, his produce
business grossed the substantial sum of $2400.

His specialty was bottled horseradish, cultivated for the
white flesh of its very pungent root and eaten with food as an
appetite sharpener and for its supposed medicinal qualities.
Freshly grated horseradish made dull food palatable and good
food — such as beef and raw oysters — better. Multitudes
swore by it as a sure remedy for grippe, catarrh, and dyspep-

sia. It grew wild, but if cultivated in carefully prepared rich soil, the root was more tender, less fibrous, and of a much finer flavor. Western Pennsylvania soil seemed especially suitable for growing superior horseradish.

From early childhood Harry had helped his mother harvest and prepare the family horseradish — cultivated roots of one year's growth, individually scrubbed and scraped, the imperfections trimmed away, the product grated and bottled in vinegar. It was a job that bruised the knuckles and made the eyes smart, and housewives did it reluctantly. A local trade had grown up in horseradish, sold always in green or brown bottles (the natural colors of glass) and often with substances contained therein that looked like, but were not, grated horseradish. Harry bottled *his* product in clear glass and peddled it to housewives, then to grocers and the managers of hotel kitchens, as of the whitest and best-quality root. Probably he would hold it up to the light; perhaps he would produce a spoon, open up a bottle, and suggest a sampling — see, no lumps, no leaves, no wood fiber, no turnip filler! When sales rose, two convictions were implanted in his mind. Though he never formally described them as such, these were the first of eight Important Ideas that would henceforth guide him on his career. Idea Number One: Housewives are willing to pay someone else to take over a share of their more tedious kitchen work. Idea Number Two: A pure article of superior quality will find a ready market through its own intrinsic merit — if it is properly packaged and promoted.

When he was twenty-one, Harry used his savings to buy a half interest in his father's brick business. Brickworks normally shut down in winter, but the new partner installed heating flues and drying apparatus so that the plant could operate through the cold months and build up inventory for the spring rush. He made a profit of $1000 and kept the plant busy for six months by capturing an order for 750,000 bricks at Flemming Station on the Ohio River. When he saw that Flemming Station was having trouble with its coal supply, he got a contract to ship coal in barges from Pittsburgh.

In 1868, when he was twenty-four, Harry engaged in his first business venture outside the family; he formed a partnership with a friend and neighbor, L. Clarence Noble, twenty, son of one of the "chief families of Sharpsburg," to manufacture brick at Beaver Falls, on the Ohio River below Pittsburgh. Noble was to live in Beaver Falls and supervise the plant operations while Harry sold the product.

In that same year, with his affairs in good hands, John Heinz voyaged to Germany for an extended visit with his and his wife's relatives. When he returned, he found that Anna and Harry had built the family a new brick house in Sharpsburg — larger, more comfortable, more appropriate to the style of the time, with a porch, an outside upper balcony, bow windows upstairs and down, dormers, and Gothic fretwork at the gables. Presumably John Heinz was pleased as well as surprised to be presented with a house on which he had not been consulted. When he expressed alarm at the cost, he was told — and no doubt was relieved to hear — that there was no debt; Henry had already paid for the house, using money that had come from debts that he, Heinz Senior, had written off as uncollectable.

Eighteen sixty-nine was a year of great events for the United States, the food industry, and Henry J. Heinz. The transcontinental railroad across the United States was completed with the joining of tracks in Utah. George Westinghouse organized the Westinghouse Air Brake Company in Pittsburgh to manufacture air brakes for steam locomotives. A velocipede was produced in Brooklyn and, despite dire predictions, it did not frighten horses and cause accidents. Petroleum was first used as a fuel in a furnace and india rubber for tires on a vehicle. A workable electric motor was designed for a sewing machine. The country's first underground railroad, running under Broadway in New York, was about to be opened. On September 15, in Philadelphia, the first issue of *The American Grocer*, a magazine for the trade, appeared. And Henry J. Heinz, in his twenty-fifth year, became a married man and renounced all other business activities to join in founding a company to grow and bottle food.

Such a business was not one a man would enter with any idea of great success or riches, but it was, next to brickmaking, what he knew best, and it was what he wanted to do most. He and L. C. Noble became partners in purveying what they called the Anchor Brand of food products. They began with horseradish as their first. They planted three quarters of an acre in Sharpsburg, took over a room and the basement of the homestead from which the Heinz family had recently moved, and engaged the services of two women and a boy.*

On September 23 he married Sarah (Sallie) Sloan Young, twenty months older than he, whose parents had emigrated to Pittsburgh from County Down, where the family — "an esteemed Presbyterian North Ireland family" — owned a mill. For a wedding present, Anna Heinz gave her son and daughter-in-law a large Bible with brass clasps.

The only record of the honeymoon is contained in a curious manuscript in the family archives dated November 13, 1901. A Clarence M. Johns lunched with Heinz on that date in the "firm's dining room" at a table that held a number of company executives and at least two Heinz sons. A transcript of the conversation, with editorial asides, was made:

> Mr. Johns: Do you know where we met for the first time?
> Mr. Heinz: I think it was at a hotel.
> Mr. Johns: No, it was on a train.

---

* The first woman hired was the wife or widow of a man who had started to work at John Heinz's brickyard at the age of eight. She visited the Heinz factory twenty-nine years later, in July 1898, and received a royal reception, H. J. Heinz conducting her through the plant, introducing her to the employees in the dining room at lunchtime, and arranging for a story to appear in *Pickles*, the company newspaper.

Mr. Heinz: Yes, that was it — the latter part of September, 1869, about the 29th day of September.

Mr. Johns: We happened to meet on the train. I had been in Boston about one week. We were on the same train and expected to arrive at New York in the morning. That was after I was married. Mr. Heinz and I were married on the same day. Instead of going on to New York we were held over in Boston, as there had been a flood, which had wiped away all the bridges between Boston and New York, and we found that we could either go to Worcester, or else stay in Boston until the bridges were rebuilt. We concluded to go to Worcester and remained there two days before the floods subsided, and then from Worcester we took a train to the place where this big wash-out occurred — some place between Worcester and New York.

The train we were on was a large one; there must have been four or five locomotives, weren't there? and about one thousand people on board. When we arrived at the place of the wash-out, of course all of the men on the train got out and ran forward and filled the wagons which the railroad people had furnished in order to connect with the railroad on the other side. As we had our wives with us, we could not hurry forward as fast as the men, so we were left.

We men made some fires out of fence rails in order to keep warm as it was a very cold night. We got tired staying there and thought we would go to the ford, some distance below, and see if we could not get across. On the way to the ford we inquired about the depth of the water. Some said it was not deep, some said it was ankle deep, and others said we could get across without getting water in our boots.

Mr. Heinz: We all wore boots in those days.

Mr. Johns: So we got there, and one of the wagons stalled. It was not the last wagon, but the last wagon was out in the stream. The stream was quite deep, but we concluded we could get as far as the wagon, which was about 150 feet, but before we got to the wagon we found that we were in about three feet of water. Mr. Heinz was ahead of me carrying his wife, and I was carrying mine.

Mr. Heinz: We had been married about one week.

Mr. Johns: About that time your Mother (addressing Mr.

Heinz's sons) was a good deal heavier than my wife, and Mr. Heinz had been getting along first rate, but she was slipping, and one foot was in the water, and he was holding her up as best he could. I got to the wagon first and threw my wife in, and I went to help you and was just in time to save your wife from going under.

When we got to Buffalo I remember that I could not get off my boots and had an awful toothache for about a week. We stopped at Buffalo for several days and went to Canada several times — took drives there, same as at Worcester. We both wanted to buy a horse at Worcester. Mr. Heinz had $1,000 and I think I ran short and had to borrow a little from him, but I think I paid it back, didn't I?

Mr. Heinz: I have forgotten. (Applause and jokes on this.)

Mr. Johns: He had more money than I had. I only had $300 or $400 and he had $1,000.

Mr. Heinz: I have something to add to your story. My sister was asked the question while we were away on our wedding trip, when her brother Henry would return. She said she did not know, but supposed he would stay as long as his money lasted. (Laughter.) I think we stayed away about one month. I wanted to get home in time for my birthday, which was in about three weeks.

On his return to work, Heinz set out to extend the trade in horseradish beyond the Pittsburgh market. He made a tour of stores in the booming Pennsylvania oil regions and returned with a carpetbag full of orders. The company was launched and he was on his way.

CHAPTER 2

The Ordeal of Henry Heinz

The bank president and the cashier told us, time would tell whether we knew what we were doing.

Henry J. Heinz,
Diary, April 15, 1875

IT IS FIVE YEARS LATER, January 1875, and the partners have, in the words of a commentator of that day, "built up the business with a rapidity seldom witnessed." Their company is now, in fact, one of the country's leading producers of a product that had largely been imported from Europe — processed, preserved, and packaged condiments.

From the first the partners had written substantial orders and had seen them repeated and increased. They expanded; they took over the entire Heinz homestead and then the house next door; they built a large shed on the grounds as a "preserving department." They added products to the Anchor Brand — celery sauce and pickled cucumbers in 1871, sauerkraut and vinegar a year or two later. They took in a third partner in 1872 — E. J. Noble, L. C.'s twenty-two-year-old brother, who bought a two-eighths share of the business, the original partners each retaining three-eighths shares. They adopted the name Heinz, Noble & Company in that year and leased a four-story factory, office, retail store, and warehouse right in downtown Pittsburgh, on the south side of Second Avenue between Grant and Smithfield streets. The commentator who praised their rapid growth added, "It may be stated as a fact, that they have never failed to meet the requirements of the trade in any article in their line; and they have made it an inflexible rule to never place in market other than a first class article. To these praiseworthy efforts may be attributed their signal success."

Now they have 160 acres in garden crops along the Allegheny River at or near Sharpsburg, twenty acres of it in horseradish. They have as many as 150 "operatives" in season. They have twenty-five horses, the Heinz homestead as a warehouse, a business office and vinegar factory in St. Louis, and a branch distributing warehouse in Chicago. They have an annual capacity of 3000 barrels of sauerkraut, 15,000 barrels of pickles, and 50,000 barrels of vinegar. And they have just written a new contract with a pickling and bottling company at Woodstock, Illinois: a commitment to take the produce of some 800 acres of cultivated land at the rate of sixty cents a bushel for cucumbers and $10 a ton for cabbage.

E. J. Noble runs the house in St. Louis and "attends to the jobbing trade in the principal cities." L. C. Noble represents the company at Woodstock and is to issue checks, payable in Pittsburgh, as the crops come in. Heinz manages the business in Pittsburgh, oversees the gardens there, and maintains the bank funds to cover all expenses, including those to be incurred at Woodstock.

The Heinzes have a daughter, Irene Edwilda, born August 5, 1871, and a son, born April 17, 1873, named Clarence Noble in friendship for the business partner. Heinz takes the short train ride daily to and from the city and generally works at home on company bookkeeping and correspondence until 11:00 P.M., writing an average of six to eight letters in an evening. Life at Sharpsburg seems to be pleasantly typical of a Pennsylvania village in the 1870s. Croquet in the backyard with friends. A spelling bee at the Lutheran Church for the benefit of the poor, at which Sallie is one of the spellers and Harry is (very wisely) the doorkeeper. Sallie putting up grape jelly in the washhouse while Harry makes out bills for his father's brick accounts. A mild quarrel with a neighbor over the children. ("Mrs. Moyle provoked at me for saying when other children were with our little ones, then they were harder to control and wanted to gad all the time and we were going to keep them in. We were a good deal annoyed by theirs in our yard.") Sallie, no termagant, is a little afraid of the hired girl. "September 28, 1875 — Kate Galacher is quite mad and saucy and threatened to leave next week. I told Sallie she (Kate) should leave tomorrow as it was then 7 P.M. Kate heard it in the next room and left at once. She has a fearful temper and Sallie would not ask her to do even what she knew she should do."

Dr. Spencer puts a filling in Harry's right eyetooth, which takes three hours and causes "fearful suffering." The tooth becomes (in a Western Pennsylvania expression) "bealed," and the ache is so severe that Dr. Brinton gives him morphine. The morphine frightens Sallie and makes him so sick that he never wants to take morphine again. Dr. Spencer puts a live leech on the gum, which (in still another Western Pennsylvania idiom) "eased it some." Sallie then poultices his cheek with hot cakes and potatoes, which relieves the pain but causes his face to swell.

Harry is evidently the disciplinarian for the entire Heinz family, for he writes of his youngest brother, "I whipped Jacob my brother for not attending school regularly, but he would stay home and drive the horse. I hope never to have occasion to whip again." He later takes Jacob to Professor Fowler, the distinguished phrenologist, to have his head examined and a chart drawn up, $9. The result so impresses E. J. Noble that he has his done too. Anna Heinz considers it nonsense and a waste of money.

A party is formed to leave at 6:00 P.M. on a twenty-mile sleigh ride to see a burning gas well beyond Bakerstown. It is "the greatest sight any of us ever saw"; 1500 people are there in sleighs. Some of the party lose their way; the others arrive safely home at 7:00 A.M.

He sells the Beaver Falls brickyard for $5000. He attends but does not comment on a meeting at the Lutheran Church called to prevent Masons and other secret orders from joining. He refuses a nomination for president of the local Building and Loan Association. ("Have not time. *I am now in the pickle business.*") Sallie has a miscarriage caused by a jolt in the buggy while driving to her mother's. He and Sallie take the children to Dabbs Picture Gallery to have a photograph made. He wakens on a morning in October to find birthday presents displayed on a chair beside the bed: a pair of slippers embroidered by Sallie, a necktie and a pair of socks from the children, and one of his old hats cleaned to look like new. The presents are given on Sunday, a day early, because he would not have time on a working day to appreciate them.

He makes a trip to Woodstock in March and spends an afternoon and evening with the directors there talking of plans for a new building and for processing increased amounts of cauliflower, cucumbers, and vinegar. The plans, he writes, "seem to frighten them." He buys a silk hat for one of the directors who has done him a service and on the train back to Pittsburgh, "Argued temperance with a soldier, an officer."

He hires a red-whiskered cooper at $10 a week, his fare to be paid from another city. He scolds the factory girls because they are disobeying orders and filling the bushel baskets with so many bottles for washing that some are falling and breaking. He promises to pay William Munholland ten cents a day extra for one year if he will "quit the use of tobacco entirely while with us." The firm wins the First Prize Medal at the Cincinnati Exposition. The stand and display at the Pittsburgh Exposition hold eighty dozen of bottled goods and "fifty packages with glass heads," all arranged in an artistic pattern and insured for $800.

He talks plainly to the vegetable salesmen and the boys who

drive their wagons, forbidding them on pain of instant dismissal from entering any tavern to sell goods. Brother Peter is in trouble again with three of the other salesmen; they have been driving around in carriages for four days in a state of inebriation. "Found them on Liberty Street. This was the worst and longest spree Peter ever was on . . . He is troubled about Bell Kernan for fear she will make him marry her. He wants to go away on that account." Peter and the others all sign the temperance pledge, agree to do better, and promise to attend church regularly.

Harry Heinz had far more serious troubles on his hands than Mrs. Moyle and Brother Peter, and the picture given of a placid life in Sharpsburg and a successful career in the city is more than a little deceptive. Heinz & Noble, despite its good sales and apparent prosperity, was short of capital, seriously overextended, and deeply in trouble. The country was in a depression resulting from unbridled inflation during the Civil War, excessive issues of paper currency, over-expansion in industry and agriculture, and wild speculation and manipulation by such characters as Jay Gould and Jim Fisk. In the fall of 1873, Jay Cooke & Company, the foremost banking house in America, had overinvested by some $3 million in western railroad projects. When Cooke was unable to meet the demands made on him, his house failed. The stock market broke, depositors withdrew their money, securities were sold off at a loss, and the New York Exchange closed for the first time in its history. A general panic was on.

The growth made by Heinz & Noble in this time was accomplished against that trend. "Mills and factories stopped," Heinz wrote in January 1875. "Hard times, money tight. No one presumes to say when things may improve." Money was to be had in Pittsburgh only at 9 percent and then only on the security of a good mortgage. Help was plentiful and cheap:

men at $1 a day, women at $.75, boys at $.50 to $.75. In April appeared a first ominous entry in the diary:

> Saw Claney and Covode at the Bank. I had the hardest day I ever had . . . and could eat no dinner owing to worry and hurry and planning. I had to raise $4,000, mostly by exchanging checks and by many new yet honest plans and favors of friends and cashiers. This $4,000 was unexpected as I expected L. C. to raise it at Woodstock and Chicago.

In the months that follow, Heinz is like a man crossing a quagmire, struggling to find firm footing, knowing he cannot turn back, and sinking all the deeper the harder he pushes forward.

On Sunday, May 2, he called on his parents with Sallie and E. J. Noble and told them of the pressure he was under to raise money. He had $4500 in notes and outstanding checks overdue at the bank, the bank officers agreeing to hold them until Monday afternoon. He asked his father to give a mortgage on his house and brickyard as collateral for a $15,000 bank loan to be paid to Heinz & Noble. John Heinz was opposed on principle to going security for anyone; he had said that he would not endorse a note even for his sons. Anna Heinz persuaded him to sign. He was, according to Hettie, the youngest daughter, "a very uncomplaining, sensitive soul who would rather endure in silence than make a fuss."

At the bank on Monday, after "the worst time I ever had in my life . . . the plainest talking I ever took from anyone," Harry Heinz got an advance on the proposed mortgage and deposited two certified checks — at ten minutes before three.

On May 8 he implored L. C. Noble to send him money instead of constantly drawing on him. He would sooner die in his tracks, he wrote, than continue in the present manner.

On May 24, Jacob Covode, a banker, his friend and neigh-

bor in Sharpsburg, endorsed a Heinz-Noble note for him for
$5000.*

On July 3: "This was one of the hardest and worst days to
finance. Payday at Sharpsburg, 53 hands for two weeks and
three large notes besides and little to meet them with." He
told Sallie he would like to carry on a small business by himself, or even work by the day, "as I am wearing brain and
body out . . . I have worked hard enough for the past five
years to have made $50,000." A neighbor, Dr. Deetrick, told
him that his pulse was only forty to forty-five, that he must
rest or break down, and that he would not have enough vital-
ity to throw off any disease that might come upon him.

Things were better through the next month, with trade
heavy and the first shipments of what promised to be excep-
tionally good crops. The crops, alas, were too good. It was a
year of phenomenal harvests, especially in Illinois and especially in cucumbers. By the end of August, cucumbers were
coming in from the fields at Woodstock and piling up at the
salting stations at the appalling rate of 2000 bushels a day.
Costs of payroll and of purchases soared. On October 9, one
of the Pittsburgh bankers refused for the first time to renew a
Heinz-Noble note, having been warned to be careful, the business had grown too large. Heinz wrote at the end of the
month, "I have been nearly killed and crazed at times meeting
and protecting checks which L. C. would issue on me from
Woodstock . . . I have paid out an average of $1,000 per day
since the 1st . . . I have . . . saved the firm from protest †
. . . I thank God I have lived through it."

* Covode was the youngest son of John Covode, "a man of great wealth" who
served four terms in the U.S. Congress, was a member of the Committee to
Inquire into the Conduct of the War, was twice a nominee for governor of
Pennsylvania, and at his death in 1871 was chairman of the Republican State
Finance Committee. Jacob Covode had joined the army at fifteen, spent
twenty months in the prison at Andersonville, and was suffering bad health as
a result. He was president and a director of the Farmers & Mechanics Bank in
Sharpsburg, established in 1871 with a capital of $2 million.

† Protest: a formal notarial certificate attesting that a check, note, or bill of
exchange has been presented for acceptance or payment and that it has been
refused.

On November 2: "L. C. writes again today that he checked for $300 and will check for $500 more tomorrow. This caused me to write and say, for God's sake quit this promiscuous checking, it is killing me."

On November 16 the Nobles suggested that their partner should try to keep matters in such shape that their nearest friends, and his, would not be hurt if the company got into trouble. "L. C. writes lamentable letters. He fears we cannot pay notes as they come due. Yet we have had nothing go to protest. We always pay. As we go on, we renew."

On November 22: "Hardest day on finances we ever had. I mean we were as near going to protest as ever we were. E. J. thought we would have to let two notes go to protest, but I managed just seven minutes before three to check on Sharpsburg through Peoples and got a certified check for $1,200."

One week later Heinz left the office to sell $300 worth of goods "on the wing besides my work." He had for the first time allowed one of L. C. Noble's checks, for $1000, to be returned unpaid. Two days later he wrote, "We are losing our credit at most of the banks."

Such pressure takes its physical effect in different ways on different people. On Henry Heinz, as with the Old Testament Job, it resulted in a rash of boils that were so painful that they kept him at home for several days, under poultices, unable to move about, when he had checks out and notes to renew. Sitting with Sallie, he told her for the first time not to be surprised if the company got into trouble. She lent him $700 from her modest personal savings to meet the Saturday payroll.

He stayed in bed on Friday, Saturday, and Sunday. On Monday, December 13, E. J. Noble arrived in Pittsburgh, rode out to Sharpsburg on the noon train, and accompanied him back to the city. They went to their office, then to the office of their attorney, B. C. Christy. In Heinz's absence, several checks had been protested. "We found matters were in such shape," he wrote, "that we could not save our business but must let it go. Oh, what a thought to give up all after working so hard for ten years, besides getting many friends and parents into trouble with us." At a family meeting that evening he told his wife, parents, brother John, and cousin Frederick Heinz that the business could not be saved. "We are in trouble," he said, "and will no doubt go into bankruptcy."

The real ordeal of Henry Heinz began at 8:00 A.M. two days later, when the Heinz store was closed on a landlord's warrant and the news spread. "People," he wrote, "keep constantly coming to see me — What is the matter? and Why can't you fix me? while I could say nothing, as we were powerless to do anything but are at the mercy of our creditors. Father and especially Mother takes it hard, while Sallie says little." That afternoon he was arrested on charges of fraud filed by two creditors. He was released on $3000 bail.

The following morning, Thursday, he telegraphed the Nobles to close up at St. Louis and Chicago. The county sheriff placed a levy on his household goods, his father's house, furniture, and brickyard and the company's food stock, horses, and equipment. When he returned home that afternoon he was again arrested and again gave bail. The Pittsburgh *Leader* that evening reported the earlier arrest under the cruel head, "A TRIO IN A PICKLE — Heinz, Noble & Co. Charged with Removing Their Goods to Defraud Creditors." The paper had been running editorials on a popular issue, protesting, "The present loose system of bankruptcy laws is undermining the foundations of all credit in the community. The tone of public morality is rapidly being lowered by the almost daily sight of men of the highest respectability taking advantage of the law to procure release from their debts by paying half or less of them . . . A corrupting tide of business demoralization . . ." Its story on the Heinz bankruptcy was not friendly. It reported that Kinder Blair, the confectioner, and

James Getty had made information that morning before Alderman McMaster against Henry J. Heinz, E. J. Noble, and L. C. Noble, charging them with removing their goods and secreting them for the purpose of defrauding their creditors:

> Messrs. Blair and Getty have claims against the firm amounting in the aggregate to four or five thousand dollars and they assert that during yesterday afternoon and last night these defendants removed from their establishment, on Second Avenue, the great majority of their goods for the purpose of defrauding them, and possibly other creditors, of their claims. It is said that some eight or nine wagons were engaged all day yesterday and last night in removing out jarred pickles, spices, sauces, etc. A portion of these goods, it is claimed, were stored in a house on Liberty street, but the great majority were taken to the depot and shipped by train to Chicago. The landlord of the building occupied as the pickle factory called there this morning, but it is said he found very little to levy upon for his rent.

The next day Heinz went with Christy to file papers in bankruptcy in the U.S. District Court — voluntary bankruptcy, on advice of counsel. (It was one of thirteen bankruptcy petitions filed in Allegheny County that week.) They then called on the editor of the *Leader* to protest yesterday's story. The editor received them, listened to what Heinz and Christy had to say, and had some second thoughts. In that evening's edition he printed a handsome retraction about twice as long, and in as good a position, as the original article. "There appears to be," he wrote, "another side to the story." The facts as now recounted were that Heinz, Noble & Company had sold to different merchants in the city quantities of pickles and other goods. Contracts had been drawn up which stipulated that the goods should remain in storage in Heinz & Noble's warehouse subject to the order of the purchasers from time to time, Heinz & Noble in the meantime paying insurance on the goods. The firm had had exactly similar transactions with the same purchasers in the previous year. The purchasers of these goods, under their contract, had simply presented orders for their goods to be transferred from the Heinz & Noble warehouse to their own. These were the goods that it was alleged by Messrs. Blair and Getty were removed "with the intentions of defrauding their creditors." Not a single article was shipped to Chicago, as alleged. When the goods were removed, Heinz & Noble was simply carrying out a contract. If it had not done so, it might have been made liable to the same kind of charges made by the purchasers as those brought by Messrs. Blair and Getty.

"This statement of Mr. Heinz," the editor concluded, "puts an entirely different shape to the story of the firm's troubles, and if proven, as he says it will be, it will doubtless cause the quashing of the charges against them referred to in yesterday's paper."

The Nobles arrived in Pittsburgh on Monday with the company's books from Woodstock, St. Louis, and Chicago. Heinz remained at the office until 11:00 P.M. on Wednesday working over the accounts. The next day — December 23 — he went with Sallie and E. J. Noble to Grace Church to help trim the Christmas tree. At a meeting at the office on Friday he opened the company safe and, in the presence of his attorney, returned personal documents to their owners. He and Sallie took the children that evening to see the tree lighted up.

On Christmas Day: "I have no Christmas presents to make. Sallie seemed grieved and cried, yet said it was not about our trouble only. She did not feel well, etc. It is grief. I wish no one such trials."

The schedule of bankruptcy, when filed, was two inches thick; the company books stood more than six feet high. Assets were $110,000, liabilities $160,000.

In the weeks that followed, his parents' furniture and house were appraised and advertised for sheriff's sale. ("Oh! what a feeling came over me, words can't find language . . . I never went near as I could not well bear it.") A lot he owned in Sharpsburg was sold. John R. Wightman, the court assignee, took possession of the company's books and stock on hand. He sold off the horses, mules, oxen, wagons, carts, and harness at Sharpsburg, all labels and crocks, the horseradish in the field, and Sallie's horse, harness, and buggy. He sold the boiler, engine, elevator, office equipment, and barrels of sauerkraut in Pittsburgh.

The Blair-Getty charges of removing and secreting goods by fraud were tried on January 31, trial lawyer Thomas Marshall representing the defendants. The verdict was returned in favor of Heinz & Noble. "Those present were convinced that we had a clear case and that we defrauded none and cancelled nothing. We had many witnesses to prove our characters but did not call them."

On the day the bankruptcy became known, Heinz wrote, "A *great many express their sympathy*." He was soon to change his mind about the attitude of neighbors, friends, and creditors, even of relatives, toward a man who has failed and taken others down with him. He wrote one week later, "I find few friends when we are known to have no cash and are bankrupt." For weeks to come, between accounts of meetings, work on accounts, the minutia of daily routine, and notice of national events ("300 whites killed by Indians" *), he recorded for his own eyes only an anguish of mind and spirit. This was the bitterest portion of his ordeal.

On Christmas Day: "I feel as though people were all pushing us down because we are bankrupt. Such is the world." On succeeding days: "A good many call to see us. They feel sore . . . I feel very sad, as though I had not a true friend in the world . . . I feel sometimes when I meet people, no matter how much confidence they may have in me, they don't seem as they once did . . . A man is nowhere without money . . .

* Including General George Custer, at the Battle of the Little Bighorn.

People care little about you without money . . . The majority
of friends are seemingly so as long as it costs them nothing or
they have no sacrifice to make. This I could not have believed
. . . It is hard to lose trade, money, friends and reputation,
and even parents in trouble . . . People talk terribly. We find
that we have but few friends left . . . I feel sad and constantly
worried. People as much as say we have money. It is hard to
bear . . . When I looked over the books today and found the
large credit I have and what Father and even Peter has compared with Nobles, and how I got my friends in, and then to
be censured by the world, it goes hard . . . Some say we drew
out $60,000 and fix father, etc. I think I am looked upon by
many as a rascal and Nobles the same. Yet I am more blamed
because I did the financing. It is hard to bear."

A Sharpsburg creditor, a carpenter named John Pfusch, to
whom $1000 was owing on a note, went to his house and "as
much as called us rascals. He said, Your liabilities are $170,-
000, where is all the money? He insisted for us to give him a
new note or say that we would make it good, which we told
him we could not do. So he went about town talking about us.
His wife even came to Sallie in my absence and threatened
Sallie if I or she did not make their note right, it might be very
dangerous, etc. They act like mad people and try to do us
more harm than any dozen creditors."

From time to time he would resolve "not to worry as much
about our trouble, as it will not better it. People will censure
us no matter how or what we do." The effort to be philosophi-
cal was not very successful, but certainly his character was
toughened under a hammering that would have broken a less
indomitable man. "I feel as though every person had lost confidence in me," he wrote, "and I am therefore reserved . . . I
begin to care less about what people say . . . Bankruptcy
changes a man's nature."

One of the galling experiences was the coolness of the Nobles. "L. C. and E. J. are very indifferent to us . . . E. J. very

quiet and L. C. keeps away from me . . . We have little to say to each other." He was to learn months later that the Nobles had told the Woodstock directors and employees that he was to blame for the failure. Far worse was the lack of sympathy from relatives outside the immediate family. "I have not yet found one relative," he wrote on December 28, "who has come and said, What can I do for you. Nor have Nobles . . . The McCrum boys * care little and have not expressed one word of sympathy as to our trouble, nor even have any of Sallie's relations asked if she was in need."

By the middle of January, Heinz was literally without money with which to buy food. A peculiar pride kept him from asking for help of friends and relatives; he decided instead "to try and see if with all the credit I once had, I could get groceries with indefinite payment or until I was able to pay." He called on three grocery stores, telling the owners "not to consent if it would inconvenience them as I could not say how soon we would be able to pay." He was turned down by all three. "I must confess while John England and Mrs. Moyle were not able, yet I am a good deal taken aback at G. W. Hahn and almost feel as though they did not fully know me, or wondered if I would ever pay, or they may wonder if I am honest. I feel confident I can get the groceries at Gibson's." (T. H. Gibson gave him groceries on credit.)

He had one staunch friend in these days: Jacob Covode, from whom he had borrowed $5000. When Heinz went to see him immediately after the bankruptcy became known, "He called me a welcome visitor and said these troubles must not make us lose the respect for each other that we have always had." Six weeks later he wrote, "Mr. J. Covode has been our best friend and I hope he may live long enough that I may be able to return by kindness, if no other way, some of his philanthropic acts toward Heinz, Noble & Co. and H. J. H."

❋

* Sallie's widowed mother had married Robert McCrum.

At a Heinz family conference held on New Year's Day, Henry Heinz gave a formal estimate of the situation and for the first time made known his thoughts on possible courses of action for the future. He had been offered, he said, two farms that he could live on and operate if he wished. He felt that the business and the garden owed him something, but at the same time he was deeply indebted to his parents. His attorney told him he could enter into no partnership with anyone until he had received his discharge from bankruptcy, which could take many months. If Brother John and Cousin Frederick * wished to rent the farms and gardens and form a new company, he was willing to work for them on salary and run the business, but with the unwritten understanding that he owned a share in it.

John and Frederick each owned six shares of stock in a building and loan association worth $800. Sallie Heinz was able to raise $1400 on some Young property she owned jointly. An agreement was reached: a company would be formed. The owners were to be John, Frederick and Anna Schmitt Heinz, each with one-sixth interest, and Sallie Young Heinz with one-half interest. Henry's salary was to be $125 a month.

F. & J. Heinz Company was launched on February 14, 1876, with $3000 capital. On that date, at age thirty-two, Henry Heinz started over again. He wrote in his diary, "John Heinz got his money out of the loan association today. I started to work for John and Fred this morning." In his pocket he carried still another notebook, this one marked "M. O.," which stood for "Moral Obligations." It listed all the creditors of Heinz, Noble & Company, with the amount owed to each.

---

* Frederick Heinz, born in Kallstadt in 1842 and trained there as a florist and gardener, had come to America at twenty-seven. He had supervised the farming and gardening work of the bankrupt company.

"Truly It Is Starting Life Over"

Am reading a book titled "The Successful Merchant."

Henry J. Heinz,
Diary, August 12, 1877

THE ROAD BACK to restored respectability and substance was rough and painful. Heinz used as much as he dared of the firm's capital and income to buy back equipment and stock of the bankrupt company: eight vinegar generators, office furniture, glass, cauliflower, salt pickles — $7000 in all. He persuaded the hands to work for half pay for some weeks, the other half to represent a short loan from them for the purchase of equipment. He persuaded a man named Anderson to lend John the use of his boilers for processing pickles. He hired one salesman and in July "started out to hunt up trade with satchel in hand such as our man could not sell to." He journeyed to Philadelphia to reopen avenues of trade, sitting up all night in the day coach to save money. He established an agency in Baltimore, advancing it $137.09 in goods as a start. By July, Fred had seen to the planting of forty-five acres of rented garden land in Sharpsburg; Heinz inspected these on foot, "which tried me very much as I used to have a horse to do it." Pittsburghers had admired the Heinz & Noble teams, matched for size, breed, and color. Now he wrote in his diary, "Bought a cheap $16 horse to help us out in a pinch. He is blind."

Young Hettie remembered that year, with some bitterness, as one of toil and sacrifice. Her mother and older sisters worked in the basement of the old homestead until after midnight putting up horseradish to help raise money. When she came home from school she would find a great heap of dinner dishes piled on the table; she had to wash these before supper could be cooked and served. Everyone was so busy that she had no companionship at home and felt neglected. She was constantly being told that as the youngest she should be seen and not heard. But no member of the family, she remembered, including their father, ever said a word of reproach to Henry or in any way let him feel that they regretted standing behind him.

That fall Heinz bravely mounted an exhibition of pickles at the Pittsburgh Exposition, and on November 6 he sent three wagons and a buckboard to take part in the Great Procession for presidential candidate Rutherford B. Hayes, Brother Peter and another employee carrying a large banner with the company trademark on it and one wagon bearing a sign, "Tomorrow We Will Pickle Tilden."

His goal was to have in four years, by 1880, "as good credit as ever Heinz-Noble had." The prospect throughout 1876 seemed hopeless. In Philadelphia in June he wrote, "Several letters from home and not at all encouraging and business is fearful dull. Here no one wants goods in our line and if you force them you can only do it at a loss. Sometimes I feel discouraged, and now F. & J. Heinz are started and dare not stop — nor me." In August and September, "Very close run for money. Can't see how to get along and not a man or friend will give us a cent, even on chattel mortgage or any other way . . . Money hard to get. Am very much worried to keep our heads above water. 45 acres of cabbage and horseradish and can't realize on any yet. It takes nice financing to get through. Have come to the conclusion that everybody is *selfish* . . . We manage with a little capital to do a business of about $3,000 to $4,000 a month, but it requires managing. Give checks and then hope in some way to meet them at Sharpsburg when they come in. (It takes two days.)" Two years later he was to write of these times, "The physical and mental strain was enough to kill more than one man."

On some of his calls he met with distrust and hostility. In Baltimore he had some words with Mr. Griffith of Griffith and Drakeley, whom he considered "mean, close and suspicious." Frederick Heinz reported in exasperation that he could not get anybody to give him money and that the reason was Henry Heinz's connection with the business. Perhaps as a break with the past, he had his hair cut short and his whiskers taken off for the first time in more than six years. He and Sallie began to attend the North Avenue Church, where they were strangers; they preferred to go where they were not known and knew no one.

At the end of the year things began to change. He was able to write, "Trade good. We bought a span of mules this day for $140 (cheap). Our glass bill for the month is $400 — biggest since F. & J. Heinz started." And, "Our trade is good and we are working hard. Truly it is starting life over, in a sense." In February 1877, on the first anniversary of his new start, he moved into a newly completed private office. In June 1877 Mr. Smythe of Bradstreets Agency advised him not to reveal the company's capital worth ($14,000), because the high return on it would cause suspicious inquiries. Profit in 1877 was $2000 better than expected. Clearly F. & J. Heinz Company was going to survive, and probably it was going to grow and prosper.

He had moved to the Garrett farm outside Sharpsburg, where Sallie earned additional family income by making and selling butter (thirty-five cents a pound). With considerable difficulty he managed to keep his parents from being evicted by renting the house they once had owned and paying the new owners, the Masonic Bank, $400 yearly. (He was able in 1878 to buy the house and its three-and-a-half acres on a $10,000 mortgage.) Harlow F. Dunham, one of his neighbors and an employee of the company, persuaded him and Sallie to be received into full membership in the Grace Methodist Protestant Church.* Jacob Covode, "the best friend I ever had outside my family," died in April 1877. Sallie gave birth to their third child in August, a son to whom they gave the name Howard Covode.

The other entries in the diary for the last months of 1876 show that his life had returned more nearly to normal; for 1877 and 1878 they cover increasingly broader activities and interests. He went with Sallie, sisters Mary and Maggie, Sallie's mother and brother George, and Dr. Deetrick on an excursion to the Centennial Exposition at Philadelphia. Dr. Deetrick seems to have behaved improperly: "Sallie and Dr. Deetrick are miffed at each other. She called him a fool. He tried to pay great attention to her at the Exposition in my absence." The following week Brother John was about to leave for his own visit to the Centennial "when Fred and I told him we could not sanction it as we could not afford to take time and spend money that way. John was determined but did not go and all was quiet." When the matter was referred to Mother Heinz "she said in a few words that John had just as good a right as the rest to go."

> *November 28, 1876:* John Heinz had a lawsuit about an old horse today and had to pay costs. He is learning that courts don't always give justice.
>
> *December 10 (Sunday):* Zero through the day. We all remained home. It is very inconvenient to attend church when living in the country.
>
> *December 14:* Very busy day. I remained in the city all night writing, getting off orders, etc. Peter slept on the office floor. Waked him at 5 A.M. and started him off for Wheeling at 6 A.M.

---

* Heinz had been reared a Lutheran, Sallie a United Presbyterian; they had been married in the Methodist Episcopal Church.

with the black horse and wagon to start bulk goods in Wheeling. Last week the Brooklyn Theater burned down and 300 were in the ruins. Horrible catastrophe.

December 25: We had a small tree for Irene and Clarence. Shoes and first gum shoes for them. Sallie necktie and wrist-bands for me, and I got a cuff, collar and note paper and gloves for her. Also small *useful* presents for our folks at home. Hettie made me a present of a book mark. How sad the thought that I was the means of putting our folks into trouble and embarrass-ment.

May 11, 1877: Sallie and Irene and Clarence to city with me driving. Our two children examined by Fowler [the phre-nologist]. He gives Irene and Clarence written charts and Sallie verbal. Paid $19.50 for the three — two written and one verbal. Mother thought it very foolish. Mustard mills moving nicely.

In September Heinz moved his family from the Garrett farm to downtown Pittsburgh, renting a row house at 200 Second Avenue, a stone's throw from the F. & J. Heinz Company plant.

November 2: Mr. J. Wilson of Chicago is in our city and spends all day until midnight with us. Had quite a confidential talk with him on our past trouble. After all of our conversation he even gave me a check to help me out of a tight place, which we mailed him one week later, which was today. He also changed our terms from cash to 30 days.

February 8, 1878: John and I had a few words because he misses the first train in the morning.

February 19: There was a meeting of creditors today of H. N. & Co. There were only about 15 creditors present. They decided to pay 11% of a dividend and then close up and declare a final one again.

February 23: Henry Goodballet took all my sisters and Jacob to the opera to see Uncle Tom's Cabin played. This was the first for my sisters to go to the opera. Cousin Henry seems very kind to us all and has proven that by *actions* during all of our finan-cial trouble.

March 4: Dr. Scott, Paster of Grace Church, calls and takes dinner with us today. Sallie falls down the cellar stairs today and feels very sore tonight.

March 12: I told the Masonic Bank I was paying small claims out of my salary, 100 cents so far as my three-eighths interest went. God help me to carry out this resolve.

April 13: Sallie and I for once went to the Opera to hear Edwin Booth play King Richard the 3rd, a historical play. I do not approve of opera-going yet my conscience did not dictate to me on this occasion.

In May, on a trip to Washington, Heinz "was almost distracted" to hear that Peter, representing the company there, had bought a saloon-restaurant and had moved a widow and her daughter into the apartment above it. After an almost sleepless night he met Peter in the park and in a long talk told him he must leave Washington. J. W. Ports, the firm's agent in Baltimore, was on his way to Washington and would buy out his territory. The saloon-restaurant would have to be sold.

May 6: Ports arrived from Baltimore and we closed on giving Ports the territory and he agreed to pay P. J. Heinz the cost for his goods with freight added, $400, his gray horse and rig, and would pay $100 for a Christmas gift next year if he succeeded.

May 7: Took stock today and made out Bill of Sale, etc. to Ports. Peter kicked hard as he did not wish to leave this place nor sell the best territory in the land. I told him we would not allow him to continue on account of women and whiskey.

May 8: Sold stand in market to other party and tried hard to close out his whiskey stand.

May 9: Worked late and early but did not yet succeed in selling out the saloon. Tried many plans to get Peter out of it and wanted him to lose some money in this Devil's Business whiskey so as to last him a life time.

May 10: Drove out with Peter to collect and closed up with Kennedy. Turned over saloon, etc. to him and he gave us a note and chattel mortgage and assumed rent and Peter turned over the keys and lost what he had paid, $250 in all, and glad to get out.

May 11: Mr. Ports again arrived. Peter was determined not to go home with me and I was determined the other way and checked his trunk and succeeded in getting him to go home willingly and I was not to tell on him.

May 12 (Sunday): We arrived home at 9 A.M., Peter quite contented. Took Peter to Dr. Pearson's Fourth Avenue Baptist Church at night.

May 17: George McNally was caught in the belts of the mustard mill at 6 P.M. and all his clothes were ripped from his back, and yet not much hurt. God be praised for his mercy.

May 18: Swing sign today across First Avenue, 18 feet long by 15 feet high, lettering viz: Heinz — Pickles, Vinegar, Mustard. The words Pickles and Vinegar read from Grant Street and the rest reads from Wood and Smithfield streets. It is all made of wire and cost $40.

May 25 (Chicago): Bought a blue business suit today, $17, trying to save.

June 5: John and I had some words in the office which I am sorry for.

June 18: George Halsinger buys goods on his Debt of Honor. I insist on him to take plenty, but no, only a few bottles of each to start his brother in a grocery in the country. I tell him he has more confidence in human nature than I have, or he would buy all he could.

June 24: Hired Joe Hite [stableman] back at $7 per week after apologizing for his actions last week. He promises to quit growling and swearing.

July 1: Had a first chat with Mr. Craig (Grocer), a creditor of H. N. & Co. Told him this 8:30 P.M. for the first time if I was ever able, and that my moral obligation to him was 100 cents on the dollar so far as my interest in the business went, and that he could have goods to the extent of $200 between this and January

1, 1879, and we would take off 25% and charge to my salary, and that would be $50 paid for a start, and that I would see what I would be able to do. He remarked he did not expect me to pay Nobles' share — if I paid my own ⅜ I would do well.

July 2: I loaned Henry Covode $50 today for 30 days. This was the first loan granted the boys. He wants to start a paper in Sharpsburg and we gave him circulars on our change of trade mark to print and some posters.

On July 4 the city was quiet, with most of the stores and businesses closed. The entire Heinz relationship left at 9:00 A.M. in various carriages and wagons to spend the day at Ross's Grove in Aspinwall, a few miles up the Allegheny River from Sharpsburg. During the afternoon, after a merry picnic dinner, it began to rain.

Directly after the rain began also the wind came up from the west and changed and came from the north and heavy lightning. We drove our barouche above the trees so that they could not fall on us, while Reithmiller's Grocery and our Chow Chow wagons (covered) were standing within 30 feet of each other and horses unhitched and all of Reithmiller's family and others got into it. Mother, Hettie, Mary and Ivor Heinz, Preacher Waltz and family and others (except Ludwig Waltz) were in our chow wagon. The storm blew down the shed, so people stood in the storm except those who were in the above-named wagons, and such a storm we never experienced. We feared we would be carried up into the air. We unhitched the horse out of the barouche when the hail began. The horse was afterwards found with part of his skull knocked in by some limbs of trees which were falling in every direction. It closed up his eye and swelled up his head. He may get over it. But we were saved of accident to all in the barouche, though wet on account of the immensity of the storm tearing curtains and soaking the little ones. Irene was praying to Jesus to stop the storm. John was then outside with me trying to hold the barouche from being thrown over.

When the worst seemed to be over, John went to see how our

fellow creatures had fared amidst falling oaks and branches of those that still stood and found Mr. Reithmiller hunting an axe and a few steps further on he told the tale. While the chow wagon was unharmed with its precious freight, the Reithmiller wagon was felled to the ground with a large oak which smashed the wagon to splinters and killed Mrs. Reithmiller and baby, 15 months old, and two Prager boys, Willie 16 years and Herman about 9 years. Both had their skulls broken. They were struck by large limbs while running away from the wagon when the tree was falling.

Tod Keefer, Saint's son, about 12 years, was caught between the forks of the tree but escaped with slight bruises. Lizzie Croft escaped with limbs bruised. Lizzie Reithmiller and her sister Emma had her thigh broken. Mr. Reithmiller had his breast hurt. George and Freddie were slightly hurt as well as Maggie and they were from 6 to 18 years of age. Annie Geisler was also hurt. Ludwig Waltz, 8 years old, was killed. He was a very smart boy. Sophie Gentleman was killed and one of our garden women was killed. One little girl had her back broken and is likely to die.

We worked for at least three-quarters of an hour till we had cut limbs of fallen trees to extricate the living from their awful position and then took out the dead, and when we had all the wounded in vehicles we found the bridge across the road at Ross Station had been washed away, so that we had to carry them over and put them into other vehicles and send them home. Physicians were along with them. Then we sent for lumber and built a bridge so that teams could cross the stream, during which time I sent my family up to Mother McCrum's. Those of our family and Cousin Fred remained with the wounded during the night and some of us only till midnight. It made many sad hearts and all the town of Sharpsburg was in a state of excitement, as so many at other picnics in the immediate neighborhood miraculously escaped having trees fall upon them, as they sheltered in houses.°

° Newspaper accounts listed seven killed and many injured, some by huge lumber piles that were scattered in all directions. Crowds gathered at the Sharpsburg Station to learn the fate of the thousands of picnickers and the dead bodies were laid on a platform there. The Reverend Waltz was brought home "laughing in an idiotic manner."

July 5: A sad day in Sharpsburg. All the funerals take place at 3:30 P.M. and all in one procession. All the bells of Catholic and other churches ringing at once and places of business closed up. Pastor Waltz and wife were unable to attend the funeral, also Mr. Reithmiller could not attend. The parents of the dead all lived within 100 feet of each other except two who lived in Etna, but all were buried at the same time. The wounded are doing well and will likely all recover except the little girl who had her back broken. All buried in one row, side by side. There were six German Lutheran preachers, five of which preached in German, one in English.

July 6: Not at all well. The wetting, scare, excitement and work of the past 4th has had its effect upon my system. Lying on lounge part of the day.

July 12: Cleaned out and fixed up all my drawers of case and desk today and labeled drawers so that I will know just where to look for each item.

September 20: Began to cut cabbage into kraut today for the first time this year. Had quite a chat with Peter about his fast life.

September 25: President Hayes at the [Pittsburgh] Exposition yesterday and today and quite a procession in honor to him. Took my family to the Exposition. Saw D. Carver shoot down and break 100 glass balls in 4 minutes and 54 seconds. About 6,000 to 10,000 people visit the Exposition daily.

On September 28 a laconic entry recorded the departure of an old enemy: "John Pfusch died of consumption."

October 5: Our payroll today is the largest we ever had in Pittsburgh — $500 in two weeks.

October 20 (Sunday): Had a plain chat with George McCrum, who is leaning on the side of Ingersoll.*

October 26: Joseph Wolfert called and was ashamed to come in. Called him in and to sit down. He remarked that I was paying

---

* George McCrum was the son of Robert McCrum, Sallie's stepfather. Colonel Robert Green Ingersoll (1833–1899) was the American lawyer, orator, and militant anti-Christian agnostic.

other's debt of honor. I told him, Yes, I was doing so in a small way and was pleased to pay my enemies first and that he could get some goods now. He was very much pleased and apologized for having persecuted me and slandered me, etc. I told him I forgive him for all, that these trials have done me good. We shook hands and I told him to call soon and bring his wife along.

November 9: Brother Jacob was hurt today by overlifting himself at the warehouse. His back pained him very much. Sallie fell down stairs.

November 10: I enjoyed this day very much. Sunday School at 9:15. Met my class. All well. Then to Christ Church to hear Dr. Morgan and to Mission Sunday School at 2 P.M. Then to hear Reverend E. M. Wood at 7:30 P.M. at Christ M. E. Church. To class at 6:15. So on the whole, my day was all taken up except about two hours which I enjoyed with my family.

November 16: Maggie Keil called at office for donation of pickles for Grace Church Festival. We supplied her with all they wanted and the church has our best wishes. Bought Clarence a suit for $6.50 and suits for the children and just wonder how some people who have a large family get along on small salary.

December 2: Had to speak plainly to the bill clerk, as he delayed some invoices last night and insisted it must not happen again.

Also called all the girls together upstairs. Told them we would not allow talking during working hours except such as was necessary to do their work, etc. All was kindly received. Good feeling throughout the house.

December 9: Met Leo Oppenheimer on train, also Smitley of Reymer Brothers. They took drinks and offered me one. When I asked for water, they handed me a tumbler of water which I drank and thanked them. Had a pleasant time and am satisfied I did not lose their respect on this account.

December 16: Watkins, the jelly man, called and was under the influence of liquor. I told him to call when his head would be clear. Mrs. Jacob Covode called today to dine with us. I loaned her $75.

December 27: Accommodated John Cook today with $300. Don't owe him that amount as due. He is in a tight place, and we are very short ourselves.

December 31: Spent happy day at office. At 5:30 our office force and salesmen presented me with a very handsome inkstand (cut glass) and a fine gold pen and pencil combined. I returned heartfelt thanks in a short speech, when we all wished each other a happy New Year and gave all a jar of pickles.

In the hard times of the summer of 1877, the Pennsylvania Railroad cut wages 10 percent and introduced measures to reduce the number of brakemen on train crews. The men struck and violence followed — nowhere worse than in Pittsburgh. In a week of rioting, three Pittsburgh militia regiments and a battery were called out and then disbanded because their sympathies were clearly with the strikers. A National Guard division was sent in from Philadelphia; it fired on what was now a burning and looting mob of 5000, killing nearly a score, and retreated to take up positions in a railroad roundhouse. In an all-night siege the mob broke into gun shops and attempted unsuccessfully to drive the troops out by running burning coal cars down on the building. By the time the violence was ended, twenty-nine people lay dead and some 1600 cars, 126 locomotives, and the railroad's buildings in Pittsburgh, including the Union Station, built in 1857, were destroyed.°

Heinz was on a business trip to Baltimore when the violence broke out:

July 20: Left Washington for Baltimore on the 5:20 train, arrived at Barnes Hotel at 7:30. Soldiers shot in among a mob out of the armory as they were stoned. About a dozen shot dead. The 6th Regiment was to go to the depot to quell the riot strikes.

July 21: Baltimore is in a terrible uproar on account of the strike.

° The city paid the railroad an indemnity of $2.75 million.

July 22: The last two days there has been the worst feeling among the Rail Road employees on account of the Rail Road Company reducing them 10 per cent and the people generally especially are in sympathy with them. It is more like war times than anything else. Even government troops are not sufficient to quell the rioters. There has been the most terrible time in Pittsburgh ever known. Sheriff Fife killed and General Pearson wounded and many others killed by soldiers guarding railroad property, and citizens, railroad men and rioters killed many soldiers. The Rail Road roundhouse and depot were burned down as well as 400 or 500 cars and 50 locomotives, and can't anyone tell where it will end. President Hayes has issued a call for 75,-000 men to quiet the mobs and protect public property. I can't leave for home — track torn up for miles, besides not safe to travel toward Pittsburgh.

August 5: Pittsburgh. Arrived at 9 A.M. and saw all the ruins caused by the mob during the Great Rail Road Strike. It is the awfullest looking sight I ever saw. Millions of property burned down.

August 6: Find about 600 men and 200 head of horses cleaning up what the rioters destroyed.

The railroad strike and riots made a profound and enduring impression on Henry Heinz. From that time forward he began to search for ways of running a business that would make such violence unlikely because it would be unnecessary.

CHAPTER 4

Life, Diet, and
"Upward Progress"

How to Manage Silver Skin Onions to keep them white for Bottling, which we discovered in Nov or Dec 1877. We first salt the Onions same as pickles but add no allum as allum makes them turn yellow or darkens them a yellowish cast. Allow them to be well cured, say 2 to 3 months. Then peal and if very salty simply put them into bbls in a 60 to 70° atmosphere and put water on them (no brine). This will start them working off the vegetable matter in a fermenting process. Then use good judgment for if they work too hard or for some cause they sometimes become soft in the ends. But should the onions not be well salted then put into weak brine instead of water to have them ferment. They should work in this manner for several weeks before ready to use to Bottle.

Recipe book of Henry J. Heinz, 1883

THE EARLY HEINZ RECIPES were kept in a series of pocket notebooks, the products listed alphabetically. Entries for Anchor spice, beans, chow-chow,* and walnut catsup are intermingled with instructions on how to make red ink, black ink, shoe blacking, and a cure for horse colic, how to write a blanket policy on stock ("$150 each horse"), how to start the vinegar generators, specifications for building a truck wagon, the ingredients of a superior cleaning fluid ("Recipe bought from a Merchant Tailor"), and 150 Bible passages memorized by H. J. Heinz.

The books make it clear that, from the first, Heinz was not simply a commercial canner of fruits and vegetables, but a

* A relish of mixed pickles and cauliflower in mustard.

processor of reciped products — of such ready-made dishes as chili sauce, tomato sauce, fruit butters, mince meat, piccalilli, baked beans with pork, macaroni with cheese, spaghetti with cheese.

The diet of Americans in 1869, when Heinz started out, was of a dreary monotony through seven or eight months of each year. The staples were bread, potatoes, root vegetables, dried fruits, and pork or beef, usually smoked or salted. Fresh fruits and vegetables were eaten only in that brief period when they were ripening, but without refrigeration these often rotted or wilted in shipment to the cities. Cucumbers and pickles were the only salad in winter. Except for meat on the hoof, there was little movement of foodstuffs from one region to the other. Few inland families ate oysters or shrimp, salmon or tuna, or any other seafood. A lemon was a luxury; an orange was something found in a Christmas stocking. Pomelo — grapefruit — was little known outside Florida, and there it was choked with seeds and was often so bitter that it had to be reamed and sugared overnight. Tomatoes were an exotic Mexican fruit for which the country had only recently begun to acquire a taste.

With such a diet, spices, sauces, condiments, and "relishes" were used to aid digestion and add interest to the plate. Even though food was plentiful, there were common physical ailments: faulty bone growth, bad teeth, sallow complexions, dyspepsia — at the worst, scurvy, goiter, and pellagra. Many European visitors before the Civil War, when diet began to improve, wrote of the poor physical appearance of Americans, using such adjectives as *lank, spare, flabby, dyspeptic, languid, wan,* and *listless.*

There were wide gaps and differences in diet in the North, South, and West; among families living on the farm, in the towns, and in the great cities; and between the employed worker and the unemployed poor. The well-to-do, of course, had rich and varied fare.* But all classes and regions shared in some degree the difference between the winter and the summer diet.

They also shared in common an almost total ignorance of what have since come to be known as the elementary principles of nutrition. It was assumed that all foods were equal in nutritional value, that diet deficiency illnesses were caused by something *in* the food, never by something missing from it, and that such illnesses were infectious. There were dietary reformers, to be sure, some of them with remarkable prescience (Sylvester Graham of "Graham Cracker" fame was one), but they had no sound scientific explanation for their theories and were commonly looked upon as cranks. There were advances in dietary practices, but they were uneven in different regions and among different social and economic classes. Prejudices long discarded by sensible people lingered on in many places and many minds, bearing out the old German

---

* Pittsburgh's finest and most famous hotel, the Monongahela House, offered the following Bill of Fare for a New England Festival held on December 22, 1856 (given in the spelling of the original menu):
Soup: Mock Turtle. *Fish:* Fresh Cod, Oyster Sauce. *Boiled:* Turkey, Oyster Sauce; Leg Mutton, Capre Sauce; Chicken, Celery Sauce; Beef Tongue. *Ornamented Cold Dishes:* Round of Beef, a la Mode, decorated with Jelly; Mayonnaise of Chicken; Ham, decorated; Boned Turkey, in Jelly. *Grosses Pieces Chaudes:* Fillets of Beef, with Mushrooms; Ham, Champagne Sauce; Baron of Beef, a la Royale. *Dishes Nationale:* Baked Beans and Pork; Chowder of Fresh Cod; Hashed Codfish with Potatoes, in Forms. *Entrees:* Venison Steaks, with Currant Jelly; Broiled Quails; Oyster Pies; Domestic Ducks, Braised, Mushroom Sauce; Prairie Chicken, Grilled, Jelly Sauce; Fried Oysters; Oysters en Escallape; Maccaroni au Gratin; Celery au Jus; Fillets of Rabbit, Broiled, Madeira Sauce; Sweet Breads, Tomato Sauce; Chicken Salad. *Roast:* Turkeys, Cranberry Sauce; Saddle of Venison, Currant Jelly Sauce; Tender Loin of Pork; Domestic Ducks; Chickens. *Vegetables:* Forms of Mashed Potatoes; Baked Potatoes; Fresh Tomatoes; Hominy. *Game:* Canvas Back Ducks; Broad Bills; Teal Ducks; Red Head Ducks; Grouse; Venison; Mallard Ducks; Partridges; Lake Ducks. *Relishes:* Celery; Cranberry Sauce; Currant Jelly; Mixed Pickles; Olives. *Pastry:* Plum Puddings; Indian Puddings; Mince Pies; Pumpkin Pies; Apple Pies; Cocoa Nut Pies; Cranberry Tarts; Charlotte Russe. *Dessert:* Vanilla Ice Cream; Strawberry Ice Cream; Madeira Jelly; Pyramids of Candied Orange; Pyramids of Maccaroons; Lady Cake; Jelly Cake; Malaga Grapes; English Walnuts; Oranges; Apples; Almonds; Raisins. Coffee and Tea.

saying, "What the peasant does not know, he does not eat." There had been and still persisted a prejudice against white flour bread in favor of cornmeal, against fresh meat (it might be "tainted") as compared to smoked or salted meat, against white potatoes as "unwholesome" in favor of sweet potatoes, against fresh green salads as "unmanly," against the tomato, a most versatile food, because it was related to the poisonous nightshade plant and was thought to cause cancer, against uncooked fresh fruits, because they were thought to cause cholera.

Whether she shared or ignored these prejudices, the housewife of a century ago ran a complex and time-consuming kitchen operation. If she could afford to own them, she used a battery of hand-operated appliances: coffee grinder, meat grinder, sausage stuffer, apple parer, cherry seeder, and, on the farm, a churn and a cheese press. She scaled and dressed the fish, plucked and drew the chickens, ground the meat, and on Saturday baked the bread. (To buy store bread was a reflection on her worth as a housekeeper.) Those fruits and vegetables that would keep she stored in her cellar: potatoes, cabbage, nuts, turnips, pumpkins, prunes, squash, apples. Some orchard fruits she dried; some she preserved with sugar in crocks in a syrup so heavy that the air could not reach them to cause fermentation. When sugar became scarce and expensive during the Civil War, she more and more took to putting up jellies and preserves (originally called "conserves") in sealed, airtight glass "fruit jars."

In the city she often bought her fresh fruit and vegetables in season at the farmers' market or from a huckster making his rounds with a horse and wagon. Her milk she bought from a street vendor who ladled the unpasteurized product into her pitcher from a large can. (Milk was not bottled until the late 1880s.) In a large city, before the introduction of state regulations and codes, she was likely to get a very poor grade of swill milk, for the wretched cows, confined throughout their lives in stables, lived chiefly on mash from the city distilleries. Consumption of milk, however, was relatively low before the growth of rail transportation and home refrigeration. She bought her meat from a neighborhood butcher, who either slaughtered once a week or procured quarters of meat from one of the local slaughterhouses to which the cattle, swine, and sheep were driven through the city streets, dropping pollution as they went. The city abattoirs were situated near the market stalls, sometimes in or near residential districts. They have been described as "These shambles, veritable pest holes surrounded by heaps of putrifying offal and pools of blood giving rise to horrible stenches." [*] They were tolerated until after the war, when city ordinances, passed over the outraged protests of the meat merchants but upheld in a Supreme Court decision in 1873, restricted them to certain districts.

For her "dry groceries" the housewife went to the nearest or most desirable grocery store. Both the grocer and his shop were somewhat less romantic than pictured in nostalgic imagination and in the restored museum villages. The typical store — especially in the cities and larger towns — was badly lighted and ventilated, for windows reduced the amount of shelf space. It had no door screen to keep out the flies; screens were not introduced until the 1880s. It smelled strongly of roasting coffee, kerosene, and dried codfish. The floor was crowded with flour in the new paper sacks and loose beans, rice, potatoes, and coffee in burlap bags. Underneath the shelves that were pathways for the rats and mice stood open barrels or bins of crackers (in which the cat loved to curl up for a nap), rolled oats, raisins, dried prunes, molasses (swarming with flies), sour pickles, sugar, and pork. Butter was spooned out of a fifty-six-pound firkin into thin beechwood boxes

[*] Richard Osborn Cummings, *The American and His Food: A History of Food Habits in the United States,* 1940.

shaped somewhat like a miniature river barge. Soap was cut in oblong pieces out of a sixty-four-pound firkin.

Store fixtures included a spitbox, a hand-operated Enterprise Coffee Mill, a coffee roaster, tin measures, a mounted roll of brown butcher paper with cutter, a balance scale, an auger or "devil" for loosening sugar and dried fruit in the barrel, a sugar grinder, a rack for paper "pokes" (in the advanced stores), canisters for tea, coffee, and spices, a feather or turkey-wing duster, a bell on the door, and a cupboard — a "safe" — made of a wooden frame covered with wire or perforated tin, where bread and cheese were protected from flies and mice. Except in rare instances, there was no icebox.

If he ran a produce department in season, the grocer bought his fruit, vegetables, and eggs in small lots from local farmers. He had an inventory of perhaps $5000 and totaled his accounts in a ledger; the first cash register did not arrive from Dayton until the 1880s. His markup over the wholesale price ranged from 50 percent to 100 percent and up, depending on the condition of the merchandise, the amount of stock on hand, the urgency of the demand, and the paying habit of the customer. He had an assistant, generally young, always tired, who wore a pencil over one ear and, unhampered by considerations of hygiene, tended the horse when not waiting on customers.

The grocer might be as honest as the day was long, but some were not and temptation was strong. It was not unknown to solder a one-ounce lead sinker on the appropriate side of the balance scale. Some miscreants put ground beans in the coffee, sand in the sugar, chalk in the bread, dust in the pepper, flour in the ginger, flour in the chocolate, hayseed in the raspberry jam, chicory in the coffee, farina in the mustard, lard in the butter, and potato starch in the lard. One social historian has recorded that pork sausage long on hand was inclined to collect mold and become unsalable. The proper remedy was to rub off the mold with a piece of cheesecloth and then rub on a coating of butter. This made the sausage look fresh, shiny, and appetizing.*

Rapid changes were taking place, however — scientific discoveries and material improvements so striking that men were beginning to see a vision of a world without fear of hunger and therefore without crime or war. Despite four years of civil rebellion, despite five years of hard times, there had been long-range upward progress in many aspects of life: in transportation and agriculture; in lighting, communication, and sources of power; in medicine, life expectancy, and the standard of living; in education and the laws for public welfare. It could be argued that science and invention could not continue to spread their benefits at such a pace, but even at a slower rate one might foresee a world that would be as different in 1900 as 1880 was different from the age of Queen Anne.

Some of the most remarkable changes were to be seen in agriculture. In the 5000 years before 1800 there had been few significant improvements in the tools men used to grow their food. The past eighty years, however, had seen an explosion of discoveries — the steel plow, sulky plow, gang plow, lister plow, steam plow (a failure but one that carried promise), the grain elevator, the spring tooth harrow, disk harrow, mechanical seed drill, mechanical reaper, threshing machine, and the beginnings of the mechanical harvester or combine — the composite machine, pulled by twenty to forty horses, that would head, thresh, clean, and bag the grain in one operation as it moved over the field. Now the farmer could plant more, and now, with the new machines, he had broken the barrier imposed on him by the need to have large numbers of harvest hands available exactly when the grain was ripe. In 1800, an American farmer could produce enough food to feed himself and family and meet one third of the needs of another person.

* Gerald Carson, *The Old Country Store*, 1954.

Anna Margaretha Schmitt Heinz, mother of H. J. Heinz.

Henry ("Harry") Heinz at age twenty-one, dressed in the height of style. Note callouses on hands.

Harry and Sallie Heinz on their wedding trip in 1869. The couple at right is probably Mr. and Mrs. Clarence M. Johns. The young ladies reflect the required feminine attitude of their day: languishing and modest.

Harry Heinz built this proper Victorian house for the family in 1868, using brick from his father's brickyard and receipts from bills his father had written off as uncollectible.

Heinz and Son Howard, eight, in 1885, in the family buggy.

H. J. Heinz in his forties.

Three Heinz wagons. The Heinz "prize team" pulls the heavy dray wagon, above. The novelty wagon, below, was used for its advertising value and for delivery of light packages. The early closed vehicle at right, with its keyhole-and-diagonal-key trademark, languishing maiden, five medallion awards, and ketchup bottles, is a choice example of a highly specialized skill: that of decorating a wagon.

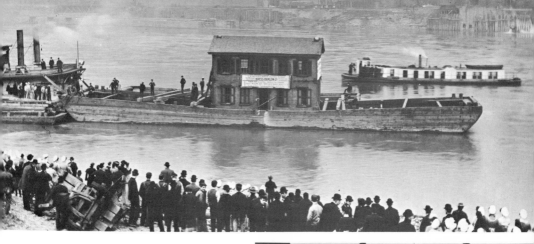

"The House Where We Began": Heinz and his young partner took over the former family residence in 1869 as their first factory. In 1904, he moved the house from Sharpsburg, despite a flood, five miles down the Allegheny River (above) to an honored place at the North Side plant (right).

Henry
Heinz
1869

Heinz and
Noble

1873

Early Heinz containers are now avidly sought "collectibles." The third bottle from the left in the top picture at the left is "Clifford's Worcester Sauce," named for the youngest Heinz son.

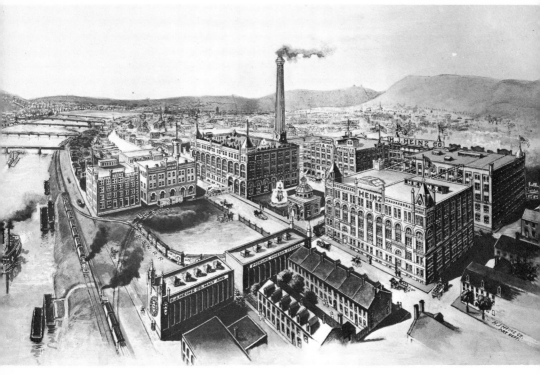

"The House of the 57 Varieties," built 1890–1898, stood (and stands) on the north shore of the Allegheny River opposite downtown Pittsburgh. The stable is the second building from the left in the background; the Time Office is in the center beside the fountain. The Baltimore and Ohio Railroad runs directly into the Vinegar Building (with roof garden). Row houses in the foreground (later replaced with factory buildings) were Heinz-owned residences.

Now the farmer and rancher could feed themselves and *five* other persons. With such a production capability, more than half of all Pennsylvanians were able to live and work in towns and cities.

It was felt that the application of science and invention to farming might continue at least as productively as it had in the first three quarters of the century. Some promising experiments were going forward, encouraged by the U.S. Department of Agriculture (created in 1862) and the Pennsylvania State Board of Agriculture (1876). Heinz was working to breed plants for such qualities as improved seed, earlier maturity, greater resistance to disease, and greater yield. He was driven by the third of his Important Ideas: To improve the finished product that comes out of the bottle, can, or crock, you must improve it in the ground, where and when it is grown. To that end he drew up agreements in April 1880 with "pickle growers" around La Porte, Indiana. He contracted to supply them with the seed and to buy their entire harvest, produced under specified conditions, at a price agreed upon at the time of the planting. Thus he insured his source of supply, improved the yield, and reduced the risks both to himself and the farmer.

The railroad, the most dramatic and visible change in America, was causing a revolution in the growth and distribution of food. By 1870 there were 5000 miles of track in Pennsylvania alone, and steps had been taken to adapt all track in the country to the same national gauge. Vegetables and citrus fruits were already being shipped in from the South, and though the spoilage rate was high and the goods carried a luxury price, they extended the market period for such products to four, five, even six months of the year. Products were coming in that northerners had never seen, or had seen only rarely and at prohibitive cost. With shipment of grain from the Midwest, flour prices in New York had dropped to one-fourth what they had been. Cattle were being transported in enormous volume by rail to the stockyards and slaughterhouses in the East.

Change was accelerated in the 1870s when the meat packers and the railroads successfully began to refrigerate goods in transit, at first in portable chests, then in freight cars insulated and packed with block ice. Now fruits and vegetables could be shipped in from the South through the entire ripening season and with minimum loss from spoilage. Now cattle could be slaughtered at the large western stockyards — even in summer — and the processed meat shipped to the eastern wholesale markets in refrigerator cars. Meat packing became the giant of the food processing industry. A complementary development, the first cold storage warehouse, was opened in New York in 1865.*

But the greatest advance in the history of food preservation, discovered in 1809 by Nicholas Appert, a French confectioner, was sterilization of the product by heat in hermetically sealed glass containers. For reasons that were not clearly understood in the 1870s, or at least not generally agreed upon, this treatment, if properly done, kept the food from changing and spoiling. Thus it was now possible to market and store a wide variety of packaged vegetables, fruits, seafood, and meats all the year round, regardless of the season. Appert's methods had been constantly improved over the past eight decades. One such improvement raised the boiling point of processing water from its normal 212° F. to 240° F. by addition of saltwater, thus reducing the required cooking time of the immersed container from five hours to thirty minutes. Another was the invention in 1874 of the pressure cooker — the closed steam pressure kettle or retort, which further reduced cooking time and eliminated the bursting of the container from the buildup of inside pressure during heating.

* "In the economic history of America, the refrigerator car was the jewelled pivot on which massive forces turned." Mitchell Wilson, *American Science and Invention*, 1954. Wilson points out that two refrigerated cars could carry as much beef as three cars containing live cattle.

The newest development in the processing industry was the use of tin-plate canisters as containers. It was a costly package best suited for out-of-season luxury items, but continual experimentation was improving the can and lowering its cost. Some decades earlier, when a mechanical fish scaler was introduced in Maine, the factory women took up their fish knives and attacked those who attended it. Now the same kind of conflict was happening in can making. Machines were developed that eliminated the craftsman with his tin shears and soldering iron; by 1880, two operators with assistants could turn out 1500 tin-lined cans a day. Pitched battles followed between craftsmen and operators. The operators won. As early as 1870, the country was producing 30 million cans per year — 1.3 cans for every inhabitant. Trade talk had it that an automatic can maker would be in operation within a few years with an unbelievably high speed and capacity. Henry Heinz continued to put up his preserves and condiments in sealed crocks, wooden tubs, and glass jars and bottles, but in March 1877 he recorded his first sale of goods in cans.

He was not aware of the fact, for the discoveries had not yet been made nor the words created, but he was engaged in controlling the two agents that act to spoil food: microorganisms and enzymes. He was preserving and selling the minerals and the family of chemical compounds, to be called vitamins, that play key roles in regulating bodily processes, are essential to human health and growths, and lead to disease if they are missing from the diet.

Preservation of food by heat in sealed containers supplanted the centuries-old custom of preserving food by chemical means — but not entirely. Certain chemicals — benzoic acid, salicylic acid, boric acid, borax, formaldehyde, and benzoate of soda, among others — were introduced as protectors against spoilage agents in canned goods. Drugstores sold little paper packets labeled "Canning Powders" for mother to mix with the food she put up in the fall. The artificial preservatives very soon appeared in commercially canned products in what was probably excessive and deleterious amounts. Their use was discovered and publicized. A crusader came forward to attack them, and a prolonged public uproar followed. The canning industry lived for years under the shadow of a bad name.

In the first decade of the new century, Henry Heinz would publicly preach the doctrine that good foods, properly processed, would keep without adulterants, and he would lead the battle among food processors to enact federal laws to ban or control their use.

CHAPTER 5

"Faithful Efforts and Good Success"

I do everything with all my might, which is too hard on me. Am trying to be cooler and easier and lazier.

Henry J. Heinz
Diary, August 4, 1880

HEINZ REACHED HIS GOAL of solvency and stability in 1879, a year ahead of his schedule. The pickle market was "much excited," with the best prices in five years. His horses, sixteen in all, were in excellent condition "and the best stock we ever owned, either old or present firm." The Sharpsburg Bank discounted $1000 of F. & J. Heinz paper and the Marine National of Pittsburgh $1500 without endorsers. ("This is gratifying.") He wrote on November 7, "All are busy and really driving a good business and profitable, more so I think than ever before in my life." And a month later, "Am beginning to be more comfortable in finances. Our returns are coming in faster."

The diaries for the next five years show a man who enjoys his family, is strong for self-improvement in himself and others, accepts more and broader responsibilities without complaining, is generous to his friends and to those who have helped him, and is clearly pushing forward to a major business success.

January 2, 1879: I worked hard all day. Seems I can't do otherwise.

January 3: This evening I gathered up all my books and placed them into my new bookcases and have enough to fill it except about eight inches of vacant space.

I find in counting up that we fed 43 tramps and beggars during the month of January 1879 in 31 days. I resolved to keep an account and had the girl mark 1 on a piece of paper for all that were fed. The majority we sat to the kitchen table and gave them coffee and warm victuals as it was very cold. We gave some of them work so as to earn money for their lodging.

January 11: Excellent sleighing, deep snow for first week. We have no sleigh nor do we care much about it.

January 31: I have finally caught up even with my work since my return on the night of the 26th. I cannot bear the idea to get behind and have work push me, but rather the reverse of this is partially my success.

February 1: Peter writes he is in New York to see Low whom he has bailed and who skipped his bail. Peter must let every fellow cheat him once.

February 4: Irene and Clarence begin going to Public School this A.M. for the first time in their lives. Irene is just 7 years, 7 months old this day and Clarence will be 6 years old on the 7th of April 1879. They express themselves as delighted and prefer it to the kindergarten. We buy them each a five cent slate and pencil at close of the first day's school and they go and pick it themselves. Neither know their letters. We have kept them from it on purpose and desire to see if they won't learn all the better.

February 26: James J. Robinson called today and I paid him $29.71, a debt of honor, which was just ⅜ of the total amount H. N. & Co. were due him when they failed. He did not even thank me. Some funny people. It would have shown courtesy at least.

March 1: Feeling comfortable and not behind in anything, took one-half day to look for a desk for my office and for a suit of clothes and a hat. It takes one dress suit every two years to do me. Then I wear it for every day.

March 7: Brother John tells me this A.M. in the private office that he can now say what a service I have been and what my services are worth or he was willing to pay me $2500 per year and asked if I would be satisfied. I replied that I would be very grateful for such a salary and that I would leave the matter entirely with them.

March 15: Gave supper to all our office boys and salesmen to-night at our house. We all spent a pleasant evening and all learned much and were highly entertained and amused. A good table was set.

March 23 (Sunday): James I. Bennett and Dr. Murray tried hard to raise $275 for the church but only raised $35. I felt like pitch-ing in but am only a member a little over a year and kept silent.

April 8: I feel this day as though I am overworked. My head feels dull, all over the top of the head and forehead. Am trying not to work too hard but fear it is almost too late. May God save my life and continue my health.

The Heinzes moved back to Sharpsburg sometime early in 1879. Heinz wrote that he was delighted with the change. "It seems more like living," he said, "than to be stuck into the dirt in the heart of the Smoky City."

April 20: Chicago. Sunday. At P.M. I went to hear Robert Inger-soll lecture on Skulls at the opera house. The house was full. He is very unfair and I felt like leaving when he began ridicul-ing the Bible, etc. He is today defying the ministers to answer him. Attended Temperance Gospel meeting at 8 P.M.

May 19 (Baltimore): Mr. Ports and I left on the new steamer Virginia for Norfolk at 9 P.M. to see Brother Peter and recruit. The boat travels 16 miles an hour which is good time. We slept in bunks below (economy) and overhead there was a number of stomping horses and a lot of Pennsylvania farmers opposite in the same room. *Stateroom next time.*

May 20 (Norfolk): Find people are nearly all prejudiced and have Southern proclivities. Don't want to live here. They think it's God's service to bleed a Northern man.

June 4: Could not get the jelly contract closed with Raher. So unreasonable, really provoking. Too small ever to do things worthy of notice. He tries to get away from the contract signed two weeks ago, and what can we make of him by forcing him? (Nothing.)

June 12: Grace Church held a Strawberry and Ice Cream Festival in Town Hall, Sharpsburg, with good success. Sallie is very active and jolly and keeps up lots of fun for others.

June 14: Hired J. W. Ulam for one year from the first of May, 1879, at $1,000 a year. Written contract, and the only written contract we have.

June 16: I paid Ingham and Son Moral Obligation or Debt of Honor in full today, $133.

He learned that T. H. Gibson, the grocer who had given him credit in the darkest days of the bankruptcy, was in financial trouble. "I have to help him," he wrote, and by a third person sent him a loan of $300. Ten days later Gibson called and asked for a loan of $1000. Heinz added $200 to the $300 he had sent earlier.

September 3: Chicago. Saw an artist very hard up. He begged me to buy a picture for $16 which was worth at least $40 to $50. Subject was a lady kneeling in prayer with her child standing locked in her arms and the Saviour standing in back of them. To me it seemed sublime. Sweet Hour of Prayer is what it represents. I expressed it home.

September 23: This is the anniversary of our tenth wedding day. I presented Sallie with a painting entitled "Sweet Hour of Prayer" which she appreciated. Bought a few pounds of nuts and candies for all.

September 26: Had a very unpleasant duty to perform. Discharged James Vance for having drunk (3rd time) stimulants to excess, so that others commented. Gave him kind advice. He gave me his hand that he would not drink. It is a loss to us but duty demands it. Rules cannot be broken and principle sacrificed for money if we can at all afford it. Office boys interceded for him. No go.

December 16: Sallie attends Grace Church Fair every evening and I go over from 8 to 11, when it costs me about $3 each evening treating to oysters and ice cream. If I go I treat others, or I can't go. I can't be little in this way. I never could enjoy myself unless I could make others comfortable in such places.

December 26: Our leaders [managers] thank us much for their Christmas presents. Kuipers gets $15 for faithful efforts and good success. Julian Soots gets $15.

December 27: Soots boy is to work three years from date of his first beginning this last fall at 50 cents per day for the first year and $25 at the close of the year if he remains; and 75 cents per day the second year and $25 if he remains; and $1 per day the third year and $150 at close of the third year provided he remains the three years under contract.

January 19, 1880: I loaned C. A. Sipe (our pastor) $50 today as the church was behind with his salary.

March 6: Philadelphia. Closed with the National Bureau of Engraving for 1,000,000 bottle and 50,000 box and bucket labels for $735 in my room at St. Charles Hotel. All to be in four printings and glossed.

April 14: Settled with Kinder Blair in the presence of G. W. Hahn. Paid him in full, ⅜ of the entire indebtedness of H. N. & Co. The Lord be praised, it makes me feel happy.*

April 23: Met old Mr. Barnet at the Hotel. He came to see me. Very poor. He wanted to pay F. & J. Heinz a bill for walnut catsup. I told him no and to get what sauce he wanted until his claim, my ⅜, was paid. He thanked me and of course was glad.

He visited Peter in his boardinghouse in Louisville in May and helped him "to get closed out to come home with me." Peter had been sick for three months with rheumatism and neuralgia, "yet succeeded well. He is quite humble . . . feels quite relieved to get away from Louisville."

May 28: Made closing entry in F. & J. Heinz books today and show net gain of $31,000. Largest showing ever made in one year.

* Kinder Blair had sued Heinz in December 1875 on the false charge of defrauding creditors. See p. 20.

May 31: I had a plain talk with Julian Soots about leaving us without notice to go with Ulam, to manufacture for him, who tries to hire our men. He (Ulam) comes into the house to get them away before we knew his tricks.

July 3: Called all hands at the warehouse together to say, if any desired to leave us and go to the new pickle factory [Watson, Ulam & Company], to get their pay and go and not deceive us through the dull season and go when things begin to be busy. Think it will have a good effect.

Told G. W. Hahn in presence of Brother John that he should have the same salary as last year and 2% of the profits of the business, all over $5,000, which we reserve for interest on the capital of the business. This he is to get provided he is faithful and remains until the end of the year.

July 9: Had my moustache shaved off for the first time in fourteen years. Seems quite odd.

On a vacation trip to Nantucket Island in July, "I paid $2 for two whale's teeth and various trinkets for home." These were the early pieces of a collection of "rare and curious objects" that was to grow and grow and become one of Heinz's consuming interests. In New York City on the way home, he and J. W. Ports "took a ride in the Elevated Cars, ten miles for five cents. This is one-half fare, because from 5:30 to 7 P.M., to help the work class to get home cheap."

August 13: Our nice buggy horse died with lung fever today. George Flaccus, Brother[-in-law] G. H. Praeger, Peter and Brother John finished him up during my absence. I trust this will be sufficient. This is the second one for them in this way. I lectured them, tried to prove to them that even horse racers seldom founder or hurt horses, but those who know little or nothing about horses do such things.

September 11: Laporte, Indiana. I began at 2 P.M. today to receive signers for the growing of pickles the coming year and had signers for 25 acres by 6 P.M. at 45 cents cash or 50 cents one-half cash, one-half January 15, 1881. This is ten cents more than last year.

September — (*Cleveland*): I saw a span of spotted mares, well matched, and inside of a half hour had tried and bought them. They will make a lovely span to advertise. Seven and eight years old, called Terastican Stock, for $250 each. Weight about 950 pounds each.

October 22: Trade good. Received new desk for my private office today. It is the Indianapolis Desk, a good one. Cost $175 but I got it with agent's discount off.

November 1: We are very busy. Sold and shipped over $20,000 worth of goods in October, little over last year's business. Trade very good. Have not been troubled much with Watson, Ulam & Co.

On November 2, presidential and general Election Day, Heinz voted for General James A. Garfield, Republican candidate, against General Winfield S. Hancock, Democrat, and that night joined a crowd at the Sharpsburg Station to watch the posting of the telegraphic returns. The next day: "A glorious victory is announced through all the press. The Pittsburgh *Commercial* heads a column by the words, GLORY TO GOD in large type."

November 8: The third of Reverend Waltz's children died of scarlet fever inside of two weeks. Very sad.

December 3: Brother Peter leaves for Cincinnati tonight to commence canvassing that city for the first time on bulk goods by wagon, in Peter's peculiar style but a very successful one. He surpasses all of our agents in this agency plan of introducing goods. We shipped him $1,200 worth of goods to Cincinnati and a span of spotted horses, new covered wagon, and harness by boat.

December 8: Brother John went up to Scott, the dentist, with Attorney John W. Hague to rescue a girl in our employ, as the dentist acted like a *crazy man.* An article in the city papers gave a statement saying Mr. H., which people took for me, as I am called the pickle man. This is very annoying to me, as Brother John so often gets into lawsuits, etc., but he is learning that it does not pay.

Heinz was now a member of the Sharpsburg school board. The borough, with a population of 3500, had 327 schoolchildren and a six-room schoolhouse. Part of the town hall was also being used to make a seventh room.

December 11: Spent one-half day at Public School as a director visiting. Talked to three of the rooms. This is pleasant work. God bless the children. I wish I was a child once more. My time is rapidly hastening away. [Heinz was thirty-six.]

On Christmas Day Heinz sent Mrs. Covode $100 on his debt to her and took Sallie and the children to spend a pleasant day at his mother's with John's family. "I see since we have fairly prospered in our business," he wrote, "I would make a number of useful Christmas presents. Sallie a set of knives and a fine large box stereopticon view, elegant for parlor, which Yeager asked $35 for. Bought it from Pitock for $15 as he was selling out."

He bought a hobbyhorse and a dog-shaped penny bank for Howard and for Irene and Clarence each a small iron safe (twelve by nine by seven inches) with a brass padlock "intended to last for life." He bought the safes, in a sentimental gesture, with $8 he had saved in a toy bank when he was fifteen years old, "which I turned over to the assignee when I was in financial trouble and he called me a fool for turning over relics and allowed it to me under state law." *

He made a careful list of gifts bought for family, relatives, and friends. ("This will prevent getting the same articles again.")

Henry Heinz Lewis, named after me, a $3.50 sled, 8 years old.
Father, 1 pair arctics.
Mother, 1 leather satchel and Sallie made her some mats.
Mary, Maggie, Lizzie, and Hettie, handkerchiefs.
Brother John, umbrella.
Brother Peter, pocketbook.

* Irene's safe is in Chicago today in the possession of her daughter, Sarah Given Larsen.

Brother Jacob, umbrella.

G. H. Praeger, brother-in-law, Cousin Fred, and Cousin William Miller, umbrellas.

Whips for drivers at warehouse and same at Sharpsburg, and a flagon bottle of Chow or Chili Sauce. All of the hands, over 125 in all, received either a five-pound pail of peach butter jelly or [illegible] of Chow Mixed or Chili Sauce, and the office force the same, except that we gave them some extra pickle goods a few days later.

February 7, 1881: at 7 P.M. young men and young ladies and teachers, about fifty in all, met at our house. At 7:40 we had three large sleds loaded. Mame Coyle, Mame Ziegler and Daisy Collier, Marsh Norton and Joseph Williams drove in the smaller sleigh and the horse ran off and threw all out and Daisy Collier fainted. But as soon as she came to she came into my sleigh with her sister Katie. All went on a success.

February 24: We had a good lecture at Grace Church tonight. Realized about $25 net. Subject: Modern Barbarisms. Irene, Clarence and I sold over one-third of all the tickets. This is the first of a course of three lectures.

February 26: Mrs. McClenen Brown delivered the second lecture in Grace Church. Subject: Our Girls. But we had a very poor audience. Sharpsburg people don't appreciate lectures.

March 5: Sallie takes Irene and Clarence to see Uncle Tom's Cabin played today.

March 8: I begin this day to have Irene practice [on the piano] 15 minutes after breakfast and 15 minutes just after school (at 4 P.M.) and 30 minutes after supper while I read the paper, and Clarence at the same time paints or writes or reads, which gives us a new system of study at home.

March 11: Mrs. Snider of Room No. 5 beat Mr. Koontz's Charley over the head at the Public School. Mr. Koontz is much provoked and will not allow Charley to go to Mrs. Snider.

Heinz appeared on May 31 with B. C. Christy, his attorney, in the office of the Registrar in Bankruptcy for a hearing on his application for discharge from bankruptcy. The charge

was heard that Heinz, Noble & Company in 1875 had allowed
T. C. Jenkins, Reymer Brothers, and Dilworth Brothers to take
goods from the premises after the petition in bankruptcy had
been filed. Heinz's defense was that the goods had been
bought and paid for several days earlier. He presented the
names of 152 creditors who had endorsed his petition and the
names of some thirty others to whom he had paid his share of
the Heinz-Noble debt. He was happy to find little opposition,
but during the ten days in which his creditors could file their
objections, Christy asked for $400 or $500 "to use as fees or as
he saw fit to quiet several and get me out of bankruptcy. I decided no. Honorably or not at all. This is and was quite a
temptation, as a small amount will quiet those who will fight
me. God help me to do right." Opposition was recorded and
his petition was denied.

June 22: This is the day of the Grocers Picnic. Our salesmen go
up in our wagon with the spotted ponies and four of our horses
haul up the band. I find about 10,000 people there, the greatest
in size I ever saw.

July 25: H. F. Dunham and I fished on the little Tionesta Creek
on the headwaters. We caught 23 trout and I was so badly bit-
ten by mosquitos I shall never forget it.

August 8: We put in a small telephone from my house to Father's this morning, a distance of 300 yards. Cost us about $10
all told, labor, etc.*

August 12: The clerks all get two weeks vacation.

October 11: We never saw such an amount of orders. Our trade
is very good. Not able to get orders filled and scarce see how to
ever catch up.

---

* The "speaking telephone" had been put into service in Pittsburgh in January
1878. The rent for the two sets was $50 a year. The first advertisement read,
"The telephone has ceased to be a novelty, and has become a recognized instrument for business purposes. Conversations may be carried on between stations several miles apart . . . NO SKILL WHATEVER is required in the use
of the instrument."

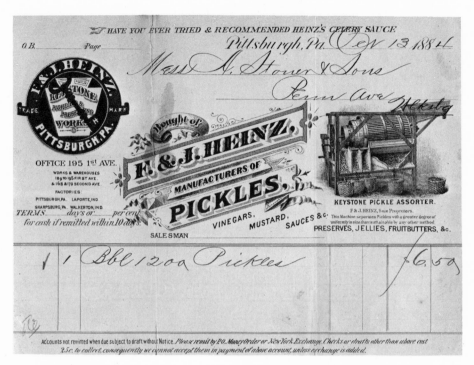

Candidate for the world's most ornate, that of F. & J. Heinz, 1884. The caption under the Keystone Pickle Assorter reads, "This Machine separates Pickles with a greater degree of uniformity in size than is attainable by any other method."

October 20: Shorthand writer, Mr. Lutz, began today. He writes 150 words per minute. Sorry I did not have one long ago as it facilitates work wonderfully. It helps me to get through as much correspondence in one hour as I could by telling others and doing part myself in five hours.

October 25: Trade very good. Employing 100 extra girls this week on citron and quinces for preserves.

January 9, 1882: We noticed Watson, Ulam & Co. putting its radish into our new flat, square American bottles made in our private mold. On the 12th we noticed that they had copied after us by adopting the same bottle. We at once consulted about patenting it and our Fancy Catsup and Dusseldorf Mustard.

January 12: I had all the wagon salesmen together in my room this 7 P.M. — a talk on temperance. The result — a handshake never to drink while in our employ. Took all to supper.

January 14: The five vinegar salesmen are so warmed up on the subject of temperance that they are about to organize a temperance society.

February 1: P. Keil, Jr. begins with us today. He is to do anything that is honorable and assist me at the home office or on the road, and to be at the warehouse at 7 A.M. and to 6 P.M. and make time count evenings or at any time, for which service we are to pay him at the rate of $1200 per annum and 2% of the entire profits of the business after deducting $10,000 for gardens or capital or both.

February 24: Had a talk with wagon salesmen and agreed to give them 5% on all wagon sales and 2½% on all orders in their line, instead of $1.50 per day and 5%.

March 8: Not feeling well. Took an electric vapor bath at Temperance House, Sharpsburg, which always seems to prove invigorating to me as well as an aid to circulation. I take them in place of the Turkish baths.

In October 1881 Heinz had bought a large, old house known as "the Roach property" on the hillside above Canal Street

near the schoolhouse. He paid $6000, with a down payment of
$1000. "Bought it for Sallie . . . It is a home for wife and
children while we are prospering and have no debts."
Throughout April he had a crew of carpenters, painters, plas-
terers, bricklayers, and laborers at work on remodeling. He
put in thirteen new single-pane window sashes ($6 each), three
slate mantels and a parlor heater ($211), and had a grainer
grain the woodwork in three rooms and a hall ($8). "We love
our new home," he wrote on May 1, "even though it is old-
fashioned. It is very comfortable and the location is delightful." But the first ceremony there was a sad one: a boy born
on May 23 died within two weeks — "our first death in our
family." Heinz stopped all business in the city and in Sharpsburg on the day of the funeral.

June 17: From 1:00 to 9:00 P.M., procession in Pittsburgh of
Labor and Mill Unions, or "Labor and Brains against Capital."
What folly.

August 11: Children are enjoying 2 and 3 months old goats in
our yard and grounds. Fun for the boys at the expense of the
goat.

August 28: Cleveland and home. Find all well and happy except
that Sallie has a very sore knee caused by running a race with
Maggie Keil and others at Cousin Kate Ingham's last Friday.

September 28: I feel overworked by working from 9 to 5 as fast
as I can go. So many things accumulated during my absence.
Am trying to take good care of myself. Retire from 9 to 10 P.M.
and sleep soundly until 7 A.M. Sound and plenty of sleep is
what keeps me up. Am trying to shift responsibilities on to others as rapidly as possible, which is a job to succeed in and make
it pay at the same time without working nearly as hard as if I
did it myself. As soon as I get them trained, it does help, but I
find it takes three or four people to do what I could do and did
myself when I had the strength.

October 4: Brother John and I had some words today in the office because he said he would not be limited as to when he re-

turned, when he went out, etc. We can't tell for hours where he is whether he will return that day or not. We both feel mortified but hope good results may follow, as the firm will now take action and mutually agree on some plan.

October 12: Irene and Clarence are both taking music lessons two times a week from Sister Hettie. Irene practices one hour each day and Clarence one-half hour each day. They dislike to practice.

November 16: Began today to pave the new brick sidewalk in front of the Roach property. Bought brick at $10.50 per thousand. I hauled them.

November 17: I helped and managed laying the pavement with a German helping me and H. F. Dunham assisting some. This is mental rest for me.

The diary for 1883 is missing and nothing is known of the events of that year except that a child, Clifford Stanton Heinz, was born on December 30. On January 8, 1884, Heinz made a major company investment; he bought "the old Crofford Foundry" in Allegheny to use as a vinegar factory. It measured 100 by 175 feet, cost $9000, and, unlike the plant on Second Avenue, was close to a main rail line. This was the core of the site he would choose five years later for what is still the Heinz factory complex.

January 22: We had our first conversation with five glassblowers to go into the glass business in our private office. My head was very tired tonight, so I took to sled riding after supper with my children in our lot on our road, 300 feet in length. This was quite a rest and settled my supper.

February 6 (Jacksonville): Go through town buying little things to take home. Six boxes of oranges at $2.75 for the best, Indian River, and $2 for the dark streaked kind. I expect to distribute them among my people at home. It is more pleasant to remember others than to be remembered.

February 14: Arrived at Jacksonville [from Saint Augustine] at 6 A.M., read and answered mail, and I left for Atlanta at 5:20 P.M.

Brother Peter and I had a good time and did not like to separate.

February 26: We had all my Sunday School officers and teachers at our house tonight. We had a nice time and enjoyed playing Scotch Carpet Ball and then changed to refreshments, including oranges brought from Florida.

March 6: We had a social gathering this evening. My sisters, brothers, and office boys and all the single men in the clerical force were out.

March 11: I paid Covodes the last I owed them of the Debt of Honor, $366.88, this being part of the interest. I feel quite glad my promise to Mr. Covode during his lifetime is fulfilled to his wife and children.

March 27: Brother Henry Praeger and I attend a Class in Elocution Monday and Thursday evenings. Began this evening.

April 17: Clarence's birthday today (11 years). Bought him his first watch, a Waterbury at $3.50. He is delighted. I scarce ever tell them what the presents cost.

May 15: Chicago. J. J. Wilson, my friend, hard up. I gave him a check for $500 to help him a little.

May 23: Bought a nice 1275-pound, seven-year bay mare. Saw her drive by, bought her inside of five minutes, $235. She will mate one we now have.

Visited Public School in the afternoon and wish I could be a school boy once more.

May 26: Closed our books. Did a profitable year's business. $43,000 are our net profits. Our sales were $381,000.

June 24: Philadelphia. Much pleased with R. M. Levering and the new place. Allowed him $100 extra for faithfulness and progress in management for a young man. Gave his salesmen a practical talk on selling goods, etc.

August 5: Finances are closer with all the banks than since the panic of 1873. We are now passing through a stock panic of 1884 caused by gambling in New York, principally, at least; that is where it had its beginning. Many private parties sleep on their few hundred dollars. A man came to me today and handed me $450 to take care of. He would not put it into the bank. He knew we laid in our stock this season of the year and could use it and would not risk the banks.

August 6: At home and through the gardens. Am pleased with our crop prospects of 150 acres on the Ross Estate. I have some anxiety in money affairs, having expended $20,000 on the new vinegar factory in Allegheny and the same amount in fruits and sugar for preserving and our bankers being close run and cannot extend us our usual loan at this season to pay for the pickle crop at Laporte and Walkerton, Indiana, where we require $40 to $50,000 inside of six weeks. It seems hard when we have $8 of assets for $1 of liabilities, but I expect to get through smoothly.

August 27: Contracted this day for one year for Bell Telephone, one for the Pittsburgh office and a private line to the Allegheny Factory, thence to my house (Sharpsburg), thence to Mother, thence to Brother John's. $525 for total cost of five instruments.

September 2: We are taking on several new clerks now. We hope to have them trained by the time we get busy the 1st of October. Five new ones in all from 17 to 22 years old. We start them at $6 and $7.50 per week and increase as they merit it.

September 8: Lice destroyed 40 acres of cabbage at Laporte, one full car load [remaining] in ¼ million heads planted and which looked splendid three weeks ago.

September 16: Chicago. Saw W. M. Johnson & Co. on the kraut question of last year, but find him extremely selfish on a small matter when I let him out on furnishing 200 and more barrels of kraut because his rotted. We bought imported at an advance cost to us of over $1,000. Such is life. Better to treat such matters on business principles and give the charity part to some poor.

September 21: Sunday. At church the death of Brother James Scott was referred to me and I was handed the collection basket, a duty which he had been performing. I felt his absence keenly. Came home, laid down, and applied a towel with ice water to my eyes for an hour and afterwards took dinner.

September 22: Philadelphia. Find affairs in bad shape. The bookkeeper's cash was short $1200. Levering carried a key to the cash drawer as well as the bookkeeper. The Father or bondsman of the bookkeeper paid us $850 and L. paid the balance on a note. But we find running after women and neglecting his own mother, wife and children, as well as his business, is all the curse of too many women and we are compelled to make a change. Women when a man has a family are worse than *Drink*.

September 27: Ports, Hopkins, and all the office boys, 20 in all, had their pictures taken in front of the Homeopathic Hospital. Each desired one or more to frame.

October 11: This is my 40th birthday. I feel as though I have just entered on the other side, crossed the line of middle life. Children presented me with socks, Sallie with a pair of elegant otter gloves.

October 22: Very sleepy and flat this A.M. after dissipating in the way of marshalling the Sharpsburg division [in a political parade] and on horseback 4½ hours. Will see that some others have such honors in the future.

November 1: The Parade by the Republicans today was a success. It required 3½ hours to pass a given point. We had eighteen two-horse wagons in line and two aids on horseback. I have not time to comment.

November 4: Election Day. All quiet. Success still doubtful but we hope for Blaine. We have telegraph reports at our Sharpsburg Station tonight. We never allow ourselves to talk or to influence our men in politics.*

November 5: A. Wood leaves with a nice new span of bay horses, harness, and peddling wagon for Cleveland. He drives all the way [150 miles]. It requires usually three days. Such an outfit as the above costs us $1,000, but it pays to start right.

November 15: I am extremely busy. I give up the idea of depending on Brother John to be regular anywhere. Instead of me going to the city at 9:00 A.M. and John at 6:15 to look after the

* Grover Cleveland, Democrat, defeated James G. Blaine, Republican, by a margin of 62,683 popular votes.

hands, etc., I go at 7:45 and John either on the 7:45 but oftener on the 8:10 or 9 train. I am in consequence worked as hard as I was four years ago, but hope to manage to get along and not depend on him except to look after the machinery and direct the vinegar man.

December 14 (New York): Visited Henry Ward Beecher's Sunday School at Plimoth Church and heard him preach in the evening to a full house, 2,500 people. A man of wonderful mind but he ought to be a *Unitarian*.

December 22: During the past six weeks, the Westinghouse Gas Co. has been laying a 12-inch gas pipe along Main Street and through Etna to Allegheny for family supply, and are now beginning to lay a 20-inch line for factory supplies. At least part of this gas is to be brought from the Murraysville wells and some may be brought from Tarentum. The Westinghouse Co. has a capital of several millions. All this is but of very recent enterprise, within one or two years. Since natural gas is found near Pittsburgh, it no doubt will be a great thing for the city.

December 25: I presented Sallie with a seal sack (39 inches long) for Christmas. Paid $175 for it. A set collar and muff for our hired girl for $5. One pair of shoes for nurse, $2.

December 31: At 4 o'clock New Year's morning we were serenaded by a brass band. After partaking of lunch, I handed each one a jar of pickles for their New Year's dinner and a happy wish for the New Year and we retired.

January 5, 1885: I had five hours drill with our salesmen today. Warm them up, etc. It exhausts me very much.

January 13: The Natural Gas Explosion at the Mill Store in Sharpsburg occurred at 11 A.M., and blew the store to atoms, all a complete wreck. A young man at the door was knocked out on the sidewalk but escaped serious injury. The store had been closed for some time as well as the mill. There was no gas in the store but was caused by a leak in the line nearby. The citizens held an indignation meeting the same evening. Westinghouse himself was present and agreed to put in all safety appliances and vent pipes so that any leaking gas may pass off. Families say they won't have it. My opinion is, inside of two years we will all have it, if we can get it.

On February 3, Heinz's application for discharge in bankruptcy came up again, this time before the United States District Court at Pittsburgh. "My enemies," Heinz wrote, "had no case at all. The judge set them down every now and then. The case went to the jury at 2:45 P.M. and returned a verdict of not guilty. The court sustained us because there was no wrong motive and could not prevent my discharge, as I had witnesses that I had declined to allow anyone to have goods. Sallie and Mother are very happy over the result, and I thank God I am once more a free man."

Two months later Heinz received word from Peter, once again in Washington, that he was about to be married. "I at once had F. J. Grubbs leave to get him away, as the lady would not be an acceptable one to us or to him either. He likes Grubbs and he can do fully as well as anyone with him." Grubbs did bring Peter safely home — "snatched him away from where he was about to be married. P. J. escaped this time." Within two weeks Peter left for a long stay in Germany, where it was hoped that the springs and baths would help his rheumatism.

April 6: Brother Jacob is now looking after the hands early in the morning and sees them started at their work instead of Brother John, who fails to get there. Brother John is successful in being behind time but is good at machinery and vinegar making.

April 23: Fire in Sharpsburg at 12:15 this early morning. The town fire bell rang. We saw quite a fire, we supposed in Etna. We retired and this morning found eleven houses, the entire block from Main to Clay Street and from Church Alley and Tenth. We hope this will stimulate the old fogies to vote for a water works, which they have opposed.

May 6: Bought a nice black 1200-pound family horse for Mother today for $175.

May 20: Working up a list of H. N. & Co. Pittsburgh creditors and began again to pay, some cash, some goods.

May 27: We set up a new five-foot (Roman) terracotta vase in our front lawn and surrounded it by a bed of colies and other flowers.

May 28 (Adrian, Michigan): I left for the west on the 11 A.M. train after presenting my hostess with a case of assorted pickles.

July 3: Very busy training salesmen how to talk vinegar. My assistant can't warm them up on the subject. Unless you charge a grocer a fair price for quality he will not appreciate the goods.

July 27: Chautauqua. We listened to a lecture on Electric Light, Autophone, and Telephone.

August 10: Watson Covode called today to loan him $500. I had no money and he does nothing about what he now has borrowed from me.

August 13: Clarence [twelve] and Howard [eight] go to the city with me to begin to work 5 or 6 hours per day in the office and factory instead of all play.

September 30: Finally settled up with R. M. Levering today. We were compelled to dissolve the partnership. He was ruining the Philadelphia agency with running after women and extravagance and negligence. He promises to do better if we allow him to work for us, which we agree to if he will do right.

October 8: Loaned Mrs. Jacob Covode $100 by note at four months.

November 12: Sallie has a number of young folks in at our house tonight, now practising for the coming concert. Sallie has charge of the wax figures, etc. She is quite young in disposition.

November 13: Had a talk at Mother's this evening asking Brother John to be at his post at 7:00 A.M. He seems quite indifferent about coming out to start his department and thinks it will run anyway. We all talk kindly, Fred, Brother John, and Mother. It may bring better results, I hope.

November 25: Natural gas turned on in our home and in Mother's.

December 6: Our church is heated with gas and it is a success. Cost but $45 for the first year.

December 8: Working hard to catch up with accumulated work during my absence. If I could stand as much or as many hours of brain work in rapid succession as I could ten years ago, when I would work 17 hours per day for a week. A short time, but 10 hours is enough now, and I do more in that time than any man we have.

December 9: I solicited life memberships at $100 each in Pittsburgh toward the erection of a new Exposition Building. Each of the 13 directors have a book.

December 11: At our meeting today they said I had more names than all put together, including our secretary, Mr. Siebeneck, whose business it is to canvass. We pay him $3,000 a year. I did more in five hours than he in a week. Luck means well directed work.

December 15: Taking German lessons this evening. Sallie and our three oldest and doing well. Two times per week.

December 27 (Sunday): The Church was beautifully decorated with evergreens and plants and some flowers. Had a large cross with gas jets burning on one side and a star burning on the other side.

CHAPTER 6

Innocence Abroad, or, Mr. and Mrs. Heinz on the Grand Tour

Cooking is one of those arts which most require to be done by persons of a religious nature.

Dialogues of Alfred North Whitehead, 1954

THE FAMILY GERMAN LESSONS were part of the preparations for a long-planned pilgrimage to Europe.

Henry Heinz was manager and half owner of a company whose letterhead now showed vegetable farms at Pittsburgh and La Porte; three packing houses and factories in or near Pittsburgh and two in Indiana; and branch houses in twelve major American cities. The business was running so well that he could safely leave for a three-month tour in Europe. He would make some business calls, visit relatives in Germany, and have the children examined by German doctors, then pre-eminent in medicine. The children would see the land of their paternal grandparents. He would see the birthplace of his father and mother and of the Reformed Lutheran Church. Sallie would go to a German spa and take the baths for the severe pains of sciatic rheumatism in her left leg.

On the evening of Tuesday, May 25, 1886, Henry and Sallie Heinz, sister Mary Heinz, sister-in-law Lizzie Praeger,* and the four children — Irene, fourteen, Clarence, thirteen, Howard, eight, and Clifford, two — assembled at the new Union

* Lizzie's brother, George Henry Praeger, had married Maggie Heinz and bought one third of Fred Heinz's interest in the company in 1879.

Depot in Pittsburgh to embark on the journey. Going to Europe was an undertaking of some importance in 1886. Henry's mother was there to bid them goodbye, as were his mother-in-law, his other three sisters, assorted other relatives and friends, and some thirty men from the plant, including John and Fred Heinz, an H. E. Pfusch, a Moses Meyers, and Joseph Hite, who, apparently having controlled his growling and swearing, was now second-in-charge of the company stables. The Reverend Ezra Morgan Wood, D.D., LL.D., pastor of the North Avenue M. E. Church of Allegheny City, who had married Henry and Sallie seventeen years earlier and was now their closest friend, mounted a baggage truck on the station platform and delivered a farewell address.° One of the company executives then read a resolution signed by thirty-four employees: ". . . recognizing his laborious services and his need of rest and recuperation, do hereby express our earnest wish that he and his family and company on their European tour may have a restful and enjoyable time and that a kind providence may have them all in his safekeeping." Heinz made an appropriate response, after which the party of eight boarded the 9:00 P.M. train for Jersey City.

The *City of Berlin* was a paddle-wheel vessel, the second largest of the Inman Line, the first German steamer to cross the Atlantic in the passenger trade. The Heinz party boarded her on a Saturday afternoon bearing some purchases Henry had made that morning: six folding chairs, two dozen lemons, and six dozen oranges. In their luggage were blankets and in the hold five packing cases of Heinz products. They had two large staterooms with a bathroom adjoining, and they occupied one family table of their own at meals.

Heinz enthusiastically wrote down in his diary the statistics one must know and record on such an occasion. He noted that

° Dr. Wood was the best-known divine of the Methodist Episcopal Church in the Middle Atlantic states. At the time of President Lincoln's funeral he delivered a sermon that made him nationally famous.

the ship was 488 feet long, 44 feet wide, and 34 feet deep. She displaced 5470 tons, had 900 horsepower, consumed 900 tons of coal every twenty-four hours, and was 11 years old. Her main mast was 180 feet high. She had 12 boilers, 36 furnaces, and 40 firemen, 11 of the men firing constantly and being relieved every four hours. There were 82 other crewmen. There were 422 passengers — 157 saloon, 125 intermediate, and 140 steerage. Liverpool, their destination, was 3160 miles from New York.

He wrote little essays on the system of watches, the method of determining speed, the significance of the Gulf Stream, and the life story of Captain F. S. Land. (Land had been thirty-one years at sea, nine years a captain, and in January 1883 had been struck by another vessel, losing his ship but no lives.) The officers were courteous and attentive. The passengers were "largely English, Scotch and Irish. Some Italians and French. The latter are quite fastidious." He did not see or did not comment on another passenger, Madame Lillian Nordica, the great operatic soprano (born Lillian Norton in Farmington, Maine), whose voice, beauty, and magnificent stature made her an ideal Brünnhilde. But a Colonel J. H. Mapleson was aboard with a troupe of singers. He had left his wife at home and "takes much interest in Madame Tota, one of the singers, who is a *live* one." The voyage lasted eight days.

In three days spent in Liverpool, Heinz was fascinated by the bathing machines on the beaches — little houses on wheels, drawn into the sea by horses. He was astonished by the immense size and weight of the draft horses and by the clumsiness of the carts, trucks, and wagons. He admired the display of specialties in the windows of the grocery, butcher, and bakery shops, but "saw no pickle displays to signify." He concluded, "I have learned little in this city which I can utilize in America to advantage."

In London, Heinz had engaged rooms at Madame Terby's, No. 70 Great Russell Street, directly opposite the British Mu-

6/18/86

London England

I drove 7 Hours to day with W. O. Cameron Clarance & Howard (while the Ladies were shoping)

I called an Broker & our Glass Men, pickle Men. I find Cross & Blackwells an Immense House. I was shown through Sir Robt Barnetts malt vinegar factory. Purchased 2 Casks of 120 Gal cask of their 24 @ 1-4^s^{d} for Eng Gal.

1st Sale in England

I then Called an Fortnum Mason & Co. I sold them 7 varieties of our finest & newest goods this being the largest House Suppling

A page from the diary of H. J. Heinz, June 18, 1886.

seum: three bedrooms and a large front sitting room for sixty shillings a week, which included meals, the Heinzes furnishing the food and Madame Terby the cooking and service. Another American, the bibliophile Alfred Edward Newton, having visited London about the same time, described the city so:

> The London of the eighteen-eighties was a much noisier and a far more crowded city than now [1925]. The streets were narrower and fewer . . . The noise of tens of thousands of horse-drawn vehicles made a confused and ceaseless roar, as of distant waves breaking upon a rocky shore. The streets were brilliantly lighted with gas lamps and alive with people surging in every direction; most men wore silk hats and carried canes: the poorer class looked very poor indeed and wore caps; soldiers, gayly dressed, with tiny round caps about the size of pill boxes, held on over one ear by a narrow strap, carrying canes about as thick as a lead pencil and two feet long, were everywhere in evidence.

For this city Henry Heinz developed an affection that was to bring him back year after year for three decades to come.

On their first full day, a Sunday, all eight drove to the Wesleyan City Road Chapel, attended morning service in the church built by John Wesley in 1777, and had the honor of sitting at Charles Wesley's reading desk and in John Wesley's chair ("I felt I was upon holy ground"). He led his family in a procession to the Bunhill Fields Burying Ground opposite the chapel and there copied the inscription from John Bunyan's tombstone and viewed the graves of Thomas Cromwell, Richard Cromwell ("He lacked mental capacity"), Susannah Wesley, Dr. Isaac Watts, Daniel Defoe, and John Wesley, from whose gravesite he plucked a small white pebblestone.

Heinz despaired of seeing "even one half of the principal places of interest" in London in two weeks' time, but he did his best. In the days that followed, attended by those of his group who were not exhausted, he:

visited and addressed a class at a Free Methodist Sunday School, taking notes on the method of teaching;

drove through Regent's Park ("alive with people") and Hyde
Park, watched part of a cricket match, and spent a half day in
the Zoological Gardens, the children taking three-minute rides
on a white camel and a large elephant;

drove around "the Queen's home, or Buckingham Palace"
("It is quite a plain structure, much in the style of the White
House in the U.S.A., but much larger")*;

visited the Old Jail, Saint Bartholomew's Hospital, the "Blue
Coat School" for boys, the British Museum and Library; the
National Gallery, the Prince Albert Memorial ("On the whole
it is the grandest affair I ever saw and must have cost millions"), the Colonial and Indian Exhibit at Albert Hall ("the
finest exhibition I ever saw"), the Museum of Natural History,
and the Smithfield Poultry and Dead Cattle Market;

attended a noon meeting of the Young Men's Christian Association;

rode ten miles on the train to see the transplanted Crystal
Palace and watch the Great Fireworks Display (Mount Vesuvius, Niagara Falls, and rockets fired from balloons);

stood through a service at Westminster Abbey and copied
the inscription on the tablet placed there to honor John and
Charles Wesley;

visited the Houses of Parliament, "a beautiful structure and
very large. We could only take a passing glance as it required
an order to see the interior, which is owing to several attempts
in blowing up the prominent buildings in London. They have
officers examine satchels and packages as they pass into the
Abbey, much to the annoyance of the ladies, but the officers
are clever and kind and very courteous."

These were times when certain preachers had "star quality,"
attracted large followings, sold enormous editions of their ser-

---

* A British acquaintance suggests that Heinz saw the rear façade of the palace, then exposed to public view and not unlike a larger White House.

mons, and became some of the best-known personalities of their day. Heinz went to hear two such divines. One was Dr. Joseph Parker (1830–1902), nonconformist pastor of the City Temple in Holborn Viaduct. ("He is a very peculiar sermonizer, but a good reasoner. He is interesting to listen to, but not to look upon.") The other was Dr. Charles Haddon Spurgeon (1834–1892), leader of the Baptist community, author of fifty volumes of sermons, and the most popular of all nonconformist preachers. They went to his Metropolitan Tabernacle.

We arrived at ¼ after 6. We were all handed envelopes in which we placed our contributions and after passing through the iron gate we dropped them into a box placed there for that purpose. As we came to the center aisle we were with others requested to remain standing until 6:25. Exactly at that time a bell sounded and all were permitted to occupy the vacant seats. Before 6:30 the house and aisles were filled and standing room. Even in the two large galleries standing room was at a premium.

The church seats 6,000 people and most times many can't gain admittance.

Promptly at 6:30 Mr. Spurgeon stepped forward and began by a short prayer. Then announced a hymn, read one verse, emphasizing the lines. They then sang, the leader standing on the left of Mr. Spurgeon. Mr. Spurgeon then talked 10 minutes on the scripture he had just read.

After singing again and making a very impressive and powerful prayer, he proceeded at his sermon, which lasted 40 minutes. Addressing the unconverted to quiet meditation and reading the word and repenting of our sins, etc. At the close we were all introduced to Mr. Spurgeon by one of the elders.

I was impressed that he is the humblest, simplest, great preacher I ever met. A child can approach him. He is whole souled to strangers and all alike. He began to preach at 16 and is now 52 but looks like a 60-year-old man in his walk and actions while conversing, but not over 52 in the pulpit.

In the course of his business calls, Heinz visited food brokers, glass manufacturers, a pickle factory, a malt vinegar factory, and the offices of Crosse & Blackwell ("an immense house"). On Friday, June 18, he brushed his whiskers, donned his best frock coat (made for him in Philadelphia by an English tailor), and put on a shiny new top hat. He took up a Gladstone bag containing "Seven varieties of our finest and newest goods," hailed a hansom cab on Great Russell Street, and directed it to a number on Piccadilly Street. He was about to call on "the largest House supplying the fine trade of London and suburbs and even shipping." The gold letters on the window over the coat of arms read, "Fortnum & Mason," and below it, "Purveyor to the Queen."

He had no letter of introduction, no name to ask for. There was, he had learned, no Mr. Fortnum and no Mr. Mason. A salesman, he must have known, should be calling, bowler hat in hand, at the service entrance, but he grasped his Gladstone bag, marched through the Georgian doorway, and announced in a firm American voice that he was there to see the Head of Grocery Purchasing. That gentleman appeared with an inquiring look. Heinz introduced himself: a food merchant from Pittsburgh in the United States of America. He began his well-rehearsed presentation. At the proper moment he whipped open his bag and displayed his goods. The Head surveyed the seven products, tasted the horseradish, the ketchup, the chili sauce. Heinz readied himself to meet the expected rebuff with the prepared counterattack. He was astonished and perhaps a little bit let down to hear the Head say, "I think, Mr. Heinz, we will take all of them."

He began the story in his diary, "1ST SALE IN ENGLAND" and ended it, "Having thus succeeded without even an introduction in opening a way for our goods on this side of the pond, I was highly delighted." Perhaps it was on that day that Important Idea Number Four was born, or at least firmly rooted: Our market is the world.

Heinz led his women and children at the end of June across the channel and on to Paris, where he engaged four rooms at the Hotel Dijon for forty francs per day, three meals included but "candles extra." Five days later, he proceeded on to Strasbourg and thence to Wildbad in the Black Forest. There the three women consulted a physician and settled in with Irene and Clifford for a month of bath town therapy. "We could lodge cheaper," he wrote, "but we have good living and no responsibility, so we all feel contented, and when any of us are away they deduct. We are delighted with the place. People from all parts are here."

He took Clarence to doctors in Wiesbaden and Heidelberg for treatment of various ailments; they gave him gas, pulled a tooth, filled a tooth, syringed his nose, cured a running ear, and removed his tonsils and adenoids. ("I had to turn away; it looked worse than sticking a pig . . . He can already breathe better than for years . . . Our Pittsburgh doctors could do him no good.") He enrolled Clarence and Howard in Professor Kroenlein's private school in Heidelberg and he then set off at his customary dogtrot on a round of visits and errands.

Through his diary we see him making detailed notes on the methods used on the small family farms, on the building of roads, on the wages paid in various occupations, on the school system, on the forms of church services in the different denominations. He sees more soldiers in uniform than in any other country he has visited and wonders if Germany is not overtaxed to support them. He is shocked by the disfiguring Heidelberg facial scars. He makes a practice of always purchasing something in any store he lingers in, "as these Germans would be displeased at our American ways of shopping." He cannot decide to buy a hand-carved cuckoo clock; "they are elegant but we think they would seem too *much* and we would grow tired of it."

At Pforzheim, where some 455 companies make jewelry, he observes a program supported jointly by the companies for training and educating employees.

At Durlach he tours a Singer Sewing Machine factory that employs 800 hands.

At Frankfurt am Main he visits the Goethe House, the cathedral, and a small picture gallery ("a miserable collection").

At Mainz he calls on the country's finest manufacturer and largest exporter of conserves. He visits a government meat-processing plant but is not permitted to view the operation. ("They are very conservative in any matters which pertain to the army.") He inspects the ruins of the Roman aqueduct and from it collects several pieces of stone. He interviews a man who has answered his advertisement for someone experienced in the manufacture of conserves. The man knows nothing of manufacturing conserves, but he thinks he could learn, and he wants very much to go to America. ("Well!!")

At Worms he observes a service in a very old synagogue, the men on one side in tall silk hats and singing, the women on the other side in bonnets and silent. He visits Dr. Luther's church and memorial monument.

At Cologne (reached by boat ride down the Rhine) he studies the cathedral and the produce market and is shown through the factory of Stolwerk Brothers, the country's largest producer of confectionery and candies (600 hands). He arranges with this company to handle Heinz specialties in Germany.

He visits Amsterdam, the Hague, Brussels, Rotterdam, and Antwerp. At Amsterdam ("most of the principal streets are water") he observes the boatloads of "the finest cauliflower in the known world," and he goes into the cauliflower district to see "how they plant, cultivate and salt it." He buys 200 casks for shipment to Pittsburgh. With a Dutch acquaintance he visits the bourse.

> I see more people than in Chicago or any other country. Each member seems to have some particular spot on the floor where he can be seen. We find representatives from all parts of the

world, representing the various stocks. The Jews are said to have a strong grip on the important products of the country and are looked upon as smart business people.

They make a small charge for visitors to enter. They have 4000 members. It is unlike the U.S. Board in that everything is bought and sold here, merchandise, stocks, etc.

He encounters a political riot:

Socialistic and fishermen's rebellious spirit cropped out yesterday and the result was the most fatal ever known in Holland. It is continued today with even more fatal results.

It appears it has been the custom of the fishermen in Amsterdam to have an annual jubilee by stretching a line across the water of one of the main canals and hanging thereon an awl fish (large one) alive and grease it with soap. Then they would get into small boats and pass rapidly under this line and jump up and catch on to the fish, hoping to capture it into their boat, but in the attempt their hold would usually slip and the man would fall into the water, and those on the shore would enjoy it.

This mode of spending the day had been forbidden, as it was considered barbarous to treat a live fish in this manner. They, however, persisted in having their fun, when the police interfered by cutting down the line, letting the fish into the water.

The following day (26th July) they followed it up. When a large police force sought to stop the sport, fishermen and Socialists tore up the paved street and wounded many of the police. Two regiments of soldiers were soon on hand to quell the riot. 24 were killed while 9 were wounded. 5 of the wounded were policemen.

Heinz arranged in Antwerp for his return passage to England, took the night train to Heidelberg, and was greeted there by his two sons, "who are seemingly quite contented and making progress." At Wildbad he found Sallie almost cured of her rheumatic troubles. To celebrate, they bought two hand-carved cuckoo clocks.

The last ten days of the German stay held three momentous events.

He and his sister Mary started out on August 2 to visit Father Heinz's birthplace and relatives in a group of communities about two hours train ride from Heidelberg. They made their headquarters at a hotel in Dürkheim, ("This town has a salt water spring and a grape cure. People come to eat several pounds of grapes per day and thus renovate the system.") They engaged there a two-horse carriage and began to tour the countryside. They called on two of their father's sisters, his oldest brother, his aunts and uncles, his nieces and nephews, his cousins, and *their* various wives, husbands, and children. Word spread that the rich American cousins of the Heinzes were in town, and the calls and visits multiplied, including several from young cousins eager to go to America and willing to work for Cousin Henry. At Kallstadt they visited the family homestead, now occupied by a George Heinz, stepbrother of Sebastian Mueller, a Heinz company employee and first cousin who was courting their sister Elizabeth back in Sharpsburg.

> We were much *impressed.* Seventy-four years ago Father was born in this, then a large, commodious home built in the 14th century. There is a large open court leading to the garden and into the wine cellar, which was built in 1529. I rested well in the old home. Eleven rooms. Arose joyfully, calling to memory many incidents connected with the family. As near as we could count, we find a total of over 100 relatives in Kallstadt.

Sister Mary separated from Henry to visit still another of their father's sisters. His ride back to Heidelberg required two hours of waiting for four changes of cars. "The chief objection to travel in this country," he wrote, "is the frequent change of cars and connections except on through routes." It was, with an acid comment on the cab drivers in Cologne, the nearest he came in three months of travel to expressing annoyance or dissatisfaction.

Heidelberg was on the point of celebrating the five-hundredth anniversary of its university, founded by Elector Rupert I in 1386, and the Heinz family assembled on August 6 with five friends and relatives to view the culmination of the Jubilee — the Grand Procession and the Castle Lighting. Heinz had taken rooms in a hotel fronting on the Neckar River opposite the castle and had engaged "a large window" for thirty marks from which to watch the events.

The streets were crowded on the great day, with wooden seats erected along the route of the Jubilee Procession and cables stretched along the curbs. The Heinz party took their seats at the window at 8:30 A.M., a half-hour early, and spent most of the day watching "a very elegant display of costumes and personages." Their relatives dined with them and then left to return to Kallstadt, since no lodgings were to be had at any cost. The six piers of the Old Bridge (erected 1788) were lighted with bonfires and fireworks. ("The reflection on the water and the boat with music passing under it at the time added to a beautiful sight.") The students and male visitors made merry until 3 A.M. with band music, singing, wine-drinking, and speechmaking in a *Fest Halle* erected for the purpose, no ladies being admitted.

The next evening, people stood shoulder-to-shoulder in the streets; carriages were unable to move. The Neckar was lined with hundreds of anchored boats. The ruins of the grandest and largest of the old castles in Germany, looming 330 feet above the Neckar, was ablaze with light for ten whole minutes. With the return to darkness, fireworks went up from the Old Bridge. The effect was so grand, Heinz wrote, that even little Clifford was speechless.

The next day Heinz led his own procession northward toward Antwerp, Liverpool, and home. They stayed for two days at the Hotel Victoria in Wiesbaden, where they met Peter J. Heinz. Brother Peter was there by arrangement "with his intended and her relatives." She was a Fräulein Pauline Merz, of whom Henry noted approvingly, "she is smart and of good family and well to do." Herr Merz (occupation not given) invited all of them to stay in his home, but they compromised on a family dinner. During the course of the evening, Henry conferred privately with Mr. and Mrs. Merz, which resulted in an honorable if foolhardy action: "I tell them plainly how P.J. is so that no reflections can be made." The Merzes professed to be aware of Peter's shortcomings and still approved the marriage.

The next day, Henry and Sallie shopped for presents for the bride and bridegroom: "P.J. a pair of fancy foxhead slippers, 20 marks, a fine album, 35 marks, a work basket, 21 marks, and Irene artificial flowers for 3 marks, total 79 marks, and sent them to the house." They called that evening to make their farewells and express their regrets that they could not remain for the wedding four days hence. Henry asked Peter to go with Mary to visit their mother's sole remaining relative in Germany, a niece, and paid their expenses for the trip. He gave Peter a present of 250 marks and a loan of 600 more with which to pay his fare back to America.

Lizzie Praeger and Mary stayed for the wedding; the other Heinzes traveled down the Rhine to Cologne, thence to Brussels, Antwerp, and London. At Liverpool they discovered that a trunk they had expressed from Paris had been sent on to New York. ("A very unpleasant affair to our ladies. Each had some of their Paris purchases in it.") They boarded the *City of Chester* anchored midway in the River Mersey. A few hours before she departed, the tender came out and delivered Lizzie, Mary, and Mr. and Mrs. Peter Heinz.

On the fourth day out on an eleven-day voyage, Sallie Heinz came to a considered judgment that reversed an earlier opinion. Heinz recorded it in his diary: "Clifford gives us more care than the other three children. Sallie is now convinced that it does not pay to travel with children."

CHAPTER 7

"I Agree to Take the Full Generalship"

The Founder always tried to place a nervous driver behind a pair of lazy horses, and a slow-going driver behind a nervous horse.

Sebastian Mueller, in a speech
to company employees,
February 9, 1926

EIGHTEEN EIGHTY-SEVEN is a year in which the company expands and prospers. On January 29 Heinz laments that he is working too hard but must continue "to keep our growing business from getting ahead of us." On March 21 he writes, "This will finish our shipments of horseradish roots; the largest crop we ever had, averaged about $90 a ton." On June 16 he buys five more horses at $240 to $275 each, making seventy head in all, thirty-six of them in the city stables. On July 20 he visits the recently opened New York office at 420 Greenwich Street and finds the manager "late as usual . . . besides taking our time to look after business for others and absenting himself." He discharges the manager. On August 17 he installs a machine at La Porte for cleaning onions and horseradish roots.

August 25: "Pickle cucumbers are coming in at the rate of 15,000 bushels a week at Walkerton and 7,000 at Laporte, the product of 12,100 acres." October 4: He has fifty to sixty girls working at the vinegar factory in Allegheny and complains that he cannot get enough help. November 4: He stumbles on "a rare chance" at Pittsburgh's East End stockyards — twenty-five railroad carloads of manure, totaling 1750 tons, which "was in their way and they gave it to us for taking it. Cost 38 cents per ton to freight it to our Ross farm." November 5: He reports that October sales were over $100,000, a record high for any month in any year.

Brother John, who had been an annoyance for his irregular hours, has now become a serious problem in company operations. In April:

> In order to induce Brother John to go to the city on the early train I start out to volunteer to do so at any time he is not well or has something else on hand. We are behind in the manufacturing department in which he manages. I am overworked, but the trouble in this one particular — to get him to see the importance of promptness — has been for ten years more than all other annoyances combined, and I believe because of what I am experiencing is and has been driving more nails in my coffin than all other cares. I have a right to expect better. I have always taken pleasure in helping him, yet he returns this great ingratitude.

On May 2 he goes to the city on the 6 A.M. train "to encourage Brother John." Brother John is not noticeably encouraged, for Brother Henry soon writes, "The more I take on, the more John slackens up." In June there is a shift of responsibilities:

> Brother John seems to realize that the Manufacturing Department at Pittsburgh and Allegheny is too much. I agree to take the full generalship and he to assist me and he to remain in the factory. I take full charge of the vinegar factory as well as all other matters, gardens, agencies, etc. I can manage all with less friction, keeping ahead of the work, than if being behind . . . God helping me, I expect to fully succeed.

The Heinzes had been shocked on their return from Europe to be met at the Jersey dock by the New York manager with word that Jacob, the youngest of the four brothers, lay ill of typhoid fever in a Philadelphia hotel. They took him with them to the family homestead, where he died within a few

days. It was, Henry said, "a hard blow, the saddest of my life."
Another followed five months later when Sister Maggie, the
wife of George H. Praeger, gave birth to a son and died of
blood poisoning within the week. All the family was at the
deathbed; almost all the adult relatives, requiring fifteen carriages, attended the funeral. A note in the diary reads: "Oh,
what a season of rejoicing when Brother Jacob and she meet
on the other side of the river!" Sister Mary, who never married, reared the Praeger children.

In January 1888 Frederick Heinz, who now owned one ninth
of the company, proposed that Cousin Henry buy one half of
his interest at book value — $16,666. The sale and transfer
were made.

The problem of John came to a head six months later. Anna
Margaretha Heinz summoned her son to the family homestead. Henry was with her. She told John that if some
friendly and mutually satisfactory agreement on running the
company could not be worked out, she and Henry would withdraw within thirty days. John could sell his one-sixth interest
to the company and step out, or he could have his choice of
some branch of the company, run it himself, and "let the rest
who see nearer alike go on with the business." Three arbitrators would be chosen to work out a settlement that would protect everyone's interests.

As his representative, Henry Heinz named G. W. Hahn,
who in 1880 had been made one of those who shared in the
company's profits — 2 percent of net income, amounting to
$200 in that year. The company named Harlow French Dun-
ham, a family friend, resident of Sharpsburg, member of the
Grace Church, who had joined the company in 1878 and now
was in charge of all salting houses. Heinz thought of him as "a
very true and trustworthy man and more, a Christian gentleman." Hahn and Dunham selected Dr. E. M. Wood as the
third member. After talking with John and his attorney, the

arbitrators deferred further action in the hope that the family could arrive at an amicable settlement.

A meeting was held at the family homestead on August 2 with John, Henry Praeger, and H. F. Dunham present, Mother Heinz presiding. Everyone advised John to take over and run the vinegar factory as his own, or the preserving factory, or the factory and gardens at La Porte. John preferred to sell his interest and withdraw, but he asked 20 to 25 percent over book value for good will. The other partners declined to pay for good will. A week later John asked for an outright payment of $60,000. He finally accepted the book value as shown on April 1, 1888, and his share of the profits to August 1 — a total of $57,000. The papers were signed and "all closed pleasantly and mutually satisfactory and a good feeling prevails ... All is now amicably settled between Brother John and our firm. He has sold out to us rather than divide, and we have paid him well in order to close up amicably."

On November 1, 1888, at the suggestion of Anna Heinz, the firm name was changed to H. J. Heinz Company. Notice was duly sent to all names on the company's books. On behalf of the firm, Henry Praeger presented Mr. Dunham with a gold watch "for his loyalty and wise counseling and as a peacemaker."

Heinz now applied himself to an ambitious project he had been discussing and planning for many months.

He had been deeply affected by the railroad strike and riots of 1877 and remembered that public sympathy at first had been with the strikers. He read and heard of the discontent among local steelworkers that was shortly to break out in the bloody Homestead strike. He had studied the orderly, progressive, benevolent paternalism of the German factories and resolved to build a community of "workpeople" who would feel so happy on the job and so privileged as Heinz employees that they would never dream of striking or rioting. This was Heinz

Idea Number Five and he expressed it so: "Humanize the business system of today and you will have the remedy for the present discontent that characterizes the commercial world and fosters a spirit of enmity between capital and labor."

He would begin by placing the Allegheny and Pittsburgh offices and factories "under one head" in a group of buildings outstanding for their utility and architectural beauty. He would build a model industrial complex "equipped with every device of mechanical or scientific character that may be used to advantage" — preserving kitchens, bottling and packing departments, a box factory with automatic nailing machines, a can factory, the latest in stables for the horses, an engine room with dynamos capable of producing 1000 horsepower of electricity or even more. He would use what he called "heart power" in considering not only the health, comfort, and convenience of employees, but even their enjoyment. He would give them a restaurant, dressing rooms, rest rooms, an emergency hospital, a roof garden, and eventually an indoor swimming pool and gymnasium, a large meeting hall, and classes where they might take practical courses to better themselves. The project would take years, even decades, to realize.

For the site of this complex he chose an area at the eastern end of Allegheny City, on the Allegheny River about a half mile above and across the river from Pittsburgh's business section. Allegheny was a neat, relatively clean community of seven square miles between hill and river; it had some 100,000 inhabitants, a high percentage of them of German extraction, with a "Millionaires' Row" of fine stone mansions on Ridge Avenue and Liverpool Street. It was connected with Pittsburgh by a Pennsylvania Railroad trestle and several privately owned toll bridges, including the covered wooden Union Bridge at The Point, where the rivers joined. Allegheny had a beautiful commons (unlike Pittsburgh, which had no parks), a university, and an observatory on Observatory Hill. It was about to receive a splendid library building on Federal Street, for Andrew Carnegie, who had grown up in this community, would place there the third of the 2811 free public libraries he was to give the English-speaking world. Allegheny had been settled by Revolutionary War veterans holding land warrants; now, in the summer of 1888, it was celebrating its centennial. The principal ceremonies were a fireman's parade and exercise; dedication of the recently completed Court House, which Heinz thought "a very imposing building"; a conclave of veterans of the Grand Army of the Republic; and a four-hour parade of traders and other societies in which the Heinz Company exhibited the manufacture and bottling of pickles on a large horse-drawn float.

The land comprised twenty-four lots in Allegheny's eighth ward, next to the vinegar factory already there. It fronted 300 feet on Main (now Progress) Street, extended almost to the river, and held a sawmill, brewery, a mission church, lime kilns, a blacksmith shop, coke ovens, and a cotton mill left over from the once-flourishing Allegheny City textile industry that had been ruined by the Civil War. He paid $50,000, one third of it down, the rest secured by a bond and mortgage. Three fourths of the land was "intended for the firm, and the one-fourth subject to a twenty-year lease I intend for myself so that if ever needed for our firm it will be in the family and can be controlled." The Allegheny Council voted twenty-seven to four to pass the ordinances granting Heinz the privilege to extend a switch from the Pittsburgh and Western Railroad. "It did not cost us one penny to grease Council as it usually does," he wrote. "We felt pleased as I was determined to get it honestly or not at all."

Several buildings went up — solid Pittsburgh Romanesque structures of glazed pressed brick — "all hard brick, no soft at all. The best of everything. Oak posts throughout." The first building, 32 by 130 feet, completed in August 1889, had storage and shipping facilities on the first floor, mustard mills on the second, and manufacture of bulk goods on the third. The Main Building was started in November:

> The first bricks were laid today on our new 70 by 130 foot five-story building in Allegheny City. We hope to build two or three stories this fall and finish it in the spring, giving the foundations a chance to settle, as the late fall or spring floods under the foundations might be too much for a five-story building, although the concrete is 2½ feet thick, best Portland cement, 300 barrels under this building, $3.10 per barrel. 3½ foot stone walls tapered to 2½ feet.

The move into the new buildings began in October 1890 and was completed in January. The changeover coincided with and apparently helped to produce a crisis in management. It was a small rebellion, classic in nature, predictable, and probably inevitable in a company that was evolving from a friendly, informal family operation into one of the pioneer organizations of large-scale production. In such circumstances, a certain managerial ruthlessness is required if the enterprise is to survive. Heinz was able to supply it.

As he told the story at some length in his diary, certain employees were selected to set up and manage operations in the Allegheny plant. When the rest of the company's operations were transferred to Allegheny, these men

> seemed to be inclined to run the new plant, while clerks, shippers and heads from Pittsburgh, who on the whole were the more competent and experienced, expected to go right on as they had done at the Pittsburgh factory.
>
> There resulted a *clash and jar* which caused several to lose heart and give notice and leave, and we had to dismiss several before matters would move off smoothly. All of which was annoying to me, yet seemed very necessary in order to make a clean start and get a good grip on the business.
>
> Several had been with us so long they had worn out their usefulness, others had swelled heads and planned to engage with Brother John, who was at the time with others arranging to locate a new plant in Indiana and some of our men were to have

an interest with Brother John. However, after George Walter, Joseph Hite, and William Climan left in April and May, 1891, and I discharged Staley the Vinegar Man in June and Johnny Climan in July, we found we had peace and ran our business at less expense, as new men worked for less money and were more anxious to please and work up in order to make themselves more valuable.

Am still weeding out some who have been with us too long. Johnny Climan lost interest because his brother William had gone away. Discharged him about the 10th of July on account of leaving for three days without notice or permission and lack of *heart power*. Harry Grissell for same and being impudent with girls, and he a married man.

Joseph Hite, who left May 1st because he could not forgive me for the wrong he had done our firm by certain neglect, left us in a very kindly way, saying he had lost heart. I told him it was a bad break and wanted him to remain, but no, it was looked upon by others as a bad break for him, but having been with me for twelve years he must make a change.

He left us May 1st and tonight, July 20th, he comes for a position and engages to go to work for $80 per month, $10 less than he left at, and we not to pay for lost time. This is a complete vindication for our firm, as he was quite a prominent figure and well liked.

At present writing I see daylight and have a stronger grip on our business, but it has been a long and steady pull for a year and all is well.

The nature of the company's operation was changing, most notably in its sales methods. Salesmen covered their territory in wagons; delivering goods to the trade as they sold. Each man had a team of fine-looking horses, a boy to drive them, and an attractively painted closed wagon with pictures of Heinz Company farms and products — especially pickles — painted on the sides. Use of the wagons continued, but on January 1, 1889, delivery of goods at time of sale was discontinued. Each salesman called on grocers, restaurants, and hotels with a sample case in one hand and an order book in the other; the products were delivered later.

The annual convention of company salesmen held in Pittsburgh with a flourish the first week of January was changed in
1888 when increasing numbers made such a gathering im-
practical. Now the salesmen convened in annual meetings
held in their districts, and the convention in Pittsburgh was
limited to sales and distributing branch managers and assistant
managers. Such was the nature of the company's growth that
in a relatively short time the managers were as numerous as
the salesmen before them.

The position of Henry J. Heinz in his community was also
changing with growth of his company. The misfortunes of fifteen years past were forgotten or forgiven. He was now an important figure — owner and manager of a national company,
member of a half-dozen boards, and the strongest of thirteen
directors in an undertaking that touched almost every Pitts-
burgher: the large Pittsburgh Exposition buildings erected on
six acres on the north shore of Pittsburgh's "Golden Triangle."
The opening ceremonies were held in May 1889, with audi-
ences of 2000 attending weeklong concerts. Henry Heinz, who
once had not approved "opera-going," had a private box and
appeared with Sallie in resplendent evening dress:

> This night closes the greatest musical festival ever held in
> Pittsburgh in the new Exposition Buildings. Our family at-
> tended every other night and other nights we invited our rela-
> tives to use our private box. It was a royal treat. Miss [Emma]
> Juch and Campani [Giuseppe Campanari] were among the
> singers who received $1,000 per night. A success and an intro-
> duction to the new Exposition.

These were the last years (1887–1889) in which Heinz
kept a diary with regular daily entries:

April 3, 1887 (Sunday): A delightful day. Services in the morning and missionary exercises at 2:30 P.M. in the Sunday School.
Collection was $25.34, the best we ever had for a quarterly oc-
casion.

Mr. Gray, superintendent of the Second Presbyterian Church, was out with four Chinaman boys who entertained us by song and speeches and reading. Full house and much interest was manifested, and indeed a profitable occasion to our church and the Chinamen as well, creating a feeling of sympathy between them and the people. I took them to my home for tea.

April 11: (Philadelphia) We discharged R. M. Levering this day because he had neglected his family and mother and taken up with another woman. I will not temporize with anyone under such circumstances.

April 29: Am reading up on roses and flowers and getting much pleasure in cultivating them. Spent over $250 for shrubs and trees and flowers this year.

April 30: Helping my boys to build a chicken coop, which rests my mind and gives them pleasure and practice.

May 11: Setting up a small fountain at our home today. A new boy figure with a leaky boot and a 7½ foot basin. This is my first experience and this is the first one set up in Sharpsburg or Etna.

May 19: Kansas City. Am amazed at the building boom. Much Eastern capital invested here.

July 8: Our clerks are having every other Saturday off from noon and all are having a vacation of one week each during the months of July and August.

August 4: Irene's 16th birthday. Bought her a neat ring with a setting of small diamonds around a pearl. She was most pleased.

August 12: Walkerton. I leave Clarence in care of Mr. Dunham to assist in taking in pickles, etc. He can do very little but he should begin sometime. [Clarence was fourteen.]

January 21, 1888: Purchased a good sized Shetland pony, dark brown and three or four large white spots on each side. Pony races under saddle and trots in harness. Paid $180, including cart and harness. Think it will be just the thing for the boys. They are delighted.

February 6: Charleston, S.C. Brother Peter canvassing trade here. Sallie, Clifford, Pauline and I walk out. We are interested in much we see here.

February 13: We take the train [from Jacksonville] for St. Augustine at 4 P.M. and arrive at the Hotel Ponce de Leon, the new and greatest hotel in America. We are amazed at its magnificence. Covers over three acres, cost, including furnishings, $2 million. [Built by] H. Flagler, stockholder in the Standard Oil Company. Paid $15 for one day, Sallie, Clifford and I (no charge for the boy). We drive and are amazed at the improvements since I was here four years ago. Property has advanced 300 and 400 per cent. In five years, four or five magnificent hotels, all full.

February 17: Orlando. Most people are anxious to sell. They ask from $1000 to $3000 per acre for groves from six to twenty years old and [indecipherable word] within one-half to three miles of the post office. The town is partially surrounded by lakes and they are beauties. Have not allowed myself to be persuaded to invest.

February 20: Polatka. We put up at the Putnam House, rate $4 per day. We are pleased with this place and the hotel is one of the best and toniest in the state.

February 21: Jacksonville. We find the place alive preparing and decorating in view of President Cleveland and wife coming tomorrow.

February 22: The President and party arrived at 2 P.M. and after dining the parade took place. We were seated on the veranda at the Carleton on Bay Street where we were in full view of all. After which we fished from the docks. Two five-pounders was the result.

February 23: We sailed on the Steamer Seminole for New York City this 1 P.M. 25 miles until we enter the Atlantic. We enjoy this variety of scenery and the change from cars and boats.

February 24: Charleston. We arrived here this morning and spend the day with Brother Peter and wife and attend Emma Abbott's musical opera. Engage a box near the stage and take little Clifford (4 years) with us, who enjoys the singing and music as much as we do.

February 25: We are detained another day because of the captain having belated himself one hour, having spent the night at a banquet and arrived too late to take the steamer over the bar as the tide was out.

February 26 (Sunday). Delightful trip. Spent the day reading. Only about 70 passengers on board and no minister on board, therefore no preaching.

February 27: Off Cape Hatteras, I was very sick — the first time in my life that I was really seasick.

February 28: We arrived at New York at 5 P.M. 16 degrees above zero.

March 4 (Sunday). At home and church and Sunday School, where we are delighted to be. I tell the school some of the incidents of our trip, which they listen to attentively.

March 5: Boys [at office] all well. I treat them with a box of choice oranges, which is one of ten boxes shipped from Orlando.

March 6: We are planning a new brick building in Allegheny. I spend from one to two hours with our Boss Carpenter planning it, etc.

March 13: Meet with a Committee of Preserves Manufacturers relative to forming a trust of all the preservers in the United States this side of the Missouri River. We prefer to remain outside.

March 22: The worst blizzards in the East ever known. Citizens in New York City had to take up lodgings at hotels, etc. within one mile of their homes.*

March 30 (Good Friday): We stop our business today. I take Clarence and Howard and go to the Lutheran Church with my Mother.

Mother keeps this as a fast day and has for 42 years. She

---

* The Great Blizzard of 1888 lasted three days throughout much of the northeast.

made the promise to God if he spared me when I was very sick (a year old). I feel I cannot show her my love and affection in any better way than to not only keep this day as all Lutherans do but accompany her to and from church.

April 5: Looking after a Jersey cow for family and to grace our back lot.

April 26: This day for the first time I bring my new Black Earl home to our new stable, which is about completed. I have the honor of giving my mother the first drive, which we both enjoy, and Sallie the second, Irene the third.

May 1: Too busy to note even important matters. Besides, I consider it of less importance, or I am less ambitious to note events.

June 1: Chicago. Busy among the pickle manufacturers. E. J. Noble calls on me at the Grand Pacific Hotel. He is a member of the Board of Trade.

November 5: Ira W. Kimmel left us after a week's notice. He thought he could do better. We pay him $75 per month and that more because of character and honesty than ability. He thanks me for friendship, etc. We were under the impression he goes to a new position.

November 7: Duns Commercial Agency calls and shows a printed card, Watkins and Kimmel, Pickle and Preserving Business. All are surprised, as Ira's business ability is limited. I wish him well. There is plenty of room at the top.

December 2: We notified our Sunday School children that our School would begin at 9:45 in the morning instead of the afternoon. Many were displeased, but like true Americans we accepted the decision of the majority. We will have more competent teachers and more scholars will remain for church.

On December 6 the Heinz family received a new member — one who was to play an important part in their affairs for the next fifty years. Sister Elizabeth Catherine, thirty, married Sebastian Mueller, twenty-eight, who had just been made the firm's general manager of manufacturing. Born in Kallstadt,

Mueller had graduated first in his class from a Latin school, worked two years in a bank, fulfilled his military service in the Bavarian and then the German army, and in 1884 emigrated to the United States. Sister Elizabeth and Mueller were full cousins. Henry and Sarah Heinz did not favor the marriage of blood relations, "but I say nothing. They have never spoken to me about it as Sister Lizzie is not in the habit of consulting anybody and all the rest of the family seem to think it right, as their Pastor, Reverend K. Waltz, approves it."

The wedding was held in the home of John and Anna Heinz with some forty relatives and friends present. "Many choice presents," Heinz noted wryly, "In fact, none of us other relatives ever fared so well." Mother Heinz insisted that her children and the children of her children spend the day with her as a kind of continued wedding, "which was done and much pleasure to the children and all was the result."

December 15: New York. Very busy but took time to purchase Irene a bracelet at Tiffanys.

December 24: I purchased the most extravagant Christmas gift of my life at W. W. Wattles today, a diamond pin (three stones), fine in plain figures, $710, but concluded a woman so modest and kind was deserving of something while I could pay cash and had no debts.

January 19, 1889; Up to this time, a mild winter. No ice over one inch thick. Pittsburgh icemen gloomy.

March 6: Washington. G. Bilderbach came from Philadelphia and in a stupor after a drinking debauch. I discharged him but sent him to the Garfield Hospital as humanity dictated and sent his wife home to Pittsburgh. I feel bad, as he was my assistant in the management of agencies, but I never temporize when an individual takes advantage of my absence.

March 9: Very busy, but much annoyed because of G. Bilderbach's bad use of whiskey. So I must train someone to take his place and straighten up some of his careless work of late.

July 8: At 9 A.M. this day Clifford had his left leg broken, both bones, one-half way between the knee and the ankle. He was sitting under a cherry tree in company with his companion, Helen Lewis, our neighbor, in rear of our house near the little locust grove on the slope. Clarence, his elder brother (16 years old) was on the tree picking cherries when a limb broke and Clarence came down head foremost, his shoulder striking Clifford on the leg and breaking both bones. Dr. Dinsmore, our family physician, attended him promptly after the accident. Clifford is quite nervous but his mama is a good nurse.

July 13: We pull down the fence between the Helmky and our own grounds this day. We purchased this property about a month ago for $5,000. We don't consider the house of much value but the grounds are desirable in connection with ours. Our children appreciate it very much and this first day's possession is to them a picnic.

July 14: Poor Clifford's limb had to be dressed this 2 P.M. Had to give him chloroform.

July 24: Denver. I look up our agency here. Find all well, but they need waking up and organizing anew, which I am now at. Hard knocks and well directed efforts will help some here at this new agency.

October 5: This has been one of the hardest weeks of my life. Business good. Agents here for new prices. Exposition duties as a director while the Exposition is in full blast, 16,000 daily attendance, and many outside matters, are too much for my small frame. I bless God when Sunday comes.

CHAPTER 8

Triumph and Tragedy

"Harry, I am going home."

Sarah Young Heinz,
November 29, 1894

SOME SEVENTEEN BUILDINGS eventually went up in Allegheny around an open grassed courtyard, beneath which was a 100,-000-gallon water tank for fire protection. Henry Heinz worked with particular care on the design and construction of one of these, the Time Office, in which employees registered when they entered and left the factory complex. He called it "the gem in the setting." *Pickles*, the company magazine, described it as "a combination of elegance, splendor and beauty."

Of composite architectural style, the Time Office seemed to be, in its outlines, a miniature model of the Library of Congress then being built in Washington (completed 1897). It was twenty-five feet square, one story high, and of terra cotta Pompeian brick laid under the personal supervision of the Founder. A portico had two columns of red Swedish granite dressed and polished at Aberdeen, Scotland. In the one-room interior, the floor was Alhambra tile, the wainscoting dark verd antique marble from Italy, the woodwork polished red mahogany. The ceiling (again in the words of *Pickles*) revealed "intertwined vines and cupids, delicate in color, graceful in poise, and artistic in their groupings." Near the ceiling were eight round stained-glass windows. These showed the house in Sharpsburg "Where We Began — 1869" and various inspiring sayings, including one by Anna Margaretha Heinz: "Labor sweetens life, idleness makes it a burden." The iron dome, overlaid with gold leaf, was surmounted by a golden eagle, wings outspread, holding in its beak a cluster of electric lights. There were three entrances: one for men, one for women, and the center passage through the portico for visitors and the general public. The Time Office, said *Pickles*, "gives tone to the entire plant . . . gives to visitors a splendid impression from the very start."

The company's model stable was the subject of national comment; one reporter called it an equine palace. This was a three-story building with Romanesque towers, turrets, and battlements. It was completely fireproof; interior iron doors were designed to close automatically at an abnormally high temperature. The wagons were kept on the first floor, the bedding and feed on the third. An inside ramp led to 110 stalls on the second floor. At the top of the ramp at day's end, the horse's harness (tailored to fit each animal) was unfastened and carried by overhead trolley to the tack room. The stable floor was cork imported from England and covered with white sand on which the hostlers every morning used their brooms to create elaborate designs.

The building was heated by steam radiators, cooled by electric fans and ventilators, lighted by electricity, and screened at the windows. The horses were fed, watered, and brushed by electrically operated machinery. There was a hospital for horses who were sick, a glass-enclosed Turkish bath for horses with colds, a warm foot bath for horses with sore hooves, a jail for horses who kicked, and a roof garden for horses who needed airing. A visiting reporter from *The American Grocer* declared with a straight face that the animals actually exhibited pride in their surroundings.

While his plant construction was proceeding, Heinz made a basic change in his own life-style. He left the Victorian gentility of the Roach house and the middle-class surroundings of Sharpsburg to move into a baronial castle in Pittsburgh's most opulent neighborhood.

He chose the Point Breeze section some six miles east of downtown Pittsburgh — almost a two-hour ride by horsecar, one hour by the railed cable car introduced in 1889, but only thirty minutes by the electric street car line to be installed in 1896. Penn Avenue traversed the area east and west as a main thoroughfare, and along it in the space of eight blocks were now or would be in Heinz's lifetime the residences of thirty-two well-to-do or wealthy Pittsburghers, at least eighteen of them indubitable millionaires. George Westinghouse occupied an entire block along the tracks of the Pennsylvania Railroad, with a siding for his private railroad car and an underpass so that he could ride west to his office in downtown Pittsburgh or east to his factory in East Pittsburgh. Henry Clay Frick had a magnificent mansion and stable (both still standing). There was Alexander P. Moore, owner of newspapers in Pittsburgh and New York City, Ambassador to Spain, and fourth husband of actress Lillian Russell. Thomas M. Armstrong, founder of Armstrong Cork Company, and his son. Joseph E. Woodwell of Woodwell Hardware. Arthur E. Braun, publisher of the Pittsburgh *Post* and the Pittsburgh *Sun* and President of Farmers Bank. Francis T. F. Lovejoy, Henry M. Curry, and Alexander R. Peacock, Carnegie partners. George Lauder, a Carnegie uncle and partner (and father of Polly Lauder, to become Mrs. Gene Tunney). Henry William Borntraeger and Carl Hermann Borntraeger, sons of Carnegie partners. Durbin Horne, President of the Joseph Horne Department Store. Joseph Bernard Shea, Horne treasurer, later president. John Grier Holmes, banker and broker. W. Henry R. Hilliard, President of the Alcania Company, tin plate. Andrew Carnegie's mother lived at Penn and Dunfermline. One block south, on Beechwood Boulevard, was the family of William Kendall Thaw, railroad and coal magnate. Richard Beatty Mellon, President of Mellon National Bank, lived nearby, as did George Mesta, president of Mesta Machine Company (and husband of Ambassador Perle Mesta).

It was a neighborhood visited a number of times by Theodore Dreiser, a young reporter-columnist working on the Pittsburgh *Dispatch* in the summer of 1894. He found Pittsburgh "to my delight . . . one of the most curious and fascinating places I had ever seen" and the prospect from Mount Washington "the finest view of a city I have ever seen." But he was shocked at the mansions he saw in Shadyside, East Liberty, and Point Breeze. "Never in my life," he wrote in 1922, "was the vast gap which divides the rich from the poor in America so vividly and forcefully brought home to me . . . Never did the mere possession of wealth impress me so keenly . . . Even the street lamps were of a better design than elsewhere."

Henry Heinz bought Greenlawn, the Hopkins mansion, for $35,000 — $10,000 in cash, $5000 payable in one year, and $20,000 in three years at 5 percent interest. His property occupied the full block (171 by 500 feet) on Penn Avenue between Lang and Murtland avenues. George Westinghouse was his immediate neighbor to the north; Armstrong and Woodwell were across from him on the south side of Penn Avenue. Greenlawn was a four-story structure in the French Renaissance style, suggesting vaguely the chateau at Blois on the Loire River. It contained some thirty rooms, each of the "sleeping rooms" being connected to a bathroom, which were seven in number.

The Heinzes moved in on April 6, 1892; on May 30 the master wrote:

> We have had 16 men at work since April 13 and have now concluded to reduce the number to 8. The principal expense inside was the peeling of old varnish off the hard wood doors and shutters and have it like new hard wood. Put in stained glass, etc., and French plate in windows in front four rooms.°

° Pittsburgh is known for the extraordinary amount and high quality of stained glass in the windows and doors of its older homes. Heinz is credited with advancing that trend by bringing to the city three brothers skilled in art glass, J. Horace, Jesse F., and Frank Rudy.

And on June 29:

> We finish up today except for painting the stable and finish up of tennis court. We are all much delighted with our new home.

Heinz took over the fourth floor as a display area for the curios and works of art he was beginning to collect. He later retained Messrs. Duryea and Patten of New York to decorate the house, with emphasis on crested tapestries and walls covered with satin damask, rose silk, and hand-tooled gilded leather. The decorators commissioned George M. Carpenter, who had worked on the decorations of the Library of Congress and the Waldorf-Astoria Hotel in New York, to produce original mural frescoes for the reception hall on the first floor and the master's bathroom on the second. The bathroom painting, entitled *Queen of the Sea,* showed a full-size nude sea nymph standing on a sea shell (supported by dashing sea horses), with flowing hair and one hand upraised to bring a conch shell to her lips as a trumpet. Greenlawn was the scene of continuing change, improvement, and addition over the next twenty-seven years, but the sea nymph stayed on to the end.

In the spring of 1893, Heinz continued the series of trips to foreign lands that over the decades took him to almost every part of the accessible world.[*] On this occasion he was a member of a junket — a group of fifty prominent North American manufacturers sent to Mexico under the auspices of the Australasian Publishing Company of New York to foster good will, better trade relations, and a flow of United States investment capital. Heinz took as his guest his old friend Dr. E. M. Wood and found the group "a nice company of gentlemen," presumably including Mr. Hiram Walker of Hiram Walker & Sons, distillers, of Walkerville, Ontario, who was one of those present. The party entered Mexico by way of Laredo, visited scores of business operations (dominated by the English in

---

[*] In the twenty-five years 1890–1914, he visited Europe every year but four.

manufacturing and by the French and Germans in trade and commerce), and were received by Thomas Ryan, the American ambassador, and Porfirio Díaz, President of the Republic. Everyone was impressed by "one of the largest engineering achievements of the age": a $5 million project by which Mexico City would collect and drain its sewage by a wide and deep canal forty miles long, including a six-mile tunnel. The canal would take the sewage to a river; which would then carry it safely to the Gulf of Mexico.

Heinz announced bluntly in Monterey, "Mexico offers a very poor field for my goods. To be profitable and to pay for working up, I should have the trade of the masses, but the duty on all our goods is so heavy that they become expensive luxuries, and are used as such here. Pickles that retail in the States at 25 cents per bottle must sell at 90 cents here. Catsup that retails at 25 cents there is sold here at $1." Back home (by way of Yucatan and Havana), he sent Ambassador Ryan a handsome box of pickles, preserves, and condiments as a gift for President Díaz and received the President's courteous thanks.

On January 30, 1894, in his fiftieth year, feeling "very tired and worn, nervous stomach and head ache . . . in need of a long rest," Heinz undertook a five-and-a-half-month journey through Egypt, Palestine, and Western Europe. Sallie, troubled with recurring attacks of rheumatism, was not up to such an adventure; he took with him Irene, Clarence, and Myra Boyd, Irene's friend and daughter of Sallie's sister Lydia. Mrs. Boyd had left her husband Harry with their three children in 1884, "selecting" (in Heinz's words) "to remain apart on account of his drinking." She had moved in with the Heinzes and was in charge of running the household. Myra had worked creditably as the company cashier for several years. She was one of the leading members of the Duquesne Ceramic Club and had exhibited what a reviewer called "several pieces of superior workmanship, a beautiful *bonboniere* with head and several toilet articles of exquisite beauty." Heinz carried £1000 and $1500 in American Express checks, and he gave $400 to Clarence and $300 each to Irene and Myra Boyd.

They sailed from New York on the S. S. *Fürst Bismarck* as part of a tour group, four of 300 salon passengers. Heinz realized the dream of a happy traveler: "A fine trip, elegant society, many prominent people. We form pleasant acquaintances on board. Never traveled with a nicer and more gentlemanly set. Food and service never surpassed."

The *Bismarck* stopped at Gibraltar and then at Algiers: "From the bay the city is the finest sight I ever saw . . . People very filthy. We wonder how they exist."

At Genoa: "An intelligent people. Few poor. No drunkenness, no boisterous talk and the better class are well housed . . . At 8 P.M. our ship started on the minute. Two tugs were employed to draw us out past the light houses, one on either side. Our immense ship, the largest that ever entered this port (502 feet), drawing 28 feet and only 28 ⅛ feet in the bay, moved out so slowly that for the first ten minutes we could scarce notice it going. The sights from our ship, the city by gaslight, was beautiful. Good night, interesting Genoa."

At Ajaccio, Corsica: "All first visit Napoleon's birthplace. Furniture and house in good preservation. Four story stone house . . . Productive soil, but lazy, indolent, and will never accomplish much anywhere."

In the Mediterranean: "Am introduced to the Purchasing Agent for this Hamburg American Packet Company, fifty odd ships in all, who does all the *purchasing*. He gave me an order to be sent to their Hoboken Docks. This is a sample order [for 35 dozen]. They expect to use the horseradish on their 50 odd ships . . ."

"Mr. [Charles Anderson] Dana, Editor of the New York *Sun*, rose to call attention to this being Washington's Birthday.

Whether on sea or land, it was but fitting to celebrate it in a proper manner. Bishop Perry of Davenport, Iowa, was introduced who made a very fine and fitting address. A judge from Chicago followed."

At Alexandria: "Not much to be seen except the Pillar of Pompey. Measures over 13 feet at the base. The round column is about 60 feet high and 8 feet in diameter, all of solid granite, polished. Over 2000 years old."

During ten days in Cairo Heinz was shocked at the low status of women ("Horse first, woman second, dog third"); at the flies clinging to the faces, inflaming the eyes, of the children; and at the unending clamor for gifts of money ("Backsheesh is the Alpha and Omega, the first word the infant lisps, continually practised by the native poor, and the final farewell to the tourist"). He visited hundreds of bazaars. He watched his three young people climb the largest of the pyramids, that of Khufu (Cheops) at Giza. He visited there the tombs of the king and the queen, marveling that the joints between the giant blocks of stone were so neatly fitted that he could scarcely see them in the candlelight. He rode a camel to the Great Sphinx at Giza and admired "the magnificent red and black granite. Measured some blocks 18 feet long, 6 feet thick, all in perfect condition." He visited and measured, at Heliopolis, the earliest and finest temple obelisk still in position.

Back in Cairo he went to a mosque to see the howling dervishes and from there to the horse races. He attended a lecture on Egyptian antiquities in the home of Dr. Grant Bay, one of the Egyptologists then beginning the golden age of archeological discovery. He bought and shipped home two rugs and some furniture and, from the Gizeh Museum, twenty-three ancient objects packed in camphor wood — scarabs, weapons, pottery, and the like. From "an authorized excavator" he bought for $50 a human mummy, encased, and had Wells Fargo ship it home. He went by train to Memphis, the ancient capital of Egypt, fourteen miles south of Cairo, to visit the Tombs of the Kings, the Priests, and the Sacred Bulls at nearby Sakkara. "We are charmed with Cairo," he wrote. "Probably not another city in the world outside the Holy Land so novel and at the same time so full of historic, interesting things."

On a nineteen-day Cook & Son tour on the Nile to Upper Egypt (£26 each), Heinz and his young companions took a steamer as far south as Aswan at the First Cataract, 590 miles from Cairo. Equipped with sun umbrellas, large straw hats, veils, "summer underwear," and a Kodak, they left the boat at various stops to visit temples, pyramids, sphinxes ("Myra is clean gone on this animal"), obelisks, cemetery ruins, and bazaars. At Aswan they swam in the Nile and, in temperatures that reached 122° F. in the sun, visited the tombs in solid rock discovered by Lord George Grenfell in 1885–1886. On the return trip they stopped five days to see the monuments at Luxor, Karnak, and Thebes, the ancient capital of Upper Egypt, site of the Valley of the Kings, where the tomb of King Tutankhamen, the richest of all discoveries in Egypt, was to lie unopened for another twenty-eight years.

> The trip to Thebes is a very comfortable one by donkey or two-wheeled cart; it takes about four hours to the tombs of the Queens and seven hours to the tombs of the Kings, including a space of time for rest and lunch at the temple of Del-el-Bahri at Thebes. We look with admiration on the colossal statue of Rameses II, the largest in Egypt. Its weight is over 1000 tons. How they ever managed to bring it from the granite quarries at Assuam in one piece and how it ever became broken without the use of modern cannon is an unsolved mystery. Its height is 57 feet. The ear measures 3½ feet. Across the face 6½ feet. Across the breast 23½ feet. First finger 3 feet in diameter, arm 4¾ feet. The bulk of granite used in the construction of this statue would be sufficient to fill 60 railroad cars each with a capacity of 30,000 lbs, or four solid trains of 15 cars each. The granite base on which it stands is 30 feet long, 18 feet wide, and 9 feet thick. (Purchased Egyptian antiquities for my private museum.)

Heinz visited the complex of temples at Karnak again by moonlight and decided that it was "perhaps the noblest effort of architectural magnificence ever produced by man." He dined with the English consul at Luxor, oriental style, with a young sheik from the desert and two other Arabs. ("Long to be remembered. One dose sufficient.")

The four travelers left Cairo again at the end of March, traveling by train with a Mr. and Mrs. W. W. Barrett and a Mr. D. A. Woodberry from Rochester. They transferred to a French steamer at Port Said and two days later arrived in Jaffa on the way to Jerusalem, then ruled by the Turks. ("I feel that our feet are treading on holy ground.") Over the next eight days he made a reverent pilgrimage to those places he had read about since his childhood: the Garden of Gethsemene, the Mount of Olives, the Brook Cherith, Jericho, the Dead Sea ("where we take a swim and gather stones from the beach"), the Jordan River, Bethany, Saint Stephen's Gate, the Church of the Holy Sepulcher. At the church he saw "thousands of candles and lanterns burning. Greeks, Catholics, Armenians, Kopts, Syrians, and Abhasians, all worshipping in different parts of the Church, each in their own language. I . . . look upon all as true worshippers in their own way."

He visited two Bedouin villages near Jericho:

> 300 population cover 300 feet square. They build a wall around their city with prickly brush that neither their dogs or chickens venture through. A few stakes on which they lay coarse shawls and old clothing to keep off the sun, one side open, no floor, no furniture, only wooden bowls, a gun and sword and blankets about their premises. A few pennies for backsheesh will cause the whole family to smile on you. They are brighter than the Sudanese and about as dangerous. The whole valley from Jericho to the Dead Sea and to the Jordan is now a barren waste, largely because it is not safe on account of the Bedouins on the hills on the other side of the Jordan.

The party sailed on a Russian steamer from Jaffa to Beirut,

Tins of baked beans are taken from one dolly, wrapped in paper, and placed on another, ready for shipment. Standing women hold labels.

Two young ladies give a public demonstration of hand-packing jars with two sizes of pickles, red peppers, pickled green beans, white onions, and cauliflower.

In the Bottling Room, 100 girls pack pickles, one at a time, into spotless bottles with a wooden paddle, giving the pickles a pattern and inserting one red pepper where it will show nicely.

When a large shipment of cherries, strawberries, or peaches came in, everyone who could move gathered to process them. This group is hulling strawberries.

Each girl had her assigned place in the Girls' Dining Room. The table in the right foreground was for foreladies.

A corner of the company Reading Room, 1900.

Every employee who handled food had a manicure at least once a week.

The women's rest room, 1904. Wooden lockers line each wall.

Mrs. Agnes Dunn, forewoman of the Pittsburgh plant,
and Miss Lillian Weizmann, her successor.

When her turn came, a girl worker could climb into this wagonette with eight others
and be driven elegantly through the city parks. The small building, the Time Office,
was where everyone checked in and out and all hiring was done.

Inside the Time Office, which the company magazine called "a combination of elegance, splendor and beauty," an elegantly dressed employee checks out by time clock. The year is 1911, and two martyred presidents, Lincoln and Garfield, look down. The motto in the window reads, "Temperance and Labor are the two real physicians of man."

One of the tables at the company's annual "family picnic." Heinz is at the head of the table, Sebastian Mueller third from right.

The stained-glass windows of the company auditorium, with their mottos exhorting employees to be prudent, loyal, temperate, earnest, and hardworking.

thence to Tripoli, thence to Smyrna. "These Russian ships," he wrote, "carry principally Pilgrims to and from Jerusalem. The Russian government pays the third class rate, £3 15/ for the round trip, four weeks going and coming on ship. They feed themselves. Wear heavy clothings. Big *caps* and *pants* in *big boots.*" At Smyrna they took an Austrian-Lloyd steamer to Brindisi. En route, Clarence celebrated his twenty-first birthday. His father gave him four characteristic presents: a Bible bought in Jerusalem, a rug bought in Smyrna for his room in Munich, where he was to go to school, a letter filled with "kindly advice," and a check for $1000 "to be used as he may elect."

They had a hard train ride, with only two hours sleep, from Brindisi to Naples. With the Barretts and Mr. Woodberry they hired a guide and took a three-day voyage to Capri and the Blue Grotto, Sorrento, Castellammare, Pompeii, and back to Naples. At Castellammare the hotel charged them 1.07 francs (sic) for candles, which they used one-half hour ("Mrs. Barrett took them along"). At Mount Vesuvius Heinz gathered up six specimens of lava weighing twenty pounds to ship back to Pittsburgh.

Rome: A paradise for a traveler with a tape measure, a notebook, a passion for curios, an interest in secular and ecclesiastical history, and an inexhaustible energy. The Colosseum, which required 65,000 captives three years to build. Constantine's Arch, Trajan's Column, the Roman Forum, the Triumphal Arch of Septimus Severus, 203 A.D. The Temple of Castor and Pollux, only three of its Parian marble columns now existing. The Triumphal Arch of Titus, 81 A.D. The Capitoline Museum. The Caracalla Baths, which could hold 1600 bathers. The Church of Saint Sebastian. The Catacombs of St. Callistus, discovered in 1854, more than 16,000 Christians buried here. The Pantheon, a round building 142 feet in diameter, no windows. The Vatican, 22 courtyards, 11,000 rooms, 23,000 windows, 10,000 statues, 1000 employees. Saint Peter's:

"We are delighted with our climb to the top of the Dome, 715 steps, and walk over the brick roofs." The Tomb of Michelangelo, "the greatest sculptor and architect of his day, also great in art and a poet." Heinz decided, "All Italian artists are *marvellous*. Italy has much to be proud of. We are all delighted." Of the country in general: "A tax ridden people but seem to enjoy it. No middle class, or few at least. Fond of show. Dress well. Use good food. Full of music and sport amongst all classes. Fine climate. Driving cheaper than in any other part of Europe. *Not priest ridden.*"

On April 30: "Clarence had a fine experience with me all day buying water colors and paintings very low — water colors which would cost in Pittsburgh $100 to $200 we bought as low as $20 to $25." On May 7: "After lunch Irene and Myra accompany Mr. and Mrs. Barrett to the Corsini Gallery and Capuchin Church while Clarence and I invest 170 francs in antiques at four places and enjoy it." Clarence's enjoyment was moderate. On that day he wrote his younger brother Howard, "Papa has the relic fever bad, and the worst of it is, I have to go about the dingy old holes hunting things with him."

At the end of a five-day stay in Venice, Myra Boyd took Clarence to Munich to get him settled in school, while Heinz and his daughter spent several days in Vienna and then went on to visit a business acquaintance, a Baron von Berg, proprietor of a 48,000-acre estate at Kapuvar, Hungary. They spent some time with Clarence and Myra in Munich, then left them there, departing with Mr. Woodberry for Switzerland. At Zurich a young man from Ohio, interested in Irene, made himself a member of the party. At Mount Rigi, Heinz was distressed to think "what a time Napoleon and his army must have had." At Lucerne, he found the hotel "full of fine music, good people, and gay company." At Geneva, he sat in silent meditation for a time in John Calvin's chair and the next day bought a seal sack for Irene and a mink-lined overcoat for himself.

At Paris he stayed at the Grand Hotel (twenty francs per day for two rooms, three francs for electricity). He bought two expensive Patek-Philippe watches. He went with Mr. Woodberry "to the famous Jardin du Paris. The first part of the show was fairly respectable. After this was over we turned toward the music in the bandstand but some gay women got to kicking and we got out." At Antwerp he arranged to display his company's goods at the Antwerp Exposition. In London, after attending to business for several days, he took Irene to the Lyceum Theatre to see Henry Irving and Ellen Terry in *Faust* ("Very fine actors and good scenery"). At the dock in Southampton he presented ten cases of sweet pickles to the steward of the *City of Paris*, who was pleased to put three-dozen bottles on the table for the first dinner. On the voyage home he met and talked with Samuel Clemens, "our distinguished Mark Twain, about 55 [fifty-eight] years, Roman nose, heavy bushy hair, dark gray, medium height, say 5 feet 7 inches." He arrived at Staten Island on July 14 and was pleased to find that all his curios and paintings — "six shipments and one mummy" — had arrived safely.

When Heinz appeared in the courtyard of the Allegheny plant, the employees staged a reception (called impromptu by the press) in which the engineer sounded his whistle and the force appeared at the doors and windows, cheering and waving handkerchiefs. Hearing the noise, a crowd of several hundred citizens gathered on the street outside the plant, supposing a terrible accident had happened. Mr. Heinz delivered a response in which he thanked the employees for "faithfulness and loyal efforts" and expressed gratification that the factory had more than fulfilled his expectations during his absence.

Heinz did not continue to make daily entries in his diary after his return from the tour; he had decided earlier to change the manner of recording his activities. "I note only the more important events and little about any private or corporation business. I find this plan preferable at my age. I find, even though I am too busy to further tax my time and strength, that there are now and then matters of sufficient importance to note for future references." He later added in a revelatory note, "So many things now crowd in upon me daily that I pass them all by. I find the world goes on all the same and my notes will likely never be read."

Heinz made a tour of his plants and of his nine salting stations, "most of them twice in order to get the grip I had lost during our oriental trip." He took Sallie for one of the programs of study sessions, lectures, and concerts at Lake Chautauqua, which pleased him "as she seldom cared to leave home and then more to please me or the children." She was very active in other affairs, however — the Children's Aid Society, YWCA, Ladies Auxiliary of the Sharpsburg YMCA, several churches, and the board of the South Side Hospital. Heinz observed that she had never looked so well and so beautiful as in the fall of 1894: "A lovely complexion coupled with a cheery disposition made her attractive and appreciated to all with whom she came in contact."

On Christmas Day 1894 he wrote in his diary a full account of the greatest tragedy of his life. It is a moving story — one peculiar to a different age, a different philosophy, a different manner of living and dying.

Monday, November 18, 1894, at 7:30 A.M., Sallie complained of a cold and feeling rheumatic pains through her body. I rose, turned on the natural gas, and suggested to rest until the room became warm and her sister Lydia came up, which she did as soon as she was able. It was no uncommon occurrence for her to complain a dozen times or more times a year of rheumatism in her shoulder blades, and after resting a while would rise and go to Dr. Johnston's the Electrician and after several treatments she would again be quite well.

I left her in care of her sister and daughter, and when I returned from the city found her still in bed and the physician of her choice, Dr. Robert McClelland (a Homeopathist) had been administering to her. On Tuesday called in a trained nurse and Dr. Johnston treated her with electricity, which Sister Lyd applied frequently as we had faith in the treatment.

On Wednesday we arranged to have the Senior McClelland, a brother of Robert, come at night while the other in the forenoon. Sallie by the third day became very sick. A high fever of 103⅖° indicated that typhoid was developing, which would have been bad enough, but by the fourth day the lower lobe of the right lung was congested.

I had gone to the city three times during the first week but when the pneumonia began to develop I remained in the house, although our darling was too sick and nervous to have anyone in the room except the nurse, Lyd and Irene. So that I did but see her three times a day and sometimes not to speak to. She realized that she was very sick and nervous and preferred not to be disturbed. She once remarked she was glad it was her and not some other one of the family. The physicians gave no encouragement, yet held out every hope, so that we were hopeful for the first seven days.

On Monday evening, just 7½ days from the time she took to her bed, she sent for me. As I came to the bed she said, "My darling, sit down. Harry, I have done too much. We have both done too much." (Referring to her busy life in charitable and church work among the poor, etc.) Continued saying, "Maybe I have been too ambitious. I thought I could paint a little. Oh, you look so smoky. Clean up, then go to Hornes and get the best gown they have in the store, and when I get better I will take you on a wedding trip. We will go alone up to Cambridge Springs. That is all, Harry." I left the room and for 24 hours felt encouraged but only to conclude that it was all done to brace us up and make us think that she expected to pull through.

We sent for a second nurse so as to have the best possible care, also for Dr. Cooper Sr. to counsel with the two doctors McClellands on Wednesday evening, the 28th November.

They gave us no encouragement, as Sallie's age (51) and her flesh (205 lbs.) when she took sick were all against her and only her pluck and physical strength in her favor, but double pneumonia, typhoid pneumonia, were going to be too much for her and we were expecting —

We slept little that night, only anxiety, the crisis would be reached tomorrow.

November 29th, our darling wife and mother no better is no better. Both lungs congested and breathing very heavy. The physicians and Mrs. Boyd (sister) insist that not even any member of the family shall go into the room, only the nurses, herself and Irene. This does seem to me cruel when we feel and the physicians that there is one chance in a thousand that she may recover.

But we obey in order that that chance may be given. We pray earnestly that our kind and loving father spare her to us.

I slip in three or four times a day from the side door unnoticed and see the awful struggle for breath but can do nothing but leave our loved one in God's hands, not ours, but His will be done. We are all preparing for the worst. Oh, what a sad Thanksgiving Day for us.

Continued Thursday, 29th. At 3 P.M. Sallie desired to see me. I ran to her room. She said, "Dear Harry, I am going home." H : "My dear, you have not given up, we have not given up hope." "My dear, I cannot suffer much longer." (Short of breath.) "This congestion" (putting her hand to her breast). "My Savior is calling me. He is my Savior. He saves me now."

The children came while I was talking to her as above.

She had a message for Howard, for Irene, and said to Clifford to look to Aunt Lyd as his Mama. Lyd and her niece Annie Barkley were also present. She then turned her face to the east and said, "Oh, my boy [Clarence] tell him to meet me in heaven." This was the message to all of us. Not a tear on her face, a dying farewell. I then prayed with her.

There was still a chance for recovery. She began to perspire freely and a little improvement and we left her in care of nurses, the doctors and Sister Lydia and Irene . . .

Alas, at 8 P.M. the 29th November (Thanksgiving) we were called up to see our loving wife and mother breath her last. She passed peacefully away . . .

November 30. A wet rainy day. A doubly dark day for us. People come and go all day. So sudden. Ten and a half days and few knew of her illness.

November 31 [sic]. Saturday. The darkest day to us in our home and the darkest day we ever knew. Gas and electric burning all day and drizzling rain. Funeral at 2:30 P.M. in charge of H. Samson the undertaker. The remains laid out on the bed, so beautiful (embalmed) and natural. Dr. E. M. Wood who married us preached the principal sermon. Reverend Shepard our former pastor from Sharpsburg also made remarks. Dr. Stephens (also once our pastor) and Reverend Greenfield, our pastor, took part. Floral tributes from friends.

We placed the remains in a vault in the Allegheny Cemetery until such time as we can arrange for a lot. At 4:30 P.M., when placing the casket in the vault, we used lanterns. So dark was it that we could not recognize even our relations at the Cemetery.

I write this January 13, 1895. It is all a dream, even now. Purchased the finest casket. Funeral services attended by hundreds of Sallie's many friends. Interment private (only the relatives) and doubly sad on account of Clarence being in Munich, Germany. (Signed) H. J. Heinz.

In a letter to Clarence telling him of his mother's death, Henry Heinz wrote: "And now, dear Clarence, I must stop to rest, as by doing this, is an awful strain on mind and body to lead you gradually step by step until you are beginning to realize the awfulness of what has befallen us. God has spoken, and we keep still."

CHAPTER 9

"We Keep Our Shingle Out"

1890

First execution by electrocution, Wm. Kemmler, Aug. 6 at Auburn Prison, Auburn, N. Y., for murder.

Castle Garden closed as immigration depot and Ellis Island opened Dec. 31.

1892

Homestead, Pa., strike at Carnegie steel mills, near Pittsburgh; conflict between 300 Pinkerton guards and strikers; seven guards and 11 strikers and spectators shot to death, many wounded, July 6. Henry C. Frick, ch., wounded in Pittsburgh, July 23, by Alexander Berkman, anarchist.

1894

Jacob S. Coxey led 20,000 unemployed from the Mid-West into Washington, April 29.

Strike of employees of Pullman Co., South Chicago, Ill., June, led Eugene V. Debs to call sympathetic strike of American Railway Union. President Cleveland called out Federal troops . . .

Thomas A. Edison's Kinetoscope given first public showing at 1155 Broadway, New York, April 14 . . .

1895

X-Rays discovered by Wilhelm Konrad Roentgen, a German physicist.

1896

Guglielmo Marconi received first wireless patent from Britain, June 2.

1897

Eugene V. Debs formed Social Democratic party.

1898

Radium discovered by Pierre Curie, Mme. Curie and G. Bemont, Paris.

1899
South African (Boer) war began Oct. 11 . . . British losses 5,773 killed, 16,171 died of wounds or disease, 22,829 wounded. Boers engaged est. 65,000, losses unknown.

Filipino insurgents (est. 12,000 under arms) unable to get recognition of independence from U.S.A. started guerrilla war.

Boxer anti-foreign uprising started in China; missionaries and Christian Chinese murdered.

The 1973 World Almanac
and Book of Facts

THE DEPRESSION OF 1893–1897, with its strikes and wandering armies of unemployed, was disrupting and painful. "Exceedingly busy during the fall [of 1893]," Heinz wrote, "although the money panic has curtailed all branches of trade. It was hard financing. Good security was no inducements to banks. We stopped discounting bills, which was equivalent to $50,000 borrowed. A great many had to suspend." He blamed a lack of confidence, the silver question, and the Democratic party, though he had called Cleveland, when re-elected in 1892, "a very safe and conservative man." A contingent of Jacob Coxey's army of angry unemployed passed through the city in the spring of 1894 on its way to Washington, camping in Exposition Ball Park in Allegheny.

In 1893 the World's Columbian Exposition in Chicago was a bright and happy episode in the midst of social turmoil. Though addressed to the theme "The Parliament of Man, the Federation of the World," visitors who inspected the massive complex of exhibits in Jackson Park tended to conclude, "Great is America and the Glory Thereof." There were nearly 400 separate structures on 700 acres, built, equipped, and maintained at a cost of $18.5 million, not including the state buildings and exhibits. The main edifices looked out on Lake Michigan. There were the Transportation Building, the Court of Honor, Machinery Hall, Livestock Pavilion, Electricity Building, Manufacturers, Women's Horticultural, Art, dozens of foreign buildings, and the battleship *Illinois*. There were the Zoopraxological Hall, the Blue Grotto of Capri, Lapland Village, Volcano Kilauea, Indian Bazaar, Japanese Bazaar, Japanese Tea Garden, Vienna Café, Eiffel Tower, Model of Saint Peter's of Rome, and Hagenbeck's trained animals. There were the Viking Ship, the *Nina, Pinta,* and the *Santa Maria,* Venetian gondolas on the lagoon, a 130-ton Krupp cannon, and on the midway "the World's Congress of Beauty, 40 Ladies from 40 Nations." The whole was beautifully designed, built, and landscaped; it gave 12 million people a view of the best that men could do in art, architecture, and technology; it gave to some of them a lasting vision of what a city might become.

The food manufacturers exhibited in the Agricultural Building, which was at the southeasterly end of the grounds just west of the casino, quite near the lake shore, and almost completely surrounded by lagoons. This was one of McKim, Mead, and White's splendid structures, long, wide, and high, with fifty-foot Corinthian columns at the entrance and a rotunda with a glass dome. It provided nearly nineteen acres of floor space and cost $618,000.

A visitor entering by the main portal found himself at once confronted by the displays of the foreign governments and of foreign companies — Crosse & Blackwell, Lea & Perrins, Fortnum & Mason, and Dundee & Croydon, among others — apparently on the American premise that if it was foreign and imported, it must be better. The state agricultural exhibits took up the rest of the first floor. Pennsylvania displayed the Liberty Bell and 166 varieties of native grass.

The American food manufacturers were on the Gallery

Floor — Knox Gelatin, Durkee & Company, Huckin's Soups, Price Baking Powder, American Cereal, T. A. Snyder Preserve Company, Schlitz Brewery, Lorillard Tobacco, H. J. Heinz, Oswego Starch, and, by some unaccountable aberration, Wise Axle Grease Company. The Heinz Company, in Section 11F to the left of the dome, was given considerably more space than any other food manufacturer. A trade paper called its exhibit "most comprehensive, showing every variety of sauce, relish, and preserve put up, many of them being original with the firm." Rand McNally's guidebook, *A Week at the Fair,* reported, "The H. J. Heinz Company of Pittsburg * has a magnificent pavilion of antique oak, hand carved and oil polished. At each end of the four corners is a small pagoda. These are tenanted by beautiful girls — one French, one English, one German, and one Spanish." "We had a good display," Heinz wrote. "8 persons in attendance and dispensed freely from our products."

Despite the variety of sauces, the free samples, the antique oak, and the four beautiful girls, the crowds did not throng to the Heinz exhibit — nor, indeed, to any of the exhibits on the Gallery Floor. Hordes came to the Agricultural Building, looked through the foreign food and state exhibits, glanced at the flight of stairs, and left to see other main-floor displays, the midway, Sandow the Strong Man, or Little Egypt doing her belly dance. They had "done" the food show and did not return.

Heinz had attended the civic parade and dedication ceremonies that opened the Fair pro forma in the fall of 1893. He returned at the real opening the following spring and found the fair "a wonderland and a great educator." He took one look at the straggle of visitors on the gallery, meditated a while, and then left for the nearest printing shop. There he

* From 1890 to 1911, Pittsburgh, by government decree, was told to drop the "h" from its name. The order was widely ignored.

designed and produced a small white card made to look like a
baggage check, with the promise on the back that if the bearer
presented it at the Heinz Company exhibit in the Agricultural
Building he would receive a free souvenir. From his smaller
display in the Horticultural Building his men handed out
checks to all who would take them, and up and down the Exposition grounds a scattering of small boys dropped them by
the thousands. By the thousands the people headed for the
Agricultural Building, swept by the foreign food exhibits, and
climbed the stairs to the Heinz display. There they viewed an
assortment of art objects, antiquities, and curiosities, sampled
Heinz products, hot and cold, on toothpicks and crackers, and
received their free souvenir: a green gutta-percha pickle one
and one quarter inches long, bearing the name *Heinz* and
equipped with a hook to serve as a charm on a watch chain.
Fair officials had to summon policemen to regulate the size of
the crowds until the supports of the gallery could be strength-
ened. The foreign food men filed an official complaint with
fair authorities, charging unfair competitive methods. The
other American food exhibitors, grateful for the crowds attracted to their own booths, gave Heinz a dinner and an inscribed silver loving cup. "A great hit," he wrote in his diary.
"We hear it from all sources."

The company gave away 1 million Heinz pickle charms at
the fair. When it was all over, the *New York Times* reported
(in a story of the kind publicity men dream about):

NARROW ESCAPE AT WORLD'S FAIR

Chicago, Nov. 14 [1893] — It has just been discovered that
the gallery floor of the Agricultural Building has sagged where the
pickle display of H. J. Heinz Company stood, owing to the vast
crowd which constantly thronged their goods or to procure a
watch charm.

This time the Heinz firm captured first medal and diplomas on
eighteen varieties of their Keystone condiments.

Heinz's solution to the Chicago crisis was based on the Sixth Important Idea he had developed in the conduct of his business: Let the public assist you in advertising your products and promoting your name. He phrased it this way in the diary in July 1892: "We keep our shingle out and then let the public blow our horn, and that counts. But we must do something to make them do this." Very few have ever equaled Henry Heinz in the finesse with which he persuaded the public to blow his horn. He contrived to use his plant operations, his horses, his treatment of employees, his collection of curios, the "pickle brooch," the annual sales convention, the number of his products, the giant and ubiquitous outdoor signs, and the Heinz Pier in Atlantic City as means to excite public attention and make people talk. In most of these, people not only looked and talked; in some way or other they participated. In the case of the plaster pickle, they voluntarily and consciously made themselves ambulatory advertisers of the Heinz name and of its leading product.

Arthur Baum, a *Saturday Evening Post* editor, called the Heinz pickle "one of the most famous giveaways in merchandising history." The historians of advertising still speak of it with admiration for (in their jargon) its "high tie-in and recognition factor." Some unknown writer likened its shape, arching downward at the ends, to "the mouth of a small child just ready to burst into tears." The brooch or charm, first introduced in 1889, developed a clasp and became a pin, and the company gave out some scores of millions in that form. For no good reason except that they were so magnificently available and it was the thing to do, an army of boys, a whole generation of children, wore Heinz pickle pins on their lapels, shirts, sweaters, blouses, caps. It seemed to be a hard thing to throw away; adults kept them in drawers or boxes, or they carried them in pockets and purses for good luck, or as a gag, or because of habit formed in childhood. Time after time, Heinz people meeting strangers would hear something like, "I visited your plant once and they gave me this pin. Darnedest thing, but I've carried it ever since."

Heinz was the first industrialist to invite the public to call and inspect the full range of his plant operations. Any visitor to Pittsburgh automatically included a tour through the "Heinz Pickle Works." A guide with a group began with the famous stables ("You will notice that these stalls are of open construction allowing perfect ventilation"). They continued through the printing department, the box factory ("We use about ten million feet of lumber every year"), the can factory ("On account of the noise, it is impossible for you to hear me very well, but over each machine you will see a sign telling what it is used for"), the Time Office (Note to Guide: Call attention to the window showing "The House Where We Began"), the dynamo room, and the factory girls' dining room. They went on through the Baked Bean Building ("The Heinz beans are not boiled but are actually baked to a rich amber brown in ovens located on the floor above, then passing through silver-lined tubes to the hoppers below, where the cans are filled at the rate of 150 per minute"). Then to one of the preserving kitchens ("All our preserves are made on the old home plan — a pound of sugar to a pound of fruit") and the Pickle Bottling Department, where several hundred spotlessly clean girls packed, inspected, corked, capped, and labeled various sizes of pickles.

The visitors were given samples to taste along the route, a farewell lecture in the company auditorium, and the Heinz pickle pin to wear on bosom or lapel. If it was in residence, they were given, as a special treat, the chance to see a very famous American oil painting hanging in the auditorium. This was *Custer's Last Rally*, from the brush of John Mulvany, who had also painted *Trial of a Horse Thief, Love's Mirror, A Comrade's Appeal*, and other lesser-known works. *Custer's Last*

Rally, 11'8" by 19'8" in size, for which Heinz paid $25,000 in 1898, was so popular that it was kept traveling on a circuit so that no one would be denied the pleasure of seeing it: the Heinz Auditorium, the New York exhibition room at Broadway and 23rd Street, the Heinz Pier, and the major fairs and food shows at which the company had displays. In 1900, twenty years from the date the original was painted, Heinz persuaded Mulvany to produce a second version for the London office. This was a replica in every detail except that this time General Custer's hair was longer.* The figures are very nearly life-size.

Some 20,000 visitors were trooping through the Allegheny factory annually at the turn of the century. The Founder sometimes conducted the important visitors through the plant himself, often persuading them to appear before his employees in the auditorium. Signatures in the *Register of Prominent Visitors* in the early 1900s included those of E. Burton Holmes of Chicago, Henry van Dyke of Princeton, Billie Burke of London, David Belasco and John Philip Sousa of New York, J. M. Studebaker of South Bend, Raymond Hitchcock of Great Neck, Long Island, Prince Axel of Denmark, Jane Addams of Hull House in Chicago, John Drew, Billy Sunday, Ernest Thompson Seton, the U.S. Marine Band, the Brooklyn Baseball Club, twenty-six Philadelphia councilmen, eighteen Japa-

---

* At the urging of his wife, Custer had reduced his visibility before he rode against the Sioux in 1876 by shortening his flowing locks. Mulvany restored them in his second version. The original version is now in the collection of the Memphis Pink Palace Museum, Memphis, Tennessee, where it is rolled on a drum and stored.

Walt Whitman gave a long account of the picture in his *Specimen Days* (1882): "I could look on such a work at brief intervals all my life without tiring. It is very tonic to me." The work was widely distributed as a colored lithograph. Mulvany took to drink, became a derelict, and committed suicide in 1906 by leaping into the East River. Robert Taft, author of *Artists and Illustrators of the Old West, 1850–1900* (1953), nominates the work as one of the two painting reproductions that have been viewed, commented on, and discussed by more people than any others. (The other is Casilly Adams' *Custer's Last Fight,* painted around 1885.)

nese businessmen, members of the cast of the Oberammergau
Passion Play, the Cincinnati Symphony Orchestra, and the Central Committee of the World's Sunday School Association.
The name of Elbert Hubbard ("Fra Elbertus") of East Aurora
was signed first in the *Register* and appeared again a few years
later.

The plant tours, of course, were a form of corporate publicity and product advertising. So, too, were a number of other
Heinz activities. Heinz had a superb talent for promotion and
showmanship. To a degree it was based on a simple and sin-
cere desire to enable everyone else to share what pleased and
excited him — for example, *Custer's Last Rally*, the company
horses, the curios collected on his travels. But his generosity
was mixed with a quite pragmatic understanding of the benefit
to company sales and reputation. In any case, he worked his
talent to the limit.

The two hundred Heinz draft horses throughout the country
were all jet black except for a fine gray. Joe Hite, with the
company off and on since 1873, now in charge of the stables
and now accepted as a character — as a man of "keen wit,
colorful language and strong personality" — chose the Pittsburgh horses. Except for those bought in Chicago, each had
to be inspected and approved by two other experts in horse-
flesh, Sebastian Mueller and H. J. Heinz. They demanded
horses that fitted a certain conformity in weight, size, and type
and were pure black with black points, the only exception
being a modest white star on the forehead or a slight whiten-
ing at the feet. The horses had brass trimmings on their harness, and they pulled white wagons with green trimmings.
Heads turned to look and perhaps to comment when they
passed. No parade in southwestern Pennsylvania was complete without a Heinz train. As the Heinz stables were a famous showplace, so was the Heinz delivery service one of the
transportation marvels of the nation.

At the start, Heinz had emphasized "point of sale" material in his advertising — pieces displayed or distributed in the grocery stores. In 1892 he wrote, "Now in N. Y. City and have contracted for more advertising matter at one time to be used inside of a year than ever before in my life, $10,000. Consisting of calendars, souvenir books, stamped-out pickle cards, pickle charms and spoons, and show cards for boxes." Within a dozen years he was spending many times that amount. In every streetcar in America there was a Heinz color card with a four-line verse. (Nevin G. Woodside, general sales manager, paid his young son William ten cents for every streetcar the boy saw without a Heinz card in it and paid out little money.) There were signs along every main-line railroad; two dozen of the country's most prominent hillsides, including a cliff overlooking San Francisco Bay, blossomed with the numerals "57," ten feet high, cast in solid concrete, and whitewashed twice yearly. ("My God!" said a foreign visitor, "They number the hills here.") Heinz owned some 400 private-rail freight cars, and each was painted bright yellow with the company name and the 57 monogram in large green characters on both sides. The Heinz Company was the first to ship vinegar and pickles in tank cars, in 1894, designing and using its own 9950-gallon cars fashioned of four-inch-thick cypress staves. A typical sign on a car, almost as large as the car itself, read: "Loaded with H. J. HEINZ COMPANY AROMATIC MALT VINEGAR for the stores of C. H. Papworth of Syracuse and Watertown."

Henry Heinz did not believe in understatement or low key in his advertising, and he did not let many natural opportunities pass by unused. When the scores of Heinz sales managers rolled into Pittsburgh each January in chartered Pullman cars for the weeklong sales conference, flags were raised at the Allegheny works and they were met with éclat. Heinz described the meeting that opened on January 5, 1892, at a somewhat inconvenient time:

Sallie and Irene give a reception today from 2 to 5. Over 100 ladies called, about 35 carriages and nearly as many more in the evening. Irene's coming-out party. The house was handsomely decorated. (I paid the bills.) Music by Gunter, five pieces. I am vain enough to be pleased it was a success.

Our Fifth Annual Salesman's Convention also commenced to-day. It met in a new room at our works in Allegheny at 10 o'clock. From that time until 12 o'clock was spent in welcoming addresses and responses. About 100 managers of Branch Houses and salesmen are here, stopping at the Seventh Avenue Hotel. The Western men came in one car and the Eastern men in two cars with streamers over the P.R.R. and were met at the Union Depot by our H. J. Heinz Company Brass Band of 21 pieces and were led from the hotel to the works this morning. The men were highly pleased. I meet with the managers in one of the offices while Kuipers and others lead the salesmen in the Convention Hall each day from 9 to 12 and 2 to 6 P.M.

Heinz relied heavily on a relatively unexplored and expensive form of advertising, that of demonstrations at grocery stores, fairs, expositions, and food shows. These were marked by generous free samples and convincing money-back guarantees, on the principle that a person ought to be privileged to try a thing before he bought it and ought to be able to return it if he didn't like it.

Electric outdoor signs were then the newest and most costly form of advertising known. New York's first large electric sign, six stories high, went up at the corner of Fifth Avenue and 23rd Street, facing the Admiral Dewey Arch, in 1900. Heinz designed the sign and explained to O. J. Gude, the great pioneer in outdoor advertising, how it was to be erected. The sign consisted of a green pickle forty feet long bearing the name HEINZ. Below it, in letters ranging from three to six feet in height, appeared "57 Varieties Exhibited at Heinz Pier, Atlantic City." Twelve hundred Mazda bulbs were used at a cost of $90 each night, at a time when a single bulb was a curiosity. By a mechanical arrangement each line flashed separately; one moment the streets were lighted with unprecedented brilliance, the next they were comparatively dark. People thronged Madison Square Park to marvel at the transformation. After a time the sign was changed to read "A Few of HEINZ 57 Good Things for the Table — Peach Butter, Tomato Soup, India Relish, Tomato Ketchup, Sweet Pickles."

In the display room below the sign, daytime visitors might watch a pretty girl demonstrating how to pack midget pickles into a bottle or, if they were lucky, could study John Mulvany's painting of the Custer massacre. The New York *World* called Heinz "an advertising and merchandising genius," but as so often happens to works of genius in Manhattan, the sign was dismantled in July 1901 to make way for a mere office building — the $4 million, twenty-two story Flatiron Building.

In March 1905 Heinz was busily decorating London with twelve-by-twenty-four-foot enameled tin signs when his son Howard wrote, "The firm think that you are putting up a good many bulletins and do not recommend getting many of those signs." We may assume that the Founder was not deterred. He never forgot for a moment that he was operating in the country's most fragmented industry, with commercial competitors on every side, nor that every housewife who owned a box of Mason jars was a potential competitor as well as a customer. The fight for shelf space in the grocery store, even before the explosion of brand-name products and the advent of the chain store and supermarkets, was as fierce as anything the commercial world had known. Advertising and promotion would help him in the good fight. The happiest arrangement was that in which the Heinz salesman simply went through the stockroom or warehouse every Monday, took inventory of Heinz goods, and wrote up his own order. Every Heinz salesman, with his derby hat, stiff collar, and stickpin, carried in his sample case a hammer for tacking up advertisements and a clean white cloth for dusting off Heinz goods on the shelves. While dusting, of course, he would try to move his competitors' products to the back or lower shelves and place his own at end aisle or eye level.

Heinz personally hit upon the "57 Varieties" slogan in or before 1892 while riding in a New York elevated train. He was studying the car cards and was taken by one that advertised "21 styles" of shoes. He applied the phrase to his own products. There were more than sixty of them at the time, but for occult reasons his mind kept returning to the number 57 and the phrase "57 Varieties." "The idea gripped me at once," he said, "and I jumped off the train at the 28th Street station and began the work of laying out my advertising plans. Within a week the sign of the green pickle with the '57 Varieties' was appearing in newspapers, on billboards, signboards, and everywhere else I could find a place to stick it."

He had only two stern restrictions on his advertising: he never posted billboards in or around Pittsburgh, and he never advertised in the Sunday newspapers. His successors have lifted the ban on Sunday advertising, but few Heinz billboards are seen today. The last giant outdoor sign stood in Wenceslaus Square in Prague, Czechoslovakia — a huge Heinz ketchup bottle outlined in electric lights. It remained lighted all during the resistance in the spring of 1968 and the Russian invasion that followed. Czechs had a fondness for the sign; they regarded it as their window on the West.

Whenever the Founder encountered resentment at the enormous signs placed on hillsides, he called upon his philosophy of persuading others to blow his horn. The Chattanooga episode is an excellent example. The rumor somehow started that Heinz had leased the side of Lookout Mountain looming over the city and intended to erect thereon the Heinz pickle and a large sign reading "57 Varieties." The rumor spread, public indignation rose, letters appeared in the press, a committee formed. Ralph J. Pfeiffer, a Heinz executive who started as

Heinz's office boy, now an octogenarian, remembers that a batch of telegrams came to the office and that one read, "IF YOU DARE TOUCH THAT SACRED SPOT WE WILL PICKLE YOU IN 57 WAYS."

At that point Heinz happened to visit Chattanooga and appeared at his office at 204 Carter Street. The committee met him and made known its views. Heinz expressed shocked astonishment. He protested that he had no such plans. Lookout Mountain was a great historic shrine, one that he would never desecrate. In some other cities, the story goes, he confessed to having such plans but willingly scrapped them and presented the city fathers with his lease to the hillside. In either case, he departed amid plaudits, expressions of good will, and friendly stories in the press.

The costliest, most ambitious, and probably most successful promotional undertaking was the Heinz Ocean Pier at Atlantic City, sometimes called "The Crystal Palace by the Sea," sometimes "The Sea Shore Home of the 57 Varieties." Heinz had paid a first visit to the resort in August 1880, when he wrote in his diary, "Took a sea bath, very exciting, breakers very high. Probably 20,000 people here daily, while the population is but 6,000 during the winter. All sorts of swings and museums in town, and shows." Now, eighteen years later, he leased (then bought for $60,000 and remodeled) the pier near the Breakers Hotel, at the foot of Massachusetts Avenue. The Heinz Pier, still remembered with gratitude by thousands of footweary or shivering visitors, was one of three in Atlantic City, the only one that stayed open throughout the winter (and closed on Sunday).

The pier presented to the boardwalk the freestanding façade of a vaguely classical triumphal arch. It was crowned with a broken pediment and (in the early years) had two large green Heinz pickles suspended horizontally and rather attractively between the columns on either side of the entrance. Just beyond the façade Heinz added (in 1901) a glass-enclosed Sun Parlor, furnished with rocking chairs, tables, twenty-five desks with free writing paper and souvenir postcards, rest rooms, magazines and metropolitan daily newspapers, displays of Heinz products ("The kind that contain no preservatives"), and a demonstration kitchen with free hot and cold samples.

The pier extended almost 900 feet into the Atlantic Ocean and had at the outer end a Glass Pavilion, white with yellow trim, on the top of which stood an electric sign seventy feet tall: "Heinz 57 Varieties." The pavilion held, among other things, an assembly hall seating 125 persons, equipped with a large map showing the location of Heinz installations and with a display of "industrial and sociological photographs" of Heinz facilities and people. There a member of the company's Sociological Department delivered a lecture with seventy-six stereopticon slides, giving a sedentary equivalent of the tour through the Allegheny plant. He ended with, "You are cordially invited to sample the 57 Varieties and will not be asked to buy. If, however, you wish an assorted case you can leave your order and it will be delivered to your home, through your grocer, at less than wholesale price. Only one case to any one home."

At the center of the Glass Pavilion was a booth with thousands of canned and bottled products artistically arranged in revolving pyramids among exotic plants. The main area, however, was given to a remarkable exhibition of 144 paintings, bronzes, tapestries, and curios, some of them lately shown at the Columbian World Exposition. Major works among the paintings included *King Lear Awakening from Insanity* by Hildebrandt, *French Government Officials Visiting a Secret Distillery* by Buland, *Decadence of the Romans* by Thomas Contour, *Stanley at the Congo* by Gentz and Koerner, thirteen by twenty-two feet in size, and, at the height of the season, John Mulvany's *Custer's Last Rally*. There were marble busts of Socrates, Caesar, Dante, Michelangelo, Shakespeare, Othello (in six colors), Milton, Louis XIV, John Wesley, Napoleon, Garibaldi, and Queen Alexandra of England. There was the mummy bought in Cairo in 1894, a mounted ram's head, a Buddhist household shrine, a framed collection of Confederate money, a couple of nine-foot elephant tusks from the Gold Coast, a chair made of animal horns with a leather seat from Omaha's Trans-Mississippi Exposition of 1898, a panel from one of Admiral Nelson's warships, and a chair General Grant had sat in at Chattanooga.

From time to time the exhibit was supplemented with other treasures appropriately publicized: a collection of ship models, the only complete whaling outfit in the United States, a model of a Navaho village. The serious visitor could buy for a nominal fee an illustrated catalogue of the collection.

In the season, as many as 15,000 people came onto the Heinz Pier daily; in winter, when the pavilion was closed, 4000 came to the Sun Parlor. In the forty-six years of its existence, an estimated 50 million people visited the pier, and every one of them was offered — and most accepted — the Heinz pickle pin. The Delaware *Record* generously called the Heinz Pier "quite unique and wonderful in its way, for it represents the rapid growth of a business built upon broad lines of dealing justly with all, and of giving royal equivalents in goods of the highest grade to all customers."

In the 1920s and thereafter, the pier offered exhibitions, lectures, and concerts of a more sophisticated nature. In 1944, however, the fates decided that the institution had outlived its purpose. The hurricane in September of that year tore out a great section of the trestle between the two buildings and cast the "5" in the "57" into the sea. The Heinz management of that day, perhaps somewhat relieved, abandoned The Crystal Palace by the Sea.

CHAPTER 10

"Kindly Care and Fair Treatment"

The much-abused epithet "Captain of Industry" . . . is given at random nowadays to a whole battalion of commercial knaves who have succeeded in getting their heads above the million dollar mark, but it rightfully belongs to Mr. Heinz . . . It is a common thing now to see big factories and large industrial plants paying considerable attention to the social welfare and health and happiness of their employees, but to Mr. Heinz belongs the pioneer honors.

Arthur Tarbell,
"Heinz — The Man,"
Human Life, August 1910

PITTSBURGH's foreign-born population doubled between 1880 and 1900. Into the area, the country's greatest center of industrial production, came immigrants from Ireland, Germany, and the Scandinavian countries, then increasingly from Poland, Russia, Austria-Hungary, Slovakia, and Italy. Their grandchildren are working throughout the city today as engineers, scientists, nuclear physicists, teachers, doctors, lawyers, administrators, but in 1900 life was hard and working conditions often wretched. The immigrants labored in the coal mines, coke plants, steel mills, glass factories, on the railroad, in construction. If they were recruited in Europe by the contract labor system (outlawed by Congress in 1885), and if they had no resources or special skills or waiting relatives, they were housed for a time in railroad cars on sidings and then dumped into the slum areas at the Point or on the Hill, in Skunk Hollow or Painter's Row, or in the steel towns along the rivers. There they lived in tenements, ten or twelve men to a room, sharing a bed in shifts; they caroused in the saloons and whorehouses; they stood in the long line on Saturday evening before the public bathhouse in Soho, where they got soap, a towel, and hot water for a nickel. They strained the city's housing, schools, hospitals, sanitation, fire protection, police protection, and the private charities that made up almost the only welfare services. They died by the thousands in industrial accidents, in epidemics, and from tuberculosis, pneumonia, and typhoid fever. Despite their hardships, they saved to bring over their wives, children, parents, brothers, and sisters.

Women of all ages came by the hundreds of thousands. The woman who sought employment was terribly limited in the work she could do. Teaching and nursing required skills she did not have and could not acquire. Most office clerks and salespeople were men. She could work as a household domestic, or as a scrubwoman, or as a prostitute, or at manual labor in some trades — in laundries, in garment and glass factories, in stogy factories, in packaged food plants. The pay was low, the hours long, the work hard and sometimes dangerous, the future uncertain.

There was always a line of applicants at the pickle works in Allegheny City, where H. J. Heinz was engaged in an "industrial betterment" program and where, according to the newspaper stories, a girl would find "kindly care and fair treatment." Lillian Weizmann, born in Allegheny on September 23, 1888, was one of those who went to work at the Heinz plant at fourteen, on graduation from grade school. She had attended the eighth-ward public school on East Ohio Street because her parents felt every child should have contact with a public school and then went for four years to Saint Mary's parochial school on Lockhart Street. "There were eight grades at St. Mary's," Lillian Weizmann says, "and we had a nun who would teach you individually if she saw you were beyond that. My dad and mother wanted me to go to a high school, but all the girls around the neighborhood worked for Heinz. They

would say, 'Why don't you come down to Heinz?' I went
down to Heinz and I stayed at Heinz."

She worked from 7:00 A.M. to 5:40 P.M., but on Saturdays
she quit an hour early, at 4:40 P.M. She began at five cents an
hour, three dollars a week. That was what other fourteen-
year-old girls got in the best factories, and she knew that she
could advance to piecework or to the regular starting wage,
twelve and a half cents an hour (half that paid to men). This
was a time when Heinz specialty salesmen began at $12 a
week; when an unskilled mill hand worked for $.15 an hour;
when the average daily wage was less than $1. It was a time
when a bakery near the Heinz plant sold three delicious mince
pies for $.25; when a woman's full silk-lined tailor-made suit at
Gusky's Department Store, "Fresh from the Best Eastern Centers of Fashion," cost $15; when a handmade cheviot skirt cost
$5; a linen handkerchief, $.05; a pair of all-wool blankets,
$2.69; a man's shirt, $1 (all shirts were negligee garments
pulled on over the head); ten bars of White Lily Floating
Soap, $.19; a forty-eight-pound sack of white flour, $.89; a
pound of Armour's ham, 10¾ cents; a pound of soda crackers,
$.04; a twenty-six-piece set of Rogers silverware in a velvet-
lined box, $5.48; a gallon of Diamond Monogram Whiskey, $3.

Lillie's day began in the dressing room below the five-story
bottling building, where she changed her street clothes and
where she had the luxury of a private locker with her own key.
As a new employee she was given a freshly laundered working uniform and mobcap each day for one month; thereafter
she made her own dresses from dark blue, white-striped cotton
that she bought at cost from the company stockroom. Her
caps, ready-made from fine Irish dimity, cost her twelve and a
half cents. She was required to begin each day in a freshly
laundered uniform and white apron. Since she handled food,
she received a weekly manicure. The dressing room had hot
and cold running water, marble washbasins, two bathrooms

with showers, a soft divan, a reclining chair, an emergency hospital with two beds, and a matron with some nursing experience. The girls had the free services of an on-call company physician and two dentists.

Lillie was assigned a seat at one of the long tables in the 600-place girls' dining room. Every morning on the way to the bottling department, where she worked, she placed her lunchbox on her chair. (It was never stolen.) She had a half-hour for lunch. Each day she dropped a penny into a box as a token payment for the cream, sugar, and pots of tea and coffee on the tables. The money went into an employees' welfare fund. Sometimes there were bottles of ketchup or relish on the tables that had been rejected in inspection that day for loose tops. While she ate she could listen to music played on the Orphenion * or by one of the girls on the piano, or she could study any of the one hundred paintings and drawings that adorned the dining room walls. These had been collected by Mr. Heinz on his travels and were of a kind that would elevate a young lady's thoughts, appeal to her aesthetic sensibilities, and exercise a refining influence on her character. The fifteen or twenty forewomen ate at their own table in a corner of the room. There were four other dining rooms in the plant: one for male factory workers, one each for male and female office workers, and one for top-ranking company officials (male, of course).

Several times during the summer Lillie's turn came to climb into a horse-drawn wagonette with eight other girls and spend a morning or afternoon, at no loss of pay, being driven through the park and the downtown areas. If she had a suggestion on how to do something better, she could drop it into a box and perhaps get a reward or even a promotion. She could use the dressing room after hours. She could sun herself

* A large boxlike instrument imported from Germany that, according to its advertisements, "renders many pieces with the effect of an orchestra."

on the girls' roof garden atop the bottling building, equipped
with rustic benches, awnings, a fountain, blooming plants, and
a conservatory. She could swim in the company natatorium
and exercise in the company gymnasium. She could take
members of her immediate family with her on the company
outing in July. This was held on a Saturday in one of the
parks within fifty miles or more of Pittsburgh as the employees
elected — Olympia, Rock Springs, Rock Point, Idlewild, Cas-
cade, or Conneaut Lake. It involved the movement of some
3000 to 4000 people in a paddle-wheel steamboat or in three
chartered trains, sometimes loading as early as 5:00 A.M.

There was considerable emphasis on self-improvement in
the company-sponsored after-hours activities. Lillian could
take free courses in dressmaking, millinery, cooking, freehand
drawing, and, "for those who desire culture in voice music,"
training by a singing master. She could have received instruc-
tion in the intricacies of becoming an American citizen. She
could read in the reading room, borrow books delivered to the
plant from the new Carnegie libraries, and attend evening lectures in the company auditorium. At noon she sometimes
heard talks by some of the great figures of the day. She heard
Russell H. Conwell deliver his famous inspirational speech,
"Acres of Diamonds," the theme of which was the sanctity of
wealth. ("Get rich, young man, for money is power, and
power ought to be in the hands of good people . . . I say you
have *no right to be poor* . . . You and I know there are some
things more valuable than money; nevertheless, there is not
one of these things that is not greatly enhanced by the use of
money.") *

Lillie was not a poor girl and was not overwhelmed by these
amenities. She recalls that she found the working conditions

---

* Dr. Conwell (1843–1925) delivered this talk no fewer than 6000 times, and
in so doing he both reflected and set the philosophic tone of his generation.
The founder of Temple University, he used his fees to send boys through college.

"pleasant." To a girl who had worked for several years stripping moist tobacco leaves of their stems, weighing and tying them in pounds for the rollers, sitting with her back to a damp wall in a cellar, working by the light of a gas jet, eating her lunch off a corner of her workbench — to a peasant girl from Central Europe who a year earlier had been living in some remote village in a cabin with an earth floor, the animals housed under the same roof on the other side of the wall, who had worked in the fields in all weather — to such a girl the physical comforts of the Heinz plant, the relatively short hours, the pay, and the companionship were a revelation and a delight.

The center of most of the educational and social activities was the Heinz Auditorium, completed in 1900, said to be the first in the country built solely for the benefit of employees. It had a musical director, 1500 opera-type seats, a gallery with two proscenium boxes, 2000 incandescent light bulbs, a pipe organ, a Pianola, a Steinway Concert Grand Piano, an Edison Stereo-Projecting Kinetoscope, and a splendid large dome with artistically designed stained glass. The dome represented the globe, on which appeared the motto, "The World Our Field." Underneath were mural paintings representing the inhabitants of the four corners of the earth: Asian, African, North American Indian, and Anglo-Saxon, William Gladstone's portrait serving to typify the last. Around the base of the dome were inscribed the eight essential qualities for success in business: Integrity, Courage, Economy, Temperance, Perseverance, Patience, Prudence, and Tact. The walls held a number of fine paintings, including (most of the time) Mulvany's *Custer's Last Rally*. Between the pictures appeared mottoes, some of them composed by Mr. Heinz himself: "To do a common thing uncommonly well brings success," "A young man's integrity in youth is the keystone of his success in after life," "Make all you can honestly, save all you can prudently, give all you can wisely." And his favorite, which appeared in offices, halls, waiting rooms, and work areas of every Heinz installation: "Do the best you can, where you are, with what you have today."

Four times a year the seats were removed in the auditorium and the floor waxed for a large dance, generally to the music of Rocereto's sixteen-piece orchestra. Each employee was permitted to bring one guest, by written invitation only. To spare Mr. Heinz's feelings, the dances were called "Promenade Concerts," and to satisfy that title there was always a grand march, usually led by Sebastian Mueller and Mrs. Agnes Dunn, the general forewoman of the Home Plant girls. "One time Mr. Heinz came," says Lillian Weizmann, "but not on the dance floor. He stayed on the balcony, waving down at us."

There were weekly organ recitals in the auditorium and concerts given by an employee Choral Society of sixty voices. There was, one evening, an illustrated stereopticon slide lecture on the 1900 Paris Exposition, with views of the city, and the following week an employee performance of *Seven Keys to Baldpate*. There were performances of plays written and directed by Karl R. Hammers, one of the midlevel executives; these were taken quite seriously by cast, audience, and Mr. Hammers, and they were, by all available accounts, creditable productions. There were, from time to time, professional performances by "recognized stars of the first magnitude" — orchestras playing at Exposition Hall, vaudeville headliners (Elsie Janis, for example, the teen-age prodigy who did imitations of public figures). The supreme event of the year was the Christmas Party, which began at 2:00 P.M. on the afternoon of the twenty-fourth. In a typical performance, Santa Claus appeared on the decorated stage, followed by Mr. Heinz, who shook his hand and made a short address on the joyous spirit of the season. The program included instrumental and vocal solos by employees, with encores, humorous recitations, a playlet, and presentation of a floral tribute to management from the girls of the factory. The audience then dispersed to its departments, each person to receive an identical Christmas gift according to sex — an umbrella, or a silk scarf, or a music box, pocketbook, leather chatelaine bag, box of linen handkerchiefs — often an article that H. J. Heinz had seen on his travels, wanted his employees to have, and on the spot ordered by the thousands. "Sometimes not all the employees appreciated them," Lillian Weizmann recalls, "because some of them were picture albums and not everybody appreciates picture albums, you know."

All such events were reported fully in the company magazine, which began in 1897 under the name *Pickles* as a publication solely for salesmen but in 1902, as *The 57 News*, broadened to become an organ of employee communication. The humor was lame. ("When does Lettuce Blush?" "When it sees Mustard dressing.") The criticism was tactful. ("The April 23rd concert exceeded the expectations of those most interested in the aims of the Choral Society.") Whatever its faults, the *News* was crammed with names, information, and features that seventy years later are invaluable company history. An employee who was ambitious, moreover, might win some recognition in the *News;* a girl in search of a husband might manage to appear there in a picture, looking her best.

The *News* exacted in full measure the price of "kindly care and fair treatment": it constantly goaded its readers to render faithful, cooperative, and loyal service to management. The editorials were moralistic and exhortative: "Find Your Place and Fill It," "Aim for What You Want," "Character as a Business Influence," "Thoughts on Success," "Keep Step," "The Power of Perseverance," "Life is Growth," "Bridging Obstacles." There was no labor trouble at Heinz — and there were no unions — for sixty-five years. The first strike came long after the death of the founder, when the Depression and New Deal ushered in new ideas and a new age.

Lillian was hired by and worked under Agnes McClure

Dunn, the plant's forewoman. Mrs. Dunn, born in Ireland, had worked for Heinz in the mid-1870s, left to marry, and returned three years later as a widow supporting her father, badly wounded in the Civil War. Fifty-four years old in 1902, she protected and disciplined her girls with evenhanded firmness. She sat in a rocking chair in her office off the dressing room, always in factory uniform despite her position, and there listened patiently to any girl who came for advice or help. If the problem was medical, Aggie Dunn would order appropriate care and turn the bills over to Sebastian Mueller, who paid them privately and personally. A Heinz executive once remarked, "I always pitied the man or boy who would say anything to a girl that was not right, if Mrs. Dunn found it out." Adolf Siegmann, a retired executive, recalls that when he was a young pay clerk he was summoned to appear before Mrs. Dunn. "I had the habit of slamming the pay envelope down, bingo, on the table or desk in front of the girl for her to pick up. I was reprimanded. Mrs. Dunn ordered me to hold the envelope out to each girl and wait until she took it. She said, 'I want my girls to be treated with respect.' I learned a lesson."

Lillian became a pickle bottler — one of 110 girls who sat and worked at long tables with Carrara glass tops, five girls to a side. She deftly inserted pickles, one at a time, into spotlessly clean bottles by manipulating a grooved wooden stick scooped at one end. "Goods carriers" brought the pickles to her from the barrels at the side of the room. When the porcelain dish before her was almost empty, she called out, "Susie! Pickles!" and Susie came running.

This was considered a good department to work in if a girl was skillful enough to meet the requirements. The pickles had to form a uniform design according to the type of bottle used and the kind of pickle being packed. The giant bottle, about nine inches high and quite wide, held the larger pickles, Size

1250. She placed exactly twelve in each bottle; more or fewer meant that the bottle would be returned to do over. Fancy pickles — midgets or gherkins, Size 1000 — were packed in vase-shaped bottles wider at the bottom. She packed these in rows around the bottle, taking the slightly larger pickles from the bowl first, using the smaller ones toward the top, and inserting a single red pepper in the pattern where it would show.

When she finished twenty-four of the larger bottles or forty-eight of the gherkins, Lillian carried them in a crate to the inspection table, where girls examined them one by one and either passed or rejected them, as for a bad design or a stem on a pickle. She then took them to the forelady for that section, who, seated at a desk, gave her a metal tally for the approved bottles and credited the work against her number — Number 597. A boy named Mike filled these with vinegar. Other girls corked the bottles and wheeled them on hand trucks to the labeling tables, where girls applied paste-saturated labels and placed them on pallets for delivery to the shipping room. The fancy midget bottles were wrapped in paper.

At the end of the day, Lillian exchanged her accumulated tallies for larger denominations and hiked up her skirt to help the other girls scrub the labeling tables and the floor around them and to clear the bottling tables of all unused and rejected stock. Twice a week she joined the others in scrubbing every inch of the tile floors and walls of the entire room.

She earned one cent for each bottle packed and approved, and within a few months she was packing twelve or thirteen dozen a day and was averaging better than $1.50. When someone suggested to Sebastian Mueller that music would make the work easier and faster, he replied, tongue-in-cheek, "I'll try anything once" and arranged to have recorded music played in the bottling department. But packing pickles required concentrated artistic attention, and the girls who were making good money on piecework objected to the distraction. The music stopped.

Girls in the other departments — more than 1000 of them in 1902 — washed bottles, cut up chickens, trimmed meat, stuffed olives, skinned tomatoes, peeled and stoned peaches, cut the eyes out of potatoes, filled cans with beans and tomato sauce, sorted pickles by size, passed cans to men who affixed the lids. Immigrants just off the boat were put to peeling onions, which they did in a resigned or happy spirit until they learned they were doing work no one else wanted to do. In the "kitchen season," when the produce came into the plant by the trainloads, everyone who could move worked overtime at stemming strawberries or handling tomatoes or at whatever other work was urgent.

In an age blemished by sweatshops, firetrap factories, callous indifference to industrial accidents, and many filthy food-processing plants, people came from thousands of miles to see this model factory. Henry Heinz went personally in 1900 to receive two gold medals conferred at the mammoth *Exposition Universelle Internationale* in Paris, one for the quality of the products exhibited, the other "for the policy of the firm tending to the improvement of factory conditions . . . for the sociological features of its business as exhibited by means of photographs." Interviewed by a New York reporter on his return to the United States, Heinz opined that Paris was a poor place in which to hold an exposition, because "of all the cities of the world it is the most attractive, a permanent exposition in itself." Asked whether he thought his company got its money back for its services to employees, he said, "I have never given that side of the matter any thought. We are fully repaid when we see our employees enjoying themselves and spending their noons and evenings in a manner profitable to themselves." Pressed further, he said, "Very well then, if you don't like the sentiment that attaches to the plan, I want you to distinctly understand that it is good business as well. It 'pays,' it increases my output. But I don't want to put it merely on a dollar and cents basis." He received a diploma at a fair in Liége, Belgium, "for consideration given employees in lighting, warming, ventilation and sanitary arrangements" and a grand prize medal at the Louisiana Purchase Exposition in St. Louis in 1904 "for placing factory conditions on a higher plane and developing their employees into comfortable, happy, ambitious and more intellectual workers." The company's "industrial betterment work" received the ultimate accolade, however, when a Harry W. Sherman, Grand Secretary of the National Brotherhood of Electrical Workers of America, attended a convention in Pittsburgh, visited the Heinz plant, and in an interview with a New York reporter called it "a Utopia for working men" and said, "The most advanced philanthropic ideas are in practical operation there."

Lillian Weizmann was tall, pretty, hardworking, and smart, and she attracted favorable attention. She had learned a fluent German from her parents. She finished several yearlong courses at night school at Duff's Business College.

> I was the firm's waitress for a while. When the regular waitress was out I was asked to go over to the firm's dining room, so I went. Now it's called the executive dining room. I would go over there. It was always considered an honor to be selected, but some of the girls were too shy to do that work.
>
> You never knew when Mr. H. J. was coming in. The members of the board would come in pretty regularly on time — right after twelve o'clock. But no one knew when Mr. Heinz was coming.
>
> That kitchen served the office men's dining room at one end, and the office women's dining room at the other end, and the firm's dining room in the middle, and they were very careful not to have a lot left over at each meal. If they had reached the end of their line in the kitchen and Mr. Heinz came in, I'd say, "Mr. Heinz, there isn't a whole lot left over. For instance —." And he'd say, "Well, give me 'for instance.'" So I said, "Mr. Heinz, the only thing that comes to mind is prunes." He said, "Prunes

nough for anyone; bring them in." So I did that. I'm
⟋ this so you can get an idea of the kind of man he
⟋ was a man who was easy to know and very easy to talk

I didn't do anything particular to make Mrs. Dunn like me,
but when I finished my training at Duff's Business College she
came to me one day and said, "Lillian, I have to tell you this.
Mr. Anderson * said there's a job for you over in the office if
you want it." At that time there was a wide gap between factory
and office workers and never the twain should meet. She said,
"You know, you and I have been friends. Do you mind me saying this?" She was a lot older than I was. I said, "No, Mrs.
Dunn, I don't mind if you say anything." She said, "You can go
to the office side of the street, but I think your forte is right here
in the factory." And I said, "Well, I don't think you need to say
anything, Mrs. Dunn. I've already made my choice. I don't
want to go to the office, I want to stay right here in the factory."
I was eighteen then. And she said, "Good for you."

Immediately after that they asked me to go to the Pittsburgh
Exposition, where we had an exhibit, and demonstrate bottling.
So I was on a platform there, with a fence around me, and I
worked over there for the month of September. There was always someone to bring me and take me home. The manicurist
looked at my nails every morning.

Now, around the front of the exhibit we had demonstrators
who would pass out samples of our foods. At the side we had a
small lecture hall, and at given times an illustrated talk would
be given about the business and the goods and so on. Around
the back they would come to watch me bottling pickles.

At the other end of the hall there was a concert hall, and if
you pleased, for your twenty-five cents admission you could hear
Sousa, Rocereto, Victor Herbert, Walter Damrosch, and this
other Italian conductor who when he was through, he was exhausted. Even in those days he wore long hair. When Walter
Damrosch Week was on, those doorkeepers had to watch, and
nobody, but nobody, was allowed to go through that door when
he was conducting a piece.

It was quite an honor to be chosen for that work, because you

---

* H. C. Anderson, Senior Vice President.

were in close contact with the members of the firm. That's how I got to know Mr. Heinz. I really got to know him then, more than in my working in the factory. And I knew the sons Howard and Clarence. I knew them all.

We always had visitors going through the plant. In those days we had men — they were mature men, they were probably retired businessmen, because they were really imposing men — who took these visitors through. As they made the tour through the plant, they ended in the Auditorium. Then we took them into the demonstration room, where there were linen tablecloths, linen napkins, everything was linen. And they would get a sample of the various products we made. I used to love to go over there and wait on those visitors. The girls in the bottling department said to me, "You don't care how much you earn — you'd rather go over into the Auditorium and be on day work." I said, "I'd rather go over and be with people."

But it was very helpful to me because afterwards I was chosen to work in the factory employment office. I graduated from the bottling department to the employment department. I accepted that because it was something new. We didn't really have an employment department before that. If Sally Jones had a friend she thought would make a good employee, she would bring her along with her to work, and that was handled in the Time Office.

Miss Weizmann worked with "Colonel" J. S. Foster, H. J. Heinz's administrative assistant, on employee Christmas presents.

The Colonel and I — we started about a month ahead of time, and we would allot so many presents to Bowling Green, so much to Muscatine, so much for California, and so forth — and then we would get someone over from the railroad and send them out. They were sent to the personal address of the manager, to his home, very much under cover.

One year we had fur-lined gloves for the men. The first day after Christmas when we came back to work, I was in my office in the employment department when the Colonel stuck his head in the door and said, "My God, Miss Weizmann, what do you think they said down in Florida and out in California when they got those fur-lined gloves?" We both started to howl, but neither of us ever said a word about it.

It was quite odd how the nationalities of the girls changed. When I started in the bottling department they were overwhelmingly of German and Bohemian parentage. Afterwards the Polish girls came in, and still later the Italians. Before I started there had been Irish girls. When I would get awfully upset about something that was happening among the girls, Mr. Heinz would say to me, "Don't worry, Lillie. When the Irish were here they used to run at each other."

Miss Weizmann became forewoman of the bottling department in 1918, at age thirty, shortly before going to the employment department; she continued to hold both positions. When Mrs. Dunn died of pneumonia in 1924 at age seventy-six, all Heinz offices, warehouses, factories, and other plants were closed the afternoon of the funeral, and the main plant was closed all day. Lillian Weizmann succeeded to her position as general forewoman. She retired in 1953, after fifty-one years of service. Two years later she was asked to become one of two managers of Eden Hall Farm, a 375-acre institution twenty miles north of Pittsburgh, set up in the wills of Sebastian and Elizabeth Heinz Mueller, whose lives had been saddened by the early deaths of their three children. It was run for all Heinz girls and alumnae in the United States and Canada as a combination vacation resort, country club, and convalescent home. It had quarters for twenty-five girls, who were picked up at the plant on Friday evening and returned Sunday night. The original emphasis was on health, provision being made for all Heinz women to receive free surgical and convalescent care. There were horses, skating, archery, swimming, and buffet suppers that people still talk about with a dreamy look in their eyes. Miss Weizmann was still working at a very active institution in the spring of 1973.

CHAPTER 11

"The Pickle King"

*Any one of our present buildings in Pittsburgh is as large as
the entire plant of any other concern in the same business in
this country.*

H. J. Heinz Company
statement, 1901

IN LESS THAN ONE THIRD of a century Heinz had built one of
the country's largest and most profitable businesses. He was
manufacturing more than 200 products. He was the largest
producer of pickles, vinegar, and ketchup; the largest grower
and manufacturer of sauerkraut, pickling onions, and horseradish; the second largest producer of mustard; the fourth largest
packer of olives. He was operating nine branch factories in six
states, thirty-eight salting houses in nine states, a branch house
in London, and agencies around the world. He was the only
pickler who manufactured his own bottles or who had his own
private railroad freight and tank cars. He employed 2800 full-
time people, 400 of them "travelers." Some 20,000 others
cared for the crops grown for the company on 16,000 acres.
He had built the business without mergers and with purchase
of only two or three small companies.

Into the Allegheny factory sidings came long trainloads
from the farms and salting stations. From foreign lands came
cars filled with produce — raisins and green olives from Spain,
figs and dates from the groves of the Near East, currants from
Greece, casks of cauliflower from Holland, fresh fruits and
sugar from the West Indies, whole spices from the East Indies,
mustard seed from England, France, and Italy. From American distilleries came scores of thousands of used oak kegs and

barrels, fifteen- and thirty-gallon size, their insides to be scraped clean of charcoal for reuse for kraut and vinegar. (Federal law forbade a second use for whiskey.)

A group of eastern financiers proposed to buy the business, advising Heinz to cash in on his years of hard labor and enjoy a well-earned leisure. He replied, with an eye on press and public, "I do not care for your money, neither do I nor my family wish to go out of business. We are not looking for ease or rest or freedom from responsibility. I love this business. To stop work is death — mentally and physically. This business is run — not for my family or a few friends — but for what we call the Heinz family — the people who make our goods and sell them . . . We are working for success and not for money. The money part will take care of itself." To English parties who made him an offer he replied more bluntly: "I don't want to water the stock and then appear rich."

Daily operating procedures of the company were supervised in these years by an eight-to-ten-man Advisory Board, Sebastian Mueller, Chairman, that met daily. Henry Heinz attended once a week when he was in the city. The recorded minutes for 1896–1899 indicate that most decisions were neither difficult nor momentous. Among weightier matters, the committee members moved and carried resolutions to place advertisements in the city's Manchester Street car line (two cents per card per day); to appoint a committee to formulate plans for caring for beggars; to appoint a charity committee with authority to disperse $2000 annually, aside from Mr. Heinz's private charities; to buy a suitable cap and coat for the boy driving the bean wagon; to buy 500 copies of Elbert Hubbard's *A Message to Garcia;* to present Queen Victoria in her Diamond Jubilee year with a sample case of goods; to sell 5000 pickle charms to T. B. Coyne of Chicago at $10 per thousand, plus $1 for freight; to entertain 2100 Knights Templars at lunch in the Girls' Dining Room; to charter a city street car to transport sales managers in convention between plant and hotel, at a cost of $5 an hour; and not to approve "Mr. Pierce joining the Order of the Jolly Fellows at the firm's expense." On Saturday, October 9, 1897, no quorum could be recorded, "as most of the members are attending the horse show." On December 4, 1897, Heinz sent the board a letter: "I hereby notify the members that I have ceased building and extending the Main Factory at Pittsburgh and that any further suggestions for building must come from members of the Committee." In September 1896 Heinz had raised the wages of all the women in the Pittsburgh plant 12½ percent; he seems not to have consulted the committee on that decision.

Heinz received a $25,000 salary as president, the same as it had been a decade earlier; he had refused an increase to $50,-000. In a news story he was listed as one of twenty-five Pittsburghers who carried between $250,000 and $500,000 in life insurance. He was first called "a millionaire" — an ultimate accolade in Pittsburgh — in 1896; he was everywhere known as "The Pickle King." An English magazine referred to "Pittsburgh's Peerless Pickle and Preserve Purveyors."

From time to time Heinz had given his "leaders" a share in the profits of the company as partners, adding a new name as a veteran retired or died. He had expressed the fear around 1900 that the business, if it grew too large, could not continue to produce good food with the same careful handling and selection; he talked for a time of setting a $15 million limit on annual sales. Now, in 1905, he decided that a company so large needed the perpetuity of existence provided by incorporation. The six existing partners became the sole stockholders of the new corporation: Henry J. Heinz as president and general supervisor; Frederick Heinz, his cousin and original partner, in charge of the farms and gardens; Sebastian Mueller, his brother-in-law, in charge of the manufacturing department and branch factories; W. H. Robinson, finance; R. G. Evans, sales; and Howard Covode Heinz, his son, assistant to the president.

As he grew older, Heinz became less receptive to changes in company operations, but in one incipient revolution he was in the vanguard. He visited a trade show in New York's Madison Square Garden in 1899 and there saw "an electric mercantile wagon" made and exhibited by Pope Manufacturing Company. He bought it forthwith and shipped it to Pittsburgh. There it was used chiefly as an advertising device; it delivered the light goods donated as Christmas presents to churches, fire halls, police stations, political rallies, homes, and charitable organizations. The wagon was steered by a tiller and could go fifteen miles an hour on the level, thirty miles on a single battery charge. It presented two main problems: it had to be rescued at frequent intervals by a team of Joe Hite's horses (who for a decade to come were to continue as the company's main source of motive power), and it could hardly operate for the pressure of the curious and excited crowds that gathered around it.

Both difficulties subsided and Heinz electric delivery wagons multiplied — Popes, American Electromobiles, Columbia Electrics. They were the first in Pittsburgh and Chicago and among the first in New York — beautifully painted in cream and green with pictures on the sides, the earliest with a large green pickle mounted on the top. London had a Heinz pickle, but Paris was favored with both a pickle and a wagon built in the shape of a Heinz tomato chutney bottle.

The time came when the electrics had to give way to trucks with combustion engines. Heinz wanted to try them; Joe Hite was dead set against them: "They'll never do in our business. Our salesmen have too many stops to make, a dozen stops on a single street, and then crank up again every time they stop." Heinz answered him patiently, "Now, Joe, now, Joe, let's just try them and see how they work." He bought the first gasoline wagons in 1910 — four Mack Trucks, chain drive, two-and-a-half ton, solid tires, hand-cranked.

One of the electrics in Pittsburgh was involved in a mild scandal when a Heinz salesman who had imbibed too much alcohol with his noon meal rode with it from Etna to Pittsburgh's Golden Triangle. He did so sitting astride the pickle atop the wagon, waving his hat and singing a ballad normally reserved for company dinners and sales meetings, the refrain of which ran

> Heinz's, Heinz's, Heinz's, Heinz's, Heinz's pickle-man,
> Of "57" brands he sells as many as he can,
> All the world he travels o'er from Denmark to Japan,
> Heinz's pickle, Heinz's pickle, Heinz's pickle-man.

The punishment he received is not a matter of record, but the whole Pittsburgh force, at least below the top management level, was amused.

In the years since the Heinz Company and the Heinz family moved from Sharpsburg, "The House Where We Began" had remained standing, forlorn but not forgotten. Early in 1904, Heinz paid it a visit, tape measure and notebook in hand, a speculative gleam in his eye. He had helped his father to make the brick and build the house just fifty years earlier. He had lived in it from the age of ten until his marriage there at twenty-five. He had grated and bottled his first horseradish in its kitchen. He and Noble had started the business there in 1869. Now he would move the house, his first rung on the Ladder of Success, five miles downriver to a place of honor beside his present factory buildings, there to serve as a museum for some of the curios and relics he had collected and as a memorial where everyone could read at a glance every step in the evolution of the company. If it could be done, it would attract national attention and it would demonstrate that there

was sentiment — a soul — in business. His partners thought so
highly of the idea that they offered to buy the house from him
and pay for moving it. Heinz declined with thanks; he would
handle the operation himself and ask the company to accept
the house as a gift.

He was unwilling to have the house torn down and reconstructed. He consulted various house-moving companies.
They told him it could not be moved intact because of the nature of the terrain between Sharpsburg and Allegheny. What
about floating it down the river? A frame house, they said,
might be so moved, but a brick house — let alone one weighing 169 tons — had never been moved such a distance by
water. It might end up at the bottom of the river, or it might
crack and crumble to a pile of bricks. They declined to undertake the operation.

Heinz approached Kress-Hanlon Company, a new concern
founded by two Pittsburghers in their twenties who had attracted international attention by successfully moving a mammoth tank down the river for one of the oil companies. They
agreed to do the job and to bond themselves heavily to deliver
the house uninjured.

They jacked up the house on blocking timbers, trussed it
with cables, dismantled the two chimneys, and on March 1
began to roll it the 800 feet from Main Street to the right bank
of the Allegheny River. The ground was so soft that they
could cover only fifty feet a day. During that time there were
two uncommonly high floods and the house stood for some
days in swirling waters that reached almost to the second-story
windows. Blocks of ice and a floating tree stump knocked out
one of the hearths.

Using a process they kept hidden from view and would not
discuss, Kress and Hanlon slid the house onto the largest coal
barge that could be procured on the rivers. The barge settled
under the weight to become embedded in the muddy bottom

of the river. Days passed before the rains came, the river rose, and the barge floated. Barge and house started down the river guided by a large river towboat. The barge buckled in the middle and began to leak; another towboat was procured for the sole purpose of using its steam pumps to pump out the bilge water. At the 43rd Street Bridge — the lowest of four bridges that had to be navigated — the barge was moored for three days. Some six feet of house extended above the level of the bridge floor.

By this time the operation was attracting wide press coverage in the daily papers and in engineering and scientific journals. The Heinz Company operated a towboat for press representatives, complete with meals but presumably with no spiritous liquor on board. Kress and Hanlon waited several days for the river to drop, and while they waited they allowed the barge to fill with water to the point where it sank six feet lower in the river. The House Where We Began cleared the 43rd Street Bridge with four inches to spare. The barge was pumped out again. It passed under the other three bridges, through a lock, and on April 13 approached the Heinz landing, one of its maimed chimneys showing smoke from a fire lighted in the grate by workmen.

For a mile along the shore crowds gathered to watch the majestic arrival — curious spectators and some 1500 Heinz employees, most of them women in their blue dresses and white aprons. The two towboat captains blew their whistles. Other watercraft and the engineers of passing locomotives responded. A plant employee tied down the Heinz whistle. The girls took off their aprons and waved them in the air and cheered.

Over the next several weeks the house made a 500-foot journey up the riverbank, across the West Penn Railroad tracks (it had to be done within one hour on Sunday), and onward, safe and whole, to its old foundation, which had been dug up and

rebuilt on the plant grounds. There it stood next to the Covode Building, a settlement house for children named for Jacob
Covode, who had been kind to Henry Heinz during his troubles in 1875–1876.

Heinz repaid Sharpsburg for the loss of the House with a
succession of gifts: First, a cast bronze fountain and watering
trough fed by springs on the hill and surmounted by a life-size
statue of the Indian Chief Guyasuta, placed before the Farmers & Mechanics Bank at the corner of Main and North Canal
streets. Then a 125-foot flag staff of the best finished steel with
an American flag forty feet long. The local paper reported
that this gift was received with joy by the borough council,
and it ended its story, "For a rich, racy relish with your meats
and salads, use Heinz's Keystone Dressing." Then the Lewis
Homestead, largest house in Sharpsburg, as a boarding home
for homeless children. Then a building for the Sharpsburg
Y.M.C.A. constructed to hold a bowling alley removed from
the old stable at Greenlawn. Later, an organ for the Grace
Methodist Church.

Heinz did not remarry. An anonymous letter written by "A
Friend" warned him, "Some of your Church members see you
are getting sweet on Widow L — and we feel sorry for it. She
is a very nice lady in some respects but I know her designs on
you are for money *only*," etc., etc. If she had designs, the
Widow L — did not realize them. Heinz lived at Greenlawn
with the children when they were at home, a staff of servants
in attendance and Sister Henrietta in charge. Hettie was single; as often happened to youngest daughters, she had stayed
at home to nurse her aged and invalid mother until her death
of pneumonia in 1899 at age seventy-six. She was devoted to
her brother and was his companion on many of his annual
trips to Europe. But he could never understand, she said later,
the strain put upon her health as his housekeeper, nor the
drain on her income when she traveled with him, dressing as

became his sister and her station. Sallie had been dead so long, she felt, that he had forgotten what women's clothes cost, and he never realized that a woman no longer could dress as cheaply as she had in 1896. In traveling, moreover, she was rushed from one place to another without a chance to rest. For several years past he had forgotten to give her a Christmas present, excusing himself by saying that he could not think of anything. Then he gave her $5000 on a Christmas, suggesting that she spend half of it on a pearl ring and the rest on clothes.

Clifford, the youngest child — "all the members of the family and relations are fond of Clifford," he said — entered Lafayette in the fall of 1905. Irene, twenty-six, the oldest, announced in April 1898 her "matrimonial engagement" to John La Porte Given, a Cornell man, telegraph editor of the New York *Evening Sun*. The wedding was held eighteen months later at Greenlawn, after the addition of a music room and a billiard room and enclosure of the porches made space for some 150 guests. Miss Myra Boyd served as maid of honor.

Clarence, the oldest son, returned from school in Munich and went to work for the company; by 1902 he was listed briefly as advertising manager. He had the temperament of a dreamer and poet, however, and did not mature with the toughness required to stand up to the pressures of business life in a family-owned company. He left for several years to strike out on his own, unsuccessfully, in other cities, then returned to the company. "I am happy to say," Heinz wrote to a colleague in England in 1907, "that while Clarence in former years, when you knew him as a boy, gave me a great deal of concern, he has during the past two years or more invented over a dozen things which have all been of practical use, and that the firm has advanced his salary no less than three times during the last three years, when I was absent from home, and that he has, too, since been made a member of the firm." But the unhappy fact was that Clarence did not continue to show "the proper spirit"; he could not assume the shape into which he was being forced and could not meet the demands put upon him by a fond, dynamic, exacting father. He retired from business in 1914 in poor health.

His brother Howard was made of a tougher fiber. A. S. Fowler the Phrenological Analyst had written of him in 1883 (in the midst of much phrenological nonsense), when he was six years of age: "He is quite a young whirlwind . . . A natural boss and dominating over everybody. Will be a conspicuous man among men if he doesn't blight young . . . Will lead a blameless life . . . Is a handsome, fluent speaker but his controlling feature is originality and power of intellect and originality along with the highest sense of duty. His business talents are well developed . . ."

In 1885, at the age of eight, Howard signed the pledge at the Grace Methodist Church never to use intoxicating beverages. That summer he went to work, six hours a day, in the factory. "The children had to learn the business, in overalls," Lillian Weizmann says. "Mrs. Dunn used to tell me that Howard would come into her office so tired that he laid right down on the floor." He wrote his first business letter at seventeen — a report to Papa on his work at the Wooster, Ohio, salting house. At eighteen he toured Europe with a friend, bicycling from Amsterdam to Munich, averaging forty to sixty miles a day, carrying a revolver in his knapsack, returning from Paris in time to enter Yale as a freshman. He made a trip to Bermuda as a Yale senior, writing on board ship, in one of many short-lived diaries, a sentence very much of his generation: "There is a Miss Burr aboard, but so far Allan and I have not cared to meet her for she is not much on looks even though someone said she has been to several Yale Proms." He was graduated in June 1900, visited the Exposition in Paris with his father during the summer, and in October began to work for the company, at which time his father stopped his allowance ($200 a month) and doubled his holding of stock in the company. Howard's first assignment was to take charge of the Heinz exhibit for the McKinley-Roosevelt political parade. He wrote in his diary:

Suggested idea of train of cars & locomotive on wheels which was accepted by firm.

Prepared for 3 box cars, 2 pickle tank cars, engine tender & caboose.

Engine built of light wood covered with pasteboard & cloth, half regular size engine. One man in boiler to guide & two in cab to guide. Cars put on push carts, two men in each car. Took 3 elegant painters all week and until eleven at night to finish. Also 4 carpenters.

Nov. 3. Great Parade. Started train from factory at 10 o'clock with man at each side and end of car making 45 men to run train & five men as lieutenants, say 50 men on train.

We also had a large globe on float, six-horse spike team pulling. On globe was "The World Our Field." At four corners were boys dressed as Indian, Chinaman, European, and colored man. These four men threw out advertisement envelope on which was printed "McKinley-Roosevelt-Prosperity." Inside was a pickle charm, two stamped out pickles, a sailor boy card & picture of plant. These were eagerly seized by crowd. 40,000 were given out.

We also had a large gold dollar 10 ft. high on float hauled by 4 horses . . . We had a motor wagon also. We had some 250 men in line also with yellow-rimmed Roosevelt hats & a band of our own. On the top of the cars was printed "The 57 for McKinley & Roosevelt" & on top of tank cars "Sound Money & Prosperity."

This was my first great effort and I put all my thought & ability on train to make it a success. I realize that I must win respect. I thanked God that my first effort with the firm had been so successful.

"No exhibit in the entire parade," said the Pittsburgh *Leader,* "attracted more attention than that of the H. J. Heinz Company."

Howard was then assigned to the pickle assorting department, rising each morning at five-thirty to make the early shift. After several days of transferring pickles from tank cars into barrels with a long-handled net, "I had a shoot made from car to barrel and thereby the men had lighter labor, kept pickles and brine off the floor, and filled many more barrels in same time."

In December he signed his first check for the company, for $50,000. On April 6, 1901, he took an opera party of young people to Duquesne Garden to hear Jean de Reszke, Milka Ternina, and Madame Schumann-Heink in *Tristan and Isolde.** On April 23 he went to New York to attend the wedding of Percy A. Rockefeller to Miss Isabel Goodrich Stillman, daughter of James Stillman, at Saint Bartholomew's Church, afterward going to the reception at the house at 7 East Fortieth Street. William Sloane Coffin, his Yale roommate, was an usher. In July he was in charge of extensive grading and remodeling at Greenlawn while his father was in England and Scotland. In October, in the first floor of an apartment building the company owned, he began a club for indigent newsboys. In January 1902 he addressed the annual sales managers' convention on "The Sociological Work Connected with the Factory":

> Outsiders brought it to our notice that we were sociological workers and that good would accrue therefrom. In doing sociological work there is always a limit to the amount that can be done. There is also a limit to the amount that can be done at one time; it is a matter of growth and development. On account of our employees living in different parts of the city, away from our factory, our efforts had to be confined to what we could do for them while they were at the "home of the 57." Our chief idea

---

* On this occasion the Pittsburgh *Post* reported: "Never has the dressing been so universally gay . . . an array of the most brilliant plumage ever seen at an evening's entertainment in Pittsburgh, and the coiffures were ornate and elaborate. Full evening dress prevailed, and pretty necks were the rule, the whole combining to make a display of the first order of social brilliance."

in doing what we do is to make those hours as pleasant as possible, and you can see if they enjoy their work they are bound to have more interest in it and thus all concerned are benefited . . .

Remember, gentlemen, that you will do the firm a favor if you will give the simple facts when you are asked questions about our sociological work.

A young man of reserve and self-control, Howard Heinz had one inordinate passion: gasoline automobiles. He bought one in Paris in the summer of 1900 — a two-cylinder, six horse-power Panhard-Levassor built in 1898 — and drove it in the Century Run, reaching a speed as high as forty miles an hour. It was bright red. It carried four persons. The rear wheels were larger than the front wheels. It manufactured acetylene gas for the lamps in a tank under the driver's seat. It had a steering wheel instead of a tiller, a Daimler Phenix engine, a transmission and differential, a platinum hot-tube ignition, and a double sprocket chain drive. It was a beautiful machine; it was nicknamed "The French Flyer" and "The Red Devil," and when it appeared on the streets of Pittsburgh it created a sensation.*

Howard Heinz drove the car daily from Greenlawn to the factory, eight miles each way, faithfully keeping his "Odometer Record Book" and suffering recorded anguish from punctures caused by horseshoe nails, trouble with the governor, trouble with a loose sprocket chain, and double trouble with a shaft that would not turn because no oil was reaching the cylinder. He helped to found an Automobile Club with one hundred other "leading citizens." A newspaper account read:

> The object of the club is to promote club runs, arrange for races, and promote the sport generally in this city. The purpose, too, is the advancement of the welfare of the general public in

---

* Panhard-Levassor had begun to manufacture gasoline-fueled automobiles in 1889, having obtained the rights for marketing Daimler engines in France. It was the first company to put the engine in front of the car and the first to put pneumatic tires on an automobile.

matters of better thoroughfares and rigid enforcement of all laws for the protection of life and limb, and placing pedestrians, motorists, and drivers of other vehicles on a proper basis for the law.

Foolhardiness is henceforth to be discouraged and a pleasant and legitimate pastime encouraged by rules and regulations that will be welcomed by the public in general.

The intense interest shown in the meeting last night was quite a contrast to the meeting called for a similar purpose at the Duquesne Club October 21, 1900. Then there were only 15 automobiles in Pittsburgh and only three motorists appeared at the meeting.*

In June 1901 Howard drove young Clifford to the company's annual outing at Maple Grove, covering the seventy-two-mile round trip in only six hours. In September he drove to Buffalo on a business trip and there stood in line for hours with 100,000 other people to walk past the body of the murdered President William McKinley, displayed in City Hall.

With his Red Devil, his Yale degree, his extensive travels, and his position in the family firm, Howard Heinz made an impression in Pittsburgh social life and on mothers with marriagable daughters, as reflected in the society pages of the city's eight daily papers. He recorded a momentous social event on November 26, 1901:

> I met Miss Elizabeth Rust of Saginaw, Mich., at a skating party held at Duquesne Garden by Miss Edna McKay. On the 29th Miss McKay, Miss Rust, Miss Edna McKay and Miss Gilchrist lunched with me at the office. I got very well started on an acquaintance with Miss Rust and made a date with her to go walking Sunday. On that evening I unexpectedly met her at the Orchestra Concert which only made us better know each other.

---

* A main reason for forming such clubs was to set up service stations where paid-up members might get repairs and buy gasoline. Repairs were made by local blacksmiths or at bicycle shops; gasoline was commonly bought in open cans at hardware stores.

Elizabeth Granger Rust, twenty, was the heiress of an old Michigan family that had made its money in lumbering. She had graduated from the posh Ogontz School for Young Ladies in Philadelphia the year before.

> Miss McKay asked me to join them to theatre Monday. Sunday we took a long walk to the Phipps Conservatory (a most muddy walk). We seemed to understand each other very well and had a good sensible talk. She asked me if I didn't want to come down Sunday night as she was going away soon. I went and we had a great long talk by ourselves which resulted in our promising to write. We hedged ourselves by suggesting that we let nature take its own course and we would stop if either changed their opinion.
>
> On Monday night I called with our carriage and we got to know each other very well indeed. We agreed to exchange photos. The show was Floradora. I had a most perfect time with her at the theatre. (We walked between the 1st & 2nd acts.) The drive home was indeed heavenly and — well I think she is perfect.

Howard Heinz and Elizabeth Rust were married in Saginaw on October 3, 1906. A private car carried officers of the company to Saginaw, as well as a number of intimate friends and members of the family, including Irene, Clarence, Clifford (an usher), John, Hettie, and Sebastian Mueller. Henry Heinz's gift to the bride was a string of oriental pearls; Howard's was a sixteen-karat sapphire pendant set in diamonds. William Sloane Coffin was the best man.

Howard had a long talk with his father on the morning of the wedding, which he recorded in a short-lived diary:

> He told me how much I had meant to him and how much he thought of Betty and how glad he was that she was to be my wife . . . I asked him to promise me (as a wedding gift to me) not to work so hard. That he meant everything to his children and they wanted him to take care of himself so we could live with and enjoy him for may years to come. That we children

didn't want the money he might make by working so hard — we wanted him. He then promised he would take better care of himself and then handed me a check for $100,000 as my wedding present with which to build a house. Well — I was more than surprised and almost overcome. I knew that Irene had only received $50,000 on her wedding day so I told father that I did not think I could accept the whole amount — that I felt all his children should be treated alike and therefore I would take only $50,000. He said that was very generous and that as soon as he could afford to give Irene another $50,000 he would then give me the extra $50 M. The $50 M which he gave me I deposited with HJHCo where it is drawing interest at 5% until such time as we find a lot and decide to build a house.

The afternoon of the wedding, all 1500 employees of the company at the Main Plant were invited as guests of the bridegroom to a reception and dinner given in the auditorium, work being suspended for several hours.

After the reception in Saginaw, the bride and bridegroom rode in a brougham to the Court Street Station, where a special engine was waiting with the "palace car" (inlaid mahogany, electric fans, a dining room, a large brass bed with a canopy and draperies all around) of the president of the Père Marquette Railroad. The car was hooked to the express to Cincinnati, and in it the couple rode to Hot Springs, Virginia. Over the next two weeks, in a suite in the Homestead Hotel, Betty Heinz wrote 200 of her thank-you notes, including one to the company's female employees for a silver fruit dish and one to the office force for a cut glass punch bowl. On November 8 they sailed on the *Kaiserin Augusta Victoria*, the largest passenger vessel afloat, for a two-month tour of Europe. The three-hundred-seventeenth and last thank-you note was written in Vienna. When Howard appeared in the Girls' Dining Room to thank them for the wedding present, "a regular pandemonium ensued for the girls cheered and yelled, waved handkerchiefs and some of them beat tin pans: this kept up several minutes."

Irene Given had made Henry John Heinz a grandfather by producing a girl, Sarah Isabelle, in 1904, and a boy, John L., Jr., in 1907. On July 10, 1908, he became a grandfather again with the birth in nearby Sewickley of a son to Howard and Elizabeth — a six-pound, eleven-ounce namesake.*

---

* Henry John Heinz II is today chairman of the board of the H. J. Heinz Company.

CHAPTER 12

Battler against
"The Hosts of Satan"

I appreciate the loyalty with which your father and all of his staff stood by me in the darkest hours of my fight for pure food. I feel that I should have lost the fight if I had not had that assistance.

Dr. Harvey W. Wiley
to Howard Heinz, 1924

H. J. HEINZ was the host at a luncheon given in 1898 for all male employees in the Pittsburgh Works. The men ate a hearty meal, listened to expressions of appreciation for faithfulness and earnest efforts, and lined up to shake the hand of the Founder, who greeted each by name as he came up. It was the last affair of its kind. The company was too big, there were too many men, and the Founder could no longer pretend to know all the names, even with the whispered prompting of the plant foreman and the payroll clerk.

Sales were good through the next decade, profits were up, and the canning industry perfected its most exciting development since Nicolas Appert — Sanitary Can Company's "open-top" container. For several decades processors had been inserting the food through a hole about the size of a silver dollar in the top of the can, which was then capped and soldered shut. Now a machine deftly fashioned a cylinder open at both ends, the sides being rotated together and crimped in a lapped double-lock seam. It then crimped and double-locked a bottom to the can and did the same at the top after the can had been filled and was ready for the pressure cooker. The only

solder used was along the side seam — on the *outside*. One machine could turn out 40,000 of these cans air-tight, with no
"leakers," in a ten-hour day.

The development was typical of advances being made in the
whole processing industry. The new machines could automatically hull and shell peas (the pea viner, 1892), husk corn
(1892), cut green corn off the cob (1899), even dress salmon for
the can (the "Iron Chink," 1903). The "big three" of canning
were still tomatoes, corn, and peas, but now, with the open-top
container, companies were canning white asparagus (1891),
sardines (1900), ripe olives (1901), sliced pineapple (1903),
white cherries, Bartlett pears, and horse mackerel, now renamed tuna. For years canned goods had been produced without brand names, each wholesaler affixing his own meaningless
label, but the new trend was for the processor to can, label,
and sell goods under his own registered brand name, as Heinz
and a few others had been doing. The identification made the
canner responsible for his product and brought him back into
contact with the consumer. Other food products were more
and more being packaged as a unit under brand names — soda
crackers, for instance, put out in wax paper in 1898, sealed,
moisture-proof, and free of contamination. Pillsbury XXXX
Flour, Domino Sugar, Uneeda Biscuits, Quaker Oats, Baker's
Cocoa, Heinz — such brand names and consumer unit packaging, with the great increase in use of refrigeration, were producing a quiet revolution in the grocery business, changing
the appearance of the store and its stock, freeing the grocer
from the need to weigh and package bulk merchandise.

In the laboratories, the chemists were developing a practical understanding of the reasons why food spoiled and of the
steps to be taken to prevent it. At a convention in Buffalo in
1898, in fact, two M.I.T. biologists made the first public demonstration of the harmful effects of invisible, unfriendly germs,
or microbes, or bacteria, in imperfectly sterilized canned

goods. The first canners' research laboratory was established in 1902 in Aspinwall, just east of Sharpsburg, near the Heinz gardens there. (Professor E. W. Duckwall, the first director, later became a Heinz Company processor.) The Association of Packers of Pure Canned Goods was organized in Pittsburgh in 1905.

Despite these advances, the food processing industry had never before been under such constant attack. It was being condemned because many commercial processors of food and drink were using chemical adulterants in their products, were labeling them falsely, and were advertising them dishonestly.* Some chemicals they used to improve flavor and color, some as artificial preservatives to stop fermentation or decay, some to conceal cheaper ingredients or poor quality, some to restore decomposed material to salability. Vegetables were being canned with sulphate of copper to give them a vivid green color. Sugar was bleached with sulfur dioxide as the reagent, corn with sulfite of sodium. Jams were colored by aniline dyes. Most of the chemicals were harmless when used in very small quantities, so far as the processor knew, though the amounts ingested were certainly no longer small when taken in combination with other adulterated products in a daily diet. Foods were also being adulterated simply to cut costs by substituting cheaper materials — butter with coconut oil, oleomargarine with paraffin, lard with cottonseed oil and beef stearin, Demerara sugar with dyed beet root crystals, cocoa with finely ground cocoa shell, maple syrup with cane syrup, plum preserves with starch glucose, olive oil with oil of cottonseed and sesame seed, cayenne pepper with ground wood and cornmeal. Some foods were being totally mislabeled — "imported French sardines," so described in French text, were often Maine herring.

* It has been suggested that the bad name borne by the early food processing industry was one reason why Heinz erected such elaborate buildings.

Whiskey-making was a part of "commercial food processing." Some rectifiers were simply mixing artificial color and flavor with pure alcohol and selling it as whiskey. The proprietary ("patent") medicines were also considered commercial processors. Some of their concoctions for curing obesity, "lost manhood," "female weakness," consumption, and cancer were physically harmless but medicinally worthless and psychologically cruel. Others were addictive. The tonics were generally alcoholic drinks, some with as high a proof as corn whiskey.* Their headache powders, painkillers, catarrh cures, cough remedies, and soothing syrups for infants contained cocaine, morphine, or opium.

About half the states, urged on by their food and dairy department chemists, had passed pure food laws by 1895. They were laxly enforced, however, partly because of the pressures brought to bear, partly because the state laws varied and the state commissioners were powerless without a uniform national law. A bill for such a law was introduced into the United States Senate in 1889 and in every session thereafter; it was so often by-passed that it became the subject of cynical ridicule over the next fifteen years.

Into this situation came an elemental force named Harvey Washington Wiley. He was a Civil War veteran, a doctor of medicine who never entered practice, a former teacher of college Latin and Greek, the first professor of chemistry at Purdue University at its opening in 1874, and state chemist of Indiana. His baptism came with a study of adulteration of table syrups, made for the Indiana Board of Health. Nine years and scores of studies later he was appointed to a post with wider opportunities, that of chief chemist (at $2500 a year) of the new Bureau of Chemistry of the United States Department of Agriculture in Washington. There he played a major role in

---

* One such tonic, Peruna, was forbidden to be sold on Indian reservations because of its high alcoholic content.

the development of agricultural chemistry. He founded the Association of Official Agricultural Chemists (1884), of which he was permanent secretary and editor, and served for two years (1893–1894) as president of the American Chemical Society.

Wiley was a 200-pound giant, a lucid and persuasive writer, a resonant-voiced lecturer of the caliber of the Chautauqua orators, a passionate, sometimes belligerent believer in a True Cause, a skilled in-fighter with an eye for the jugular, and a master at the art of using "pitiless publicity" to gain an end. These talents he devoted to the crusade for pure food. He began with a campaign of public education, citing case after case of chemically adulterated foods that were at the least deceptive and at the worst poisonous. He found the public apathetic or doubting, and so he doubled his efforts, dramatized his programs, and heightened his rhetoric against what he called "the powerful vested interests" and "the hosts of Satan." In so doing he incurred the active enmity of self-seeking persons in industry, the press, and Congress, the more so when they realized that they had erred in looking on the pure food crusaders as ineffective cranks and reformers. Wiley wrote:

A campaign of personal denunciation and disparagement was inaugurated of a magnitude that can only be appreciated by those whose activities and principles were directed toward the cleaning of the Augean stables of trade. I [was] the target of a veritable fusillade of poisonous arrows from every trade journal, newspaper and magazine which the adulterating interests could control. There was hardly a week that some interested organization or mercenary interest did not demand my removal from public office. Detectives were placed on my trail and every possible means employed to prejudice my scientific standing and official integrity.

The western meat packers fought Wiley, and so did the distillers, the makers of patent medicines, the producers of the

adulterants used in food, drink, and drugs, those processors
and canners who were preserving food by means of chemicals
and intended to continue doing so, and most United States
senators, then appointed by the state legislators and normally
strong defenders of the interests of "big business." The editor
of *Leslie's Weekly* declared in a public confrontation that he
would not "take the hand of the man who is doing all he can
to destroy American business." On the higher intellectual
level, it was held that a national law on pure food, while perhaps good in its intent, would be a transgression against personal liberty and a violation of states' rights.

Henry Heinz flung himself into this controversy with characteristic energy — on the side of Dr. Wiley. He was gripped
by the seventh of his Important Ideas. He knew that use of
deleterious chemicals by unscrupulous food processors was
hurting all other manufacturers in the industry by creating
suspicion of the quality and purity of all products on the market. He felt that his industry would not grow to major estate
until it had earned public confidence. The way to earn that
confidence was to work in partnership with a federal regulatory agency. Regulation would make the industry respectable
and trusted — an achievement beyond any price. He was
amazed that the other food processors could not see this. He
knew, moreover, that there was really no *need* for harmful
chemicals — that good foods, properly processed, would keep
without the addition of artificial preservatives. The speed of
processing, the autoclaves, the whole state of the art, had advanced beyond such need. Processors either did not realize
this, or they were unwilling to make the required capital investment in machinery, or they were preserving inferior materials by using chemicals.

He had no fear of working with governmental agencies. He
had been working for decades with the state and federal agricultural research stations and with the county agents in a com-

mon effort to raise the quality and yield of his farming operations.

For these reasons, Heinz called openly and forcefully for federal regulation of the production, labeling, and sale of processed and preserved foods.

Like so much of Henry Heinz's philosophy, the stand on pure food legislation was idealism and noble purpose compounded with pragmatic self-interest. It was "good business" for a manufacturer of unadulterated quality foods to curb those operators who were giving the whole industry a bad name — and undercutting his prices — with their dangerous and dishonest practices. In any case, it was a hazardous as well as an unpopular position for the Founder to take. The late Herbert N. Riley, Heinz Executive Vice President, said the year before his retirement in 1957, "There were those who charged that Heinz was blacklegging* the industry. He was risking his own business and his own position in the trade, because he knew in the long run it would be for the good of the food business and its best chance of survival."

He assigned to Sebastian Mueller, his son Howard, and a midlevel executive named Loren S. Dow the responsibility for the company's active and public support for a pure food and drug law. They called at the White House to ask for needed regulatory legislation and to offer their support to the President. Mr. Roosevelt was skeptical of maverick businessmen espousing an unorthodox cause. Howard Heinz gave a forthright statement of his father's and his company's philosophy.

Heinz was not completely alone in his industry in supporting federal legislation. A few other industry leaders took the same position, some publicly, most privately. The National Association of Canned Food Packers, meeting in Cleveland in 1898, offered to Congress the outline of "a bill govern-

* Blackleg is a British term that means to refuse to support (a union, union workers, or a strike).

ing the labeling and packing of hermetically sealed goods."
The association did not push the matter, however, and it
never met again. In the words of a historian of the industry,
"It was a little too far ahead of the times. The great body of
canners did not support it morally or financially. The average
canner was too individualistic, too secretive, and not clannish
enough to become part of a solid front for the growing
industry." *

Then a rush of events, some natural, some engineered, determined the course of history.

1. In the 1898 war against Spain, charges were made that
the American forces fighting in Cuba and Puerto Rico were
being fed wormy biscuits and spoiled canned beef. The fault
lay chiefly with an inexperienced and inept army command for
its careless handling of provisions, delayed transportation, and
long exposure of goods to the tropical sun. Press and public
resentment, however, was directed against the meat packers.
The citizenry for the first time began in audible numbers to
worry about its own meat and to demand a law to insure its
quality.

2. Congress had appropriated a modest sum in 1894 ($10,-
000, then $15,000 a year) for the Department of Agriculture to
use in "human nutrition investigations." Congressional committees went further and began to hold hearings on adulteration of food, drink, and drugs. They found widespread abuses.

3. Dr. Wiley (who in 1898 was raised to $5000 a year) was
aware that one of his handicaps in the fight for pure food was
the almost total lack of accurate scientific knowledge about the
harmful effects, if any, of chemical additives to food. In 1902
he obtained authority by a special act of Congress to investi-
gate "the character of food preservatives, coloring matters and
other substances added to food, to determine their relation to
digestion and to health, and to establish the principles which

* Earl Chapin May, *The Canning Clan*, 1938, p. 325.

should guide their use." He did so by feeding the chemicals to human guinea pigs. He set up a small kitchen and dining room in the Bureau of Chemistry and recruited twelve volunteers from the Department of Agriculture — "strong, robust fellows," he said, "with maximum resistance to deleterious effects of adulterated foods." For nearly five years his volunteers ate only controlled foods containing from time to time small quantities of seven chemicals commonly used as preservatives, the assistant surgeon general standing by to render any necessary succor. Borax was the first chemical tested. The results were wonderfully satisfactory: the men became nauseated, lost their appetites, had symptoms like those of influenza, and suffered from overloaded kidneys. This was front-page material for the press. "It was not necessary to ask any publicity to this matter," Dr. Wiley said happily. "Reporters were always and incessantly on hand." One from the Washington *Post* christened his group "the Poison Squad." Wiley began to be called, with a sneer or a chuckle, "Old Borax." The New York *Sun*, no admirer, named him "chief janitor and policeman of people's insides."

The periodic reports printed as Department of Agriculture *Bulletins* were highly technical and graphically unattractive, but they demonstrated clearly that the chemicals in the amounts then being used caused serious injury to digestion and health. They caught and held nationwide public attention. "I do not hesitate to say," Dr. Wiley wrote later, "that I knew something about the subject I had been working on! So did the young men of the poison squad. And so did the public."

4. At the St. Louis Exposition in 1904, the forces fighting for pure food laws staged what has been called "one of the most effective bits of propaganda ever achieved for pure food or for any other purpose." ° The crusaders, mostly from the

° Mark Sullivan, *Our Times: The United States, 1900–1925* Vol. II, *America Finding Herself*, 1927, p. 522.

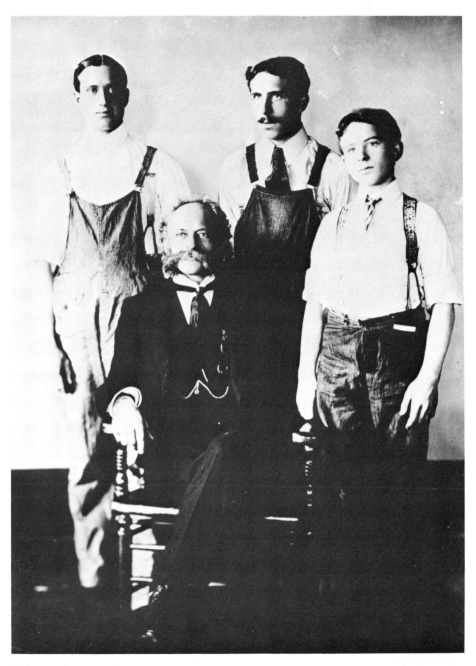

Father and sons: Clarence, Howard, and Clifford. Heinz wrote on the back of this picture, "Experience and Gaining Experience."

Heinz sales managers, back in Pittsburgh for a meeting in 1903, gather on the men's roof garden. (The women also had a roof garden.) The rug, potted palms, and *objets d'art* are tastefully emplaced, and one salesman, dimly discernible in rear center, reaches out to express his appreciation.

Right "Members of the Firm" in 1905, the year of incorporation. Seated: H. J. Heinz, Sebastian Mueller, Frederic C. Heinz. Standing: W. H. Robinson, Howard Heinz, R. G. Evans.

Above Artist at work in the company Print Shop, probably around 1903. He has recently finished the Uncle Sam poster on the easel. Of the time but not of the place are the gates-ajar collar on the artist and the fringed doily under the house plant.

As a plaster pin or a cardboard placard, the Heinz pickle was for three decades the country's best-known giveaway and company emblem. These two are from the "little ladies" series.

Another view of the Print Shop, 1901.

The Heinz Ocean Pier at Atlantic City, with its demonstrations, free samples, lectures, reading room, rocking chairs, and collection of art curiosities, was an attraction for millions of people from 1899 to 1944. The early interior shows paintings, bronze statues, porcelain vases, photographs of company salesmen by districts, a stuffed pelican (ceiling), brownies perched atop the furniture, and company products. In the rear are two demonstration booths. The sign beside one reads, "Orders taken for a Sample Assortment of the Choicest 24 of the 57 varieties . . . One order only to one home." To the right in the room with three arches is a partial view of *Custer's Last Rally*.

Custer's Last Rally

New York City's first large electric sign, erected in 1900, stood at the corner of Fifth Avenue and 23rd Street, later the site of the Flatiron Building.

Early electric wagon (1899), one of New York's first. Note the single headlight, tiller bar, carriage lamp on side, solid tires, and pickle on the roof.

Association of State Food and Dairy Departments, set up a booth near the elaborate displays of the manufacturers of canned and bottled goods. Its content was simple. State chemists had extracted the dyes contained in samples of well-known artificially colored foods and used them to dye sizable swatches of wool and silk. The swatches were exhibited, each with an attested chemist's certificate. Beside them were the name of the chemical substance extracted, the name and amount of the product from which it had been extracted, and sometimes a bottle or can of the food product itself. The exhibit was sensationally successful, attracting, in addition to the viewing public, a stream of congressmen, state legislators, press people, and delegates from women's organizations. It prompted the General Federation of Women's Clubs to join the crusade, which it did with the arsenal of weapons that women, even without the vote, were adept at using. Behind them came the National Consumers' League, the Patrons of Husbandry, the American Medical Association, and various labor unions. One of the men who organized the exhibit told Wiley, "It has kindled a fire of public interest which no power on earth will ever be able to put out."

5. *Collier's Weekly* and the *Ladies' Home Journal* began to campaign for reform with luridly illustrated but well-documented articles on the perils of adulterated food and poisonous drugs. Among other pieces, *Collier's* published "The Patent Medicine Conspiracy Against the Freedom of the Press," which cited specifically the threats the drug companies and the Proprietary Association of America — the country's biggest national advertisers — were making to editors and publishers. The *Journal* published analyses of the contents of twenty-seven of the most widely used patent medicines, and it demanded "a law in America requiring that the bottle, carton, or package should bear a label stating exactly what drugs and chemicals are in the medicine; and what chemicals, coloring

matter or preservatives have been added to the food."
Newspaper and other magazine editors joined the crusade —
partly, one senses, in retaliation for years of subjection to arro-
gant pressures.

6. Dr. Wiley's lectures were now making converts in many
quarters, including parts of the food processing industry itself.
Following an address at their annual meeting in February
1906, the largest group of canners (forerunner of the National
Canners Association) reversed its earlier bitter opposition.
"Their hearty and consistent attitude of support," Wiley said,
"did much to hasten . . . passage of the law."

In February 1905 a committee of six representatives of orga-
nized interests working for a pure food law called on President
Roosevelt and asked his help in getting such a measure passed.
Robert M. Allen, Secretary of the National Association of
State Dairy and Food Departments, was their spokesman.
Sebastian Mueller, representing the H. J. Heinz Company,
was one of the six.* The President promised to look into the
need for the law and asked them to return in the fall.

According to Wiley, Roosevelt had "a most pronounced
prejudice" against him, and he blew hot and cold on the need
for pure food legislation. Wiley decided to attack where the
President had a strong personal feeling. One afternoon he
took to the White House a portable laboratory, materials with

---

* The others were Miss Alice Lakey, representing the Consumers' League;
Horace Ankeny, Pure Food Commissioner of Ohio; J. B. Noble, Commissioner
for Connecticut; and A. B. Fallinger of the National Organization of Retail
Grocers. At the next meeting Dr. Charles A. L. Reed joined the committee as
a seventh member, representing the American Medical Association, of which
he had been president and was then chairman of its National Legislative
Council.

Mueller's position was unique in that he was the only member representing
a single company. His role was perhaps explained by Anne Lewis Pierce, editor of Bureau of Chemistry publications at the height of the battle, in a statement she made in 1922: "The Heinz Company took the lead in this reform,
did pioneer work when government officials and legislators lagged . . . The
battle for pure food was won not so much by those who claimed that dirty,
chemically preserved foods were unethical and unhealthful as by those who
proved that they were unnecessary. And the House of Heinz was Dr. Wiley's
first lieutenant in the charge over the top of this entrenched mistake."

which to manufacture ten-year-old Scotch and bourbon on the spot, an assortment of colors and flavors being used by the rectifiers, and twenty sealed bottles of whiskey, each bottle having a different analysis content, some with muck inside that would shock any serious user of drinking whiskey. He spread his exhibit on the table in the cabinet room, and for the next two hours gave the President and William Loeb, his secretary, a demonstration and lecture on the adulteration of spiritous liquors. At the conclusion, Roosevelt stepped around the table, slapped Wiley on the shoulder, and said explosively (in effect), "If a man can't get a good drink of whiskey in the evening when he comes home from work, *there ought to be a law to see that he does.*"

When the Allen committee returned to the White House in November, the President revealed in confidence that he would ask for pure food legislation, despite "some very stubborn opposition," in his annual message to Congress. His request read:

> I recommend that a law be enacted to regulate interstate commerce in misbranded and adulterated foods, drinks, and drugs. Such law would protect legitimate manufacture and commerce, and would tend to secure the health and welfare of the consuming public. Traffic in foodstuffs which have been debased or adulterated so as to injure health or to deceive purchasers should be forbidden.

The bill was reintroduced in the Senate. Powerful Republican Senate leaders opposed it. ("Is there anything in the existing condition that makes it the duty of Congress to put the liberty of all the people of the United States in jeopardy? Are we going to take up the question as to what a man shall eat and what a man shall drink, and put him under severe penalties if he is eating or drinking something different from what the chemists of the Agricultural Department think desirable?") The American Medical Association threw its weight into the balance — 135,000 physicians organized into some 2000 local units — threatening to make the issue one of partisan politics if necessary. The Senate tossed in the towel and passed the measure in February 1906 by a vote of sixty-three to four.

The House was less suggestible, and the measure seemed destined to die again in committee. The President exerted effective pressure on some of the members, upon which the Washington *Post* chastized him for "executive usurpation of power" at the expense of Congress. At that moment a book appeared that sold hundreds of thousands of copies and shocked the nation: *The Jungle,* by Upton Sinclair, published by Doubleday, Page & Company, a respected house. *The Jungle* was a novel written to expose revolting conditions in the Chicago stockyards. Sinclair had no interest in correcting conditions there — he was an idealogue who was convinced that they could be corrected only under a Socialist state — but the immediate effect was to destroy any effective opposition to pure food legislation. The federal Pure Food and Drug Act passed the House on June 23 by a vote of 240 to 17, the negative votes being cast by Democrats to protect states' rights. A meat inspection bill had been passed eleven days earlier without a roll call.°

Like other reform measures before it and since, the pure food laws fell short of the perfection expected and demanded by their most zealous progenitors. Dr. Wiley was not given the free hand he wanted in enforcing the laws, some of his recommended prosecutions were overruled, an impartial board of scientists was set up to pass on his findings, and the board ruled that several of the chemicals Wiley had crusaded against, including benzoate of soda, were harmless when used in minute amounts. Dr. Wiley called all this, perhaps with some exaggeration, "a crime against the Food Law" and "a

---

° Mark Sullivan's *Our Times,* Vol. 2, devotes a chapter of eighty-one pages to "The Crusade for Pure Food." Sebastian Mueller was one of sixteen participants in those events who read proofs of the chapter and offered suggestions and recollections.

complete triumph for the hosts of Satan," adding, to make his opinion perfectly clear, "No more outrageous and intolerable disregard of public rights and morals was ever perpetrated by the most vicious despotism described in the world's history." Wiley was investigated on a shamefully flimsy charge of having improperly employed a bureau consultant for $1600; he was cleared by President Taft, but he resigned in protest in 1912 when his accusers were not disciplined and his powers were not restored. He became an editor of *Good Housekeeping,* married a young wife at the age of sixty-seven, fathered two sons, was everywhere honored as an author and lecturer, and died in 1930 at age eighty-five shortly after publishing his autobiography. He was buried in Arlington Cemetery.

Despite his anguish, the Pure Food acts achieved their main purposes in a battle that is never won and never ends. They marked the real birth of the modern food processing industry, and they demonstrated for the first time in this country that government could regulate without controlling, to the benefit of the industry and the public alike. The meat packers, deciding that the Meat Inspection Act was not unconstitutional, inaugurated reforms, went after the business it had lost to foreign processors around the world during the brouhaha, and after some years won back the public trust. The great majority of manufacturers and dealers in food, in Dr. Wiley's words, "acquiesced at once in the conditions imposed by the new law and adjusted their business transactions with its provisions." The *Encyclopaedia Britannica,* which in 1911 had devoted thirty-two columns to the adulteration of food, declared eighteen years later, ". . . very great improvement was made in the purity of food in the markets of the United States between 1910 and 1925. No other classes of merchandise are today, on the whole, so free from adulteration and misbranding as food." *

* In an article written by one of Dr. Wiley's successors, Dr. Charles Albert Browne, chief of the Bureau of Chemistry, U.S. Department of Agriculture.

In 1946 a gathering took place in New York City to honor Dr. Wiley's memory and to commemorate the fortieth anniversary of the Federal Food and Drug Act. A number of distinguished persons from large corporations and trade associations made speeches, and others sent messages, in which they revealed that their industries and organizations had been from the very start earnestly in accord with the need for pure food legislation. Clarence Francis, Chairman of General Foods Corporation, made a crucial observation:

> The conditions created by the passage of the Act invited responsible businessmen to put real money into the food business. . . . And the food industry began to grow.

CHAPTER 13

The Plaudits of the Many, the Small Voices of the Future

OUR MOST STRICTLY INDUSTRIAL CENTRE UNDER POWERFUL MICROSCOPE. What the Kellogg Survey, Equipped by Mrs. Sage's Funds, Has Learned of the Sources of Pittsburg's Sanitary Troubles — The Terrible Ravages of Typhoid and Its Awful Cost in Lives and Money — The City Stirred to Put Its House in Order — Other Sins of the Industrial Order There — The City Overwhelmed with Business Without Big Men with Leisure Enough to Direct Its Growth — The Sudden Rise of Men to Millionaires' Estate and How Its Evils Appear in the Succeeding Generation.

Introductory lines to a review of
The Pittsburgh Survey, by John L. Mathews,
Boston *Evening Transcript*, 1909

HE WAS NOW, in his sixty-third year, an elder statesman of his industry. He was a force in his city — a city called in a serious social study of that day "the most prosperous of all the communities of our western civilization." * He was greeted with ceremony and deference on his visits to those places where his company had plants. He was quoted in the press on national issues; he was interviewed at the dock when he returned from his trips abroad. Through his friend, Senator Philander C. Knox, he could arrange to call on the President if he had an important matter to discuss or when he wished to please a body of State Sabbath School Association delegates meeting in Washington. He was a figure of modest renown, even in New York's sporting circles, for his seal brown gelding Nightshade, fifteen hands and three inches, and his pair of gray geldings,

* See page 190.

Reginald and Ronald, had been winning ribbons and sterling cups in the best shows.

There were always problems, of course. A group of grocers was threatening reprisal if his company continued to sell to the department stores. The old 1905 rumor was spreading again that he had given $10,000 to the Anti-Saloon League, and bartenders and saloonkeepers were mounting a boycott against Heinz condiments on their bars and tables. Then there was the financial crisis of 1907, for which Roosevelt incurred the hatred of much of the business community. The President said simply that the panic was caused by "matters wholly unconnected with any government action" and placed the blame on "malefactors of great wealth." But these were the normal hazards of the business life. The false rumor about the gift to the Anti-Saloon League, at least, could be straightened out. He convinced the National Retail Liquor Dealers' Association that it was not true, persuaded its secretary to write him a letter of correction, and widely distributed the letter.

His consuming interest at the Pittsburgh Works was the design and construction of the last and grandest of his structures — an Administration Building to hold the company's Home Offices. It was to have stained-glass windows with designs and quotations. The reception room would have walls of Hauteville marble, a fish pool and fountain directly under a central light dome five stories up, four balconies, and twelve mural panels showing Heinz operations around the world. The panels were by Edward Trumbull, a young muralist who, the 57 *News* explained, was painting under "the supervision and inspiration of Mr. Heinz." (Directions to the artist on panel number eight read, "Instead of a desert scene showing caravan we desire to show a scene in Java, the camels to be laden with spices emerging from a spice grove.") A critic reviewing these for the 57 *News* observed judiciously, "The artist has been lavish in the use of brilliant colors, sometimes resorting to conglomerations with impressive effects." The President's offices were on the fourth floor and the office employees' restaurants on the top floor. In what the *News* justly called "a most remarkable departure," the air would be drawn in from the roof and then washed, dried, and cooled or heated.

The cornerstone was laid in the fall of 1905 with all employees present, the Founder himself having drawn up a list of the contents. Among other objects, it held a Bible (American Revised Edition), signed photographs of all the "members of the firm," a photograph of the salesmen at the latest convention, a newspaper description of the Heinz stables, a short history of the company, and a supply of pickle charms and streetcar cards. A reception for 900 guests was held in the newly completed building in April 1908 with a fifteen-piece orchestra, banks of cut flowers, and nonalcoholic refreshments.

Heinz was now first vice president and a "life manager" of the Pittsburgh Exposition Society (he had refused the presidency). He was a director of a bank, an insurance company, a hospital, and a social service agency. He was chairman of the executive committee of the newly founded Kansas City University (Methodist Protestant in origin), to which he had given $10,000. He was president of the Pennsylvania State Sabbath School Association, the strongest in the nation, and was a leader in the city's federated church movement to stop all unnecessary work on Sunday. He was president of the Pittsburgh Branch of the Egyptian Exploration Fund. He was a vice president of the Pittsburgh Chamber of Commerce and was on the slate of the dissidents who, after a year of quiet planning, overthrew the old guard in favor of "an infusion of new blood," a more liberal policy, more attention to civic affairs, and action on civic reform measures. (The deposed managing director lamented, "Why, the men who *own* Pittsburgh voted for our ticket!") He was a member of Andrew Carnegie's committee that sought in vain to build a ship canal between

Pittsburgh and Lake Erie. He was active in (and later became president of) the Flood Commission of Pittsburgh "for determining the causes of, damage by, and methods of relief from floods . . . together with the benefits to the navigation, sanitation, water supply and water power to be obtained by river regulation." It recommended — three decades prematurely — that seventeen reservoirs be built on the upper waters of the Allegheny and Monongahela, at a cost of $20 million.

He was active in the program to reduce the city's pall of smoke. To that end he installed stokers, with a splash of publicity, in his own marble-walled powerhouse, which reduced smoke, he said, by 50 percent. He then erected, with more publicity, two of the largest gas engines in the world, each able to generate 146 horsepower. (They did not work properly and, with no publicity at all, were removed and replaced by steam engines.) He was one of the "guarantors" of the Pittsburgh Orchestra, accompanying one contribution of $2000 with a plea for support: "It has been one of the factors in giving our city such a position in esthetics as it has long held in commercialism." The orchestra, alas, declined under the six-year reign (1904–1910) of conductor Emil Paur, who, on succeeding Victor Herbert, was uncompromisingly determined to make Pittsburghers like and understand, or at least listen to, Wagner and Brahms. The orchestra died and was not replaced until 1927.

Heinz was one of the leaders in the 1905 political battle to annex Allegheny City to Pittsburgh, his voice carrying some weight in that he had his home in one and his plant in the other. He argued that other cities were consolidating and that a "Greater Pittsburgh" would move from the twelfth largest city in the nation to fifth or sixth, with accompanying benefits. The political powers of Allegheny, and most of the people, bitterly opposed annexation. Heinz knew that his Allegheny plant was subject to possible reprisals, from punitive taxation to physical damage. Nonetheless, he served as chairman of a meeting in Allegheny's Carnegie Hall called by those who favored the Greater Pittsburgh legislation. Some 4000 people attended. "Let us stand before the world as we are," Heinz called out, "a great municipality, instead of an aggregation of villages." Some rowdy elements in the audience, many of them Allegheny pay-rollers brought together for the purpose, raised (in the words of the Pittsburgh *Gazette*) "such a din and clamor that the place trembled." Heinz managed to hold the meeting under control long enough to adopt a resolution calling on the state assembly to pass the bill. Allegheny battled twice to the Supreme Court against being "taken over," but in June 1906 it participated in a hopeless election in which both cities voted collectively, the majority to decide the issue. Allegheny's 150,000 inhabitants rejected the merger by two to one but were overwhelmed by larger numbers. Allegheny City and its seven square miles henceforth suffered the indignity of being called "the North Side."

In 1908 an opportunity arose for an outpouring of civic pride in what was about to become the country's sixth largest city. In November 1758, with Colonel George Washington as one of his regimental commanders, Brigadier General John Forbes had driven the French from Fort Duquesne at the forks of the Ohio and forever out of the Ohio Valley; he had raised the British flag over what he renamed "Pittsbourgh." The best, the brightest, and the richest united in 1908 to mount a sesquicentennial celebration worthy of that event and of what Pittsburgh had since become. H. J. Heinz was second vice president of the Sesqui-Centennial Executive Committee.

The big week of the celebration took place from September 29 to October 3. Guests of the city included the Vice President of the United States (a Charles W. Fairbanks), direct descendants of William Pitt, First Earl of Chatham, and collateral descendants of General Forbes and Washington. The

week began with a parade and exhibition on the rivers of all
craft of the past 150 years, manned by crews in costume and
preceded by thirty Cornplanter Indians in a fleet of canoes.
The week continued with a street parade that marched from
Allegheny City through the Golden Triangle and east to the
new Carnegie Museum–Library–Music Hall — a parade
planned to be "beautiful and instructive . . . not too large,
which should illustrate the growth of the city from the beginning in all lines."

The seventh of the eight divisions contained floats of fifteen
manufacturing companies. The Heinz Allegorical Float, a supreme effort in a declining art, decorated in gold and ivory,
was pulled by thirty black horses, a groom in white at the
head of each. It was thirty-seven feet long, ten feet wide, held
seventeen people, and was classical in theme: "The goddess
Ceres on her throne, bearing a sheaf of wheat, surrounded by
her handmaidens, presenting to Miss Pittsburgh the fruits of
the field, Miss Pittsburgh in turn distributing the food products to the world." The float was preceded by a platoon of
heralds in costume, mounted on white horses and bearing
trumpets. Spectators estimated at more than 500,000 lined the
streets to watch.

During that week, a cornerstone was laid, a building dedicated, a statue unveiled, a loving cup presented, cannons fired
in salutes, and dozens of orations delivered. There were horse
races at Schenley Oval, flights by a "dirigible balloon," an exhibit of hundreds of pioneer relics in Carnegie Museum, tea
for 3000 ladies in Carnegie Music Hall, an enormous display of
industrial products of the district in the three Exposition
buildings, and a most un-Pittsburgh-like masquerade carnival
on lower Fifth and Liberty avenues that lasted until 2:00 A.M.

Some months later H. J. Heinz celebrated an anniversary of
his own — the fortieth year of the company he founded. The
employees, managers, and directors gave a banquet in his

honor, 1600 persons at table in the plant auditorium, described in the press as "a sight of truly entrancing beauty . . . with flowers, flags, mottoes, myriads of dazzling electric lights, and decorations." Over the head table was the legend in electric lights, "To do a common thing uncommonly well spells success." Old friends from Sharpsburg were present, and the three men from whom the Founder in 1869 had bought his first packing boxes, bottles, and corks. He made a short speech on the three fundamental principles of business success. Five veteran employees presented him with an inscribed loving cup designed for the occasion; it was gold and silver, thirty inches in height, twenty pounds in weight, classical Greek in feeling, with allegorical figures and forty flutes.

While these activities were taking place, Pittsburgh was also playing the role of a nervous host to twenty of "the leading sanitarians, economists, and civic engineers of the world." These were working under a grant from the Russell Sage Foundation in New York. They were making a survey (the term was a new one in social investigations in 1908) of the community: its hours, wages, and labor organizations in the steel industry; the household life and cost of living in a typical mill town (Homestead); working conditions and wages in the trades that employed women; the economic cost of typhoid fever and industrial accidents; and the city's child-helping agencies and institutions. For fifteen months these experts had been prowling about the community. The six volumes they published in 1910–1914, called by one critic "the most remarkable study ever made of any American community," caused Pittsburgh to be for several years the nation's most talked-about, written-about city.

Russell Sage (1816–1906), a business associate of Jay Gould, was a financier, an investor in railroads, who amassed by speculation — the source of so many American fortunes in that

period — wealth totaling $70 million. By all accounts he was a
moneygrubber with few redeeming qualities and no known
public benefactions. His embarrassed widow, Margaret Olivia
Slocum Sage (1828–1918), gave the entire fortune to worthy
causes, much of it to hospitals, colleges, social agencies,
learned societies, and museums. She also created and gave
$10 million to the Russell Sage Foundation, which in turn
made grants of $19,500 for the Pittsburgh Survey.

Those making the study tried to get additional financial support in Pittsburgh. One organization — the Civic Club — gave
$50. Four individual Pittsburghers contributed money — one
of the Thaws ($50), the wife of a banker ($50), a progressive
steelmaster ($100), and H. J. Heinz. He gave $100, allowed
the use of his name as a donor, and opened up his plant to the
researchers. Paul U. Kellogg, director of the survey, observed
that such support for "a vague and not altogether pleasant enterprise . . . required no little courage."

Pittsburghers were well known for their philanthropy, despite their Scotch-Irish reticence about such private matters
(Andrew Carnegie excepted), but those with money to give —
including H. J. Heinz — had some reason to fear public attention of the kind that might come with the Pittsburgh Survey.
The city's *nouveaux riches* — the forty-odd favorably placed
men who in 1901 suddenly happened to become millionaires
with Carnegie's sale of his steel properties to J. P. Morgan —
were a stock subject of ridicule and satire in the theater and
the press ("Are my diamonds on straight?"). So too were the
city's image as "Hell with the Lid Off," its smoky skies, and its
liquor and Sabbath laws, the most rigorous of any American
city, imposed by the Protestant Irish and Presbyterian Scots
who ruled the community and set its moral tone. Pittsburgh
society, moreover, was at this time being humiliated by a sen-
sational national scandal involving one of its sons. William
Kendall Thaw, railroad and coal magnate, was one of the city's

earliest and most enlightened philanthropists. Harry Kendall Thaw, one of his ten children, was "a wild hare." He married Evelyn Nesbit, chorus girl and model, in the parsonage of the Third Presbyterian Church in 1905; the following year, on the roof garden of Madison Square Garden, he shot and killed one of her former lovers, the architect Stanford White. The trials that followed were sordid headline affairs.

On the other hand, Pittsburghers knew and were proud that their city over the past ten or fifteen years had experienced an extraordinary renaissance. Since 1889, three splendid city parks. Two colleges — Carnegie Institute of Technology and the remade, renamed, and relocated University of Pittsburgh. Five hospitals, including one for maternity cases and one for children. A zoological garden. The world's second largest conservatory. The $6 million Carnegie Institute, with its museum, library, music hall, foyer (called by one architectural historian "the most splendid ceremonial hall in America"), and its art galleries, where the world-famous International Art Exhibition had been held each fall since 1896. A school for the blind and a school for the deaf and dumb. A water filtration and purification system that in two years (1906–1908) had cut typhoid fever cases by more than two-thirds. Skyscrapers twenty to twenty-five stories high. A new railroad station. "The world's most perfect playhouse."

Pittsburgh, moreover, had removed the railroad tracks from Liberty Avenue. It had built a fine paved boulevard from the downtown area to the East End, cut out of the side of a hill. It was buying the bridges across the three rivers and making them toll-free. It was building one of the country's most beautiful sports arenas in the Schenley Farms area. It had just established a Bureau of Smoke and a corps of fast-moving policemen on bicycles. Its public school system was reorganized as one of the best in the country. Money had been raised to cut away a monstrous "hump" of earth and relay streets at the eastern end of the Golden Triangle. All these comprised a body of improvements and additions that any city would be proud to have.

The Pittsburgh Survey first appeared, in part, in a magazine with the unwieldy name *Charities and the Commons* (later renamed *The Survey*) and then was published in a succession of six volumes.° They descended on Pittsburgh with a stunning impact.

The authors credited the city with having made "great material progress," with having "a mighty under-current of moral capacity," and with showing "a new, quickening public spirit." But they found and documented shocking conditions — what the Pittsburgh *Dispatch* called "A catalogue of Pittsburgh's plague spots; a bold charting of some of the city's most glaring municipal, civic, institutional, and housing defects; a downright denunciation of housing conditions, both within the city proper and in the mill suburbs, and a sound scolding for a half-dozen corporations."

They found:

1. Incredibly long hours of work.
2. Low wages compared with the city's prices.
3. Still lower wages for women.
4. Bad effects of absentee capitalism — wealthy Pittsburghers who had left the city.
5. "A continuous inflow of immigrants with low standards, attracted by a wage which is high by the standards of southeastern Europe, and which yields a net pecuniary advantage because of abnormally low expenditures for food and shelter and inadequate provision for the contingencies of sickness, accident, and death."
6. The destruction of family life by more than 1000 deaths each year from typhoid fever and industrial accidents.
7. Archaic social institutions.
8. "The contrast . . . between the prosperity on the one hand of the most prosperous of all the communities of our western civ-

° See Bibliography.

ilization, with its vast natural resources, the generous fostering of government, the human energy, the technical development, the gigantic tonnage of the mines and mills, the enormous capital of which the bank balances afford an indication; and, on the other hand, the neglect of life, of health, of physical vigor, even of the industrial efficiency of the individual."

Certainly, the authors said, no community before in America or Europe had ever had such a surplus, and never before had a great community applied what it had so meagerly to the rational purposes of human life. The surplus should come back to the people of the community in which it is created — not by gifts of libraries, galleries, technical schools, and parks. It should come, rather, by the cessation of toil one day in seven and sixteen hours in the twenty-four, by the increase of wages, by the sparing of lives, by the prevention of accidents, and by raising the standards of domestic life.

The adverse social conditions described in the survey, the authors said, were such as not infrequently accompany progress. They were incidents of the production of wealth on a vast scale due to haste in acquiring wealth, to inequity in distribution, to the inadequacy of the mechanism of municipal government. They were, however, remediable whenever a community thought it worthwhile to remedy them.

Elizabeth Beardsley Butler, author of *Women and the Trades,* had been secretary of the Consumers' League of New Jersey. She was a trained sociologist and reporter who could put into words what she found and thought. She was also a woman some decades ahead of her time — a relentless advocate of equal women's rights. Indignation shows through her professionally restrained accounts of working conditions and pay. Sixty percent of the working women in Pittsburgh are earning no more than $.50 to $1 a day. Only 20 percent are earning the $7 or more a week that, in Pittsburgh in 1908, is considered the minimum below which a working girl cannot live decently and be self-supporting. Slavic women are being given the most disagreeable, socially inferior jobs.

But there is worse. Girls starting out to work at fourteen are paid only half the wage paid to boys of the same age doing the same work. Women who pack crackers, for example, are paid $.50 for their ten-hour day, but unskilled laborers, employed to fetch and carry in the mills, are paid $1.30 to $1.65 for ten hours' work. Men hold all the responsible jobs; women do the menial work. Many employers try to employ girls or women who are members of families so that their fathers or husbands can help to support them. "The social fact of woman's customary position in the household," Mrs. Butler says, "her position of a dependent who receives no wages for her work, thus lies behind the economic fact of her insufficient wage in the industrial field. It is expected that she has men to support her."

Mrs. Butler is relatively kind to the Heinz Company:

> Another factory, the largest in Pittsburgh, occupies eight buildings. The walls of light brick, scrupulously clean, stand out against the murky background of the city; and within doors, the light walls, wide windows, and spotless white of work tables bear out first impressions that the management has high standards both for the surroundings of its work-people and the quality of its product. From the central building, bridges connect with the neighboring buildings on upper floors; and allied processes are grouped together in common units of space. Tin cans are made in one building, boxes and barrels are nailed together in a second, and in a third pickles are sorted, bottled and labeled preparatory to shipping; in other buildings fruits are stemmed, hulled, washed and sliced, mustard grains are ground in mechanical presses which crush a slow yellow mass into the receiving tubs, beans are baked and prepared for shipment, and the cooking and sealing for a condiment-loving people go forward with speed and ingenuity.

Canning of vegetables in factories, she said, is not pre-eminently a woman's trade, but women are in the majority. They number 55.8 percent of the plant's workers, 728 altogether as compared with 618 men. The men, of course, do all the responsible work, such as the actual cooking and preserving of fruit, the pickling of cucumbers, and the baking of beans.

They attend to the shipping and plan new methods of sale and of process. The women workers do not compete with the men, but have a division of the trade distinct and characteristic. They wash bottles and scrub floors and help about the kitchens. They sort and bottle pickles, prepare raw materials, label and fill the jars of preserves. Their work, in other words, is secondary and comparatively mechanical.

The author writes of working conditions at the plant — the first description by a trained and sophisticated sociologist.

In two establishments, however, the system of welfare work is extensive.* One of these, a factory, has a force of 600 girls. They are given excellent workrooms, clean, well-ventilated, well-constructed. The stairways are marble, and on the walls are engravings of action and battle and plunging horses. The stained-glass windows in the halls display mottoes about work and industry. In the auditorium is a large painting, rich in color, of Christ before Pilate. The girls are often summoned to the auditorium at noon to hear an address by some visitor or to sing; in this case they have an hour's recess, instead of half an hour. This does not involve financial loss to the day girls, because they are paid their day rates in any case, but the piece workers lose just so much in possible earnings. A roof garden for summer use has been erected above one of the buildings. There is a natatorium, with schedule so arranged that most of the girls may have a chance to swim once or twice a week after hours. The dressing rooms in the general factory building are beautifully kept, and the rest room is well equipped with necessities for those who are ill. The large lunch room, filled with long tables, can seat all the 600 girls at once, and for one cent a day, each girl is furnished with coffee, milk and sugar. In one corner

* The other was McCreary's Department Store (now defunct) in downtown Pittsburgh.

stands a piano, and the walls are bright with pictures. Throughout the building everything is bright and trim and clean. The girls wear fresh blue and white aprons and trim white caps. They are as well-kept in appearance as the place in which they work.

But Mrs. Butler is also critical. She wants more. She raises for the first time a voice that will become louder and more insistent in the years ahead, for this is a new century with rising demands, and the paternalism that seemed so splendid in the last century is no longer good enough. Excellent building construction, thorough cleanliness, dressing rooms, rest rooms, natatoria are good in and of themselves, but their service to employees is of little effect if it obscures the facts that women are being paid a lower wage than men, are doing the menial work, and must respond to the pace and pressure of an inexorable machine. A girl who cuts onions at seventy-five cents a day is unable to appreciate an engraving on the wall and cares very little for the polished upright piano in the lunch room or for the roof garden that is reached only after a hard climb. When higher wages are paid, even if fewer gifts are given, women employees have the precious opportunity to work out their own lives, with their margin above a living wage.

The situation of women, Mrs. Butler feels, is one that demands close study and close thinking. It can be improved. One answer, she thinks, is women's unions, which have succeeded in improving wages and working conditions in several trades. Another is the work of the consumers' leagues, which in some cities have demanded higher standards for women's pay. Still another is the minimum wage legislation being proposed in certain countries. The action of progressive employers here and there has established higher rates.

"And can we reasonably be content if the standard of wages be raised merely to the level that makes existence possible? Shall we call sufficient a sum less than enough to make possi-

ble a life decent, healthy, colored, and individualized by recre-
ative leisure?"

The *Pittsburgh Survey* was discussed and extracts printed
throughout the country for several years. It produced a spate
of articles about the city, most of them with the title, real or
implied, "What's the Matter with Pittsburgh?" The chief complaint of the subjects of all this attention was that the survey-
ors claimed too much credit in their final roundup for producing actions that had been started or planned before the survey
began.

The "sanitarians, economists and civic engineers" would be
pleased to know that the next two generations carried out all
the reforms they proposed. Many were accomplished in the
city's celebrated second "renaissance" in the years 1946–1960:
smoke abatement, flood control, cleaner rivers, a countywide
sewage system, slum clearance. The Typhoid Fever Commission was indeed created, but it eventually disappeared, along
with typhoid fever. There is no hospital for tubercular pa-
tients, because there is almost no tuberculosis. The municipal
hospital where cases of diphtheria, scarlet fever, and mastoiditis
had once been treated was converted to a research center in
which the vaccine for preventing poliomyelitis was found.
The seven-day week and the twelve-hour shift in the steel
mills and railway yards have disappeared, along with child
labor and the moral influence of the Scotch-Irish. The working person's wage is considerably above the subsistence level.

Mrs. Butler would be pleased to know that Slavic women
have improved their lot, that a substantial number of Pittsburgh's women hold responsible jobs, and that laws have been
passed setting a minimum wage and legally entitling a woman
to the same pay as men for similar work. She would be
pleased, and perhaps surprised, that machines have eliminated
most of the tedious handwork women had been doing in mills

and factories, that in the same Heinz buildings she visited in 1908 the work week is five eight-hour days, and that the average wage of employees there, from laborer to master mechanic, is $4 an hour, no distinction now being made and no payroll breakdown being kept on which are male and which are female. Knowing all this, finding that almost all the social, economic, and health problems she knew and worried about had been solved, Mrs. Butler would surely rejoice for a country that obviously must have achieved an unprecedented level of human happiness.

CHAPTER 14

At the Crest of the Wave: 1911-1913

I want to keep ahead of my boys. I don't want them to do anything I could do first.

H. J. Heinz, after an aeroplane flight
with Glenn H. Curtiss,
August 19, 1911

In the years 1911–1913, when he was sixty-six going on sixty-nine, Heinz seemed to be five different men pursuing five different careers: industrialist, world traveler, art patron, political campaigner, and religious leader, with an episode of dare deviltry laid on like garnish on a mixed salad. The pleasure he felt in each of these varied pursuits shows clearly in everything he said and wrote.

In January 1911 he set out with his valet, William Whatley, and Mr. and Mrs. John Bindley, old Pittsburgh friends, on a voyage to Egypt. He followed much the same route he had taken in 1894, buying art works and curios as he progressed: Gibraltar, Algiers, Villefranche, Monte Carlo, Naples, Alexandria, Cairo, Luxor (this time by train), Thebes, Aswan (where he stayed at a new hotel with 400 bedrooms and 10 bathrooms), and then to Rome.

An American friend of the Bindleys living in Rome, Charles Sumner Graham, introduced him to a German-born Norwegian sculptor named Hans St. Lerche.

> Having arrived at an age 66 years, I concluded to have a bronze bust made, life size, for 2000 lira. He has made a bust for

the Pope and one of the noblemen here. The Norwegian and his wife both speak German and some English. It required ten sittings of two hours each, and two sittings which he desired to work out and study details of about one hour each. My friend pronounces it very good in studying it from time to time. I discovered a hole and marks over my face which I never knew were there. He is to make it in bronze and ship it to our London office for reshipment to the States.

I became very fond of Mr. and Mrs. Lerchi. They entertained several times a week. Most of the gentlemen were artists, sculptors, physicians, professors from among their friends who were visiting the city, besides new-made friends while living in Rome. Mr. Graham said he was the best in Rome.

From Rome he went on to Florence, Verona, Munich, Würzburg, Bad Kissingen (for a two-week rest cure, his seventh visit to that town), and thence to London to be reunited with the Bindleys at the Savoy Hotel.

Heinz had made an early acquisition in 1905 in the Batty Company, a small firm in Peckham, England, and had been selling his products in the British Isles under the Batty name. He introduced baked beans into Britain in 1902 and first bottled and sold goods there under the Heinz label in 1910. When his fellow-directors expressed apprehensions about the Batty acquisition, he made the English company a personal venture and informed them with some vigor, "If this undertaking is in black ink by the time my grandchildren are old enough to be in it, my judgment will be vindicated."

Now, on the 1911 visit, he wrote

I was very much pleased with the system and order of the old Batty factory, now Heinz No. 11 Factory. We have increased our output 50 per cent since putting on the new style labels and bottles. We pack only for Continental Europe and export under the Batty label where the goods were introduced in 1824, while in Great Britain we offer no Batty foods for sale except when the trade demands some of the sauces that were formerly well known, we fill the order.

I was the only one who had any faith in the future development of the 57 through a branch house in England. It required courage and hard work to continue for years at a loss to introduce the goods, but after ten years the tide turned and we are now practically running the business on the same average cost as in the States. So I feel my labours have at last been rewarded in the satisfaction of having accomplished more than I set out to do. I now turn both the Heinz 57 Department as well as the Batty factory over to be directed by others who have demonstrated through ability and loyalty the fitness to continue the work. My sons and partners have the pleasures of enjoying the fruits of some of my labours, which they often feared were taking me beyond my strength, but it was a great pleasure to me, and I saw the end, otherwise I should have given up after the first five years." *

My friend John Bindley and I sail on the Mauretania May 13th for New York.

In New York, while visiting the Givens and his two grandchildren (living at 495 West End Avenue), Heinz was persuaded to have his portrait painted.

I arrange with Mr. Wm. M. Chase, the noted American artist, to paint my portrait . . . and therefore concluded to remain in New York another week and grant my children's request. I sat sitting fourteen hours in all. A splendid strong portrait, so say several judges. Mr. Chase is an exceedingly bright, clever man, a worker, a prolific painter. He is considered one of the best still life painters of fish, as well as of portraits, in New York. He lectures and writes on art. He has a striking personality, dramatic and forceful in his conversation and gestures, seems never to tire of carrying on a conversation while painting. A wonderfully argourious [gregarious?] man nearly 60 years of age.

When finishing the portrait in the presence of my private secretary, William E. D. McCafferty, he stopped suddenly, saying, "Finished. I don't think I can improve on it," laying aside his pastel [palette]. He added, "If your family care to have some lit-

---

* The English company became profitable two years before H. J. Heinz's death, when his grandchildren were thirteen, ten, nine, and five.

tle changes made, I will be pleased to do it any time." I believed he had done his best and simply said, "It is very good, thank you," at the same time realizing that he had not quite caught the spirit, that it would require some slight changes to make it a good likeness. Sent him a cheque the same morning as he was to sail in a few days.

In August of 1911, at Winona Lake, Indiana, Heinz made a flight with Glenn H. Curtiss in his newly developed hydroaeroplane — the fifth passenger to go up in the "flying boat." * He traveled (appropriately) at fifty-seven miles an hour, covered thirteen miles in fifteen minutes, and said happily to reporters on landing that he had surpassed his three sons, since they had done nothing more exciting so far than ride in an automobile.

In April 1912 Heinz made his third trip to California, traveling this time in a private railroad car and stopping at several cities along the way to visit his factories and to make public statements on behalf of Theodore Roosevelt, candidate of the progressive wing of the Republican party in the approaching convention. He continued to campaign in Santa Barbara, Los Angeles, Pasadena, and Seattle, mixing praise for Roosevelt and for the marvels of the West Coast in judicious proportions. Taft, the incumbent President, he said, was a kind and gracious man, but he had permitted himself to be overpersuaded by his associates. He would make a fine Supreme Court justice. A Los Angeles daily paper's identification of the speaker was typical: a churchman and philanthropist whose "name has become a household word for his steadfast stand for pure food products."

---

* Glenn Hammond Curtiss (1878–1930) had adapted his successful air-cooled motorcycle engines to planes. In 1908, while the work of the Wright Brothers was still being conducted in secret, he began to give the first public flights in America. He established the country's first flying school the following year and in 1910 won the $10,000 first prize in the New York *World* flight from Albany to New York City.

In 1909, the Carnegie Museum of Pittsburgh mounted an exhibit of Heinz's collection of timepieces. Most of them were of the eighteenth century, many by Parisian watchmakers, two earlier pieces being specimens of the seventeenth-century Nurnberg egg. Now, early in 1913, shortly before undertaking the longest and most arduous journey of his life, Heinz turned over to the museum for extended display almost 1000 pieces of his carved ivories, considered one of the most important collections of such work in America.

The tour was a six-month junket around the world, no less — across the Pacific to Japan, Korea, and China; 6000 miles across Siberia to Moscow and St. Petersburg; and on by way of Poland and Germany to Zurich to attend the Seventh Convention of the World Sunday School Association. He would travel with thirteen other business and professional men and a number of women Sunday School superintendents, state secretaries, and teachers, all delegates to the Zurich Convention. Some would be accompanied by members of their family, to bring the tour party to twenty-nine persons in all. Since he had proposed the tour after his visit to Japan in 1902, when he foresaw the possibilities of Sunday School work there, and since he would be chairman of the group, Heinz would pay the expenses of those who were not in a position to do so themselves. They would be a working party known as "Commission Four," making "visitations" to the centers of Christian education in the Orient, conferring with the several hundred missionaries supported there by the association, and reporting at Zurich on the conditions and prospects of the Sunday School movement in the countries they visited.

Commission Four sailed from San Francisco on March 1, 1913, on the 22,000-ton *Tenyo Maru* — "heavenly sea ship" — bearing letters of introduction and recommendation from President Taft, Secretary of State-designate William Jennings Bryan, the president of the Chamber of Commerce of the United States, the Japanese ambassador in Washington, and several important Japanese businessmen in America. Each man carried morning clothes, full-dress evening clothes, and a high silk hat in a leather case. Heinz took along a number of cases of Heinz products. He was accompanied by his son Clarence, thirty-nine, his valet William Whatley, and his nephew Henry W. Heinz, son of Brother John. Howard and Clifford were at the dock to see them off. Heinz had asked Clifford, now twenty-nine and working happily in the Pittsburgh Works, to make the tour; Clifford declined with thanks.

Frank L. Brown, former banker, now general secretary of the Sunday School Association, was administrative head of the tour. One of the group was James W. (for Wesley) Kinnear, Pittsburgh attorney, Heinz's personal legal counsel, one of the founders of Firth Sterling Steel Company, a director, with Heinz, of the Pittsburgh Chamber of Commerce, a member of the executive committees of the Pennsylvania State Sabbath School Association and of the World Sunday School Association. Kinnear had with him his wife, two college-age daughters, and his fifteen-year-old son James Junior, the only child on the tour, a sharp, camera-carrying youngster who observed in 1973, "I remember every detail of that trip better than things that happened a year ago."

The members were a cohesive group among 1079 other passengers, eating at four reserved tables, holding daily devotion services at 10:00 A.M. in the music room, to which they invited some missionaries among the passengers who were going out to charges in the Orient. They organized daily classes in Japanese words and phrases, heard lectures on Japan and China, and attended the ship's motion pictures shown each evening. On March 4 they held a patriotic meeting to mark the inauguration of Woodrow Wilson as twenty-eighth President of the United States, Mr. Heinz presiding, with speeches by a Harvard professor, a Japanese doctor, and a missionary from

Shanghai who was distantly related to the President. The voyage lasted eighteen days.

Heinz had been active in Sunday School work from the age of twelve — as a pupil, a teacher, a superintendent, a director of the county association, as president since 1906 of the Pennsylvania State Sabbath School Association (succeeding his friend John Wanamaker), as a member since 1902 of the executive committee of the International Sunday School Association, and as a member since 1904 of the executive committee of the World Sunday School Association. Throughout his life he frequently quoted and seems to have tried to follow his mother's counsel: "I have only one piece of advice to give you about your religion. Do not make it so narrow that it will be unattractive to others, and do not make it so broad that you leave yourself no foundation on which to stand."

It requires an effort to understand today the intense and widespread preoccupation with religion, how strong was the zeal, of most people between the Civil War and the First World War. The church was then the center of social and intellectual pursuit and everyone but the village atheist belonged. There were 28,011,194 enrolled members in the World Association, some 17 million of them in the United States and 2 million in Pennsylvania. Heinz and Kinnear had gone to Philadelphia the previous October to take part in the Fiftieth Anniversary jubilee celebration of the Pennsylvania Association; they watched 25,000 men march down Broad Street in a two-and-a-half-hour parade on behalf of the movement. They had gone to Dayton a few weeks before they sailed to work at business meetings of the World and International associations. "Committee worked until 11:00 P.M.," Heinz wrote in the margins of a *Book of Psalms* he carried. "None of us would do it in our business, neither can we do our best work in the Lord's vineyard by abusing ourselves in this manner . . . 4th day: Mr. Warren, Mr. Wells and others worked until after midnight. Many said they were wrecks the next morning when they left for home."

The World and International associations were basically a world peace movement, and after ninety-eight years without a major, extended war in Europe and only one in North America, there was great hope in the world for growing friendship among nations and fellowship among peoples. Heinz knew that in many countries people felt as he did. He believed — and this was one of the Important Ideas that guided him in life — that if these people could work together in the Sunday School movement and use it to teach children to believe in the Golden Rule, there might be lasting peace in the world. The philosopher Alfred North Whitehead put it succinctly years later: "Religion is world loyalty."

Heinz thought the Sunday School movement to be "the world's greatest living force for character building and good citizenship." He was further motivated by a deep, warm, and considerate affection for children — a feeling that children accepted and reciprocated. A director of his company said, "He loved children more than any man I knew. I don't think he ever saw a child without giving it something." The younger Kinnear knew Heinz as a child living in his neighborhood and as a fellow-traveler on the six-month trip around the world. After a distinguished career in the steel industry,* he remembers the old gentleman as a delightful companion and a congenial grandfatherly neighbor.

The *Tenyo Maru* docked at Yokohama on March 18, for which occasion the gentlemen of Commission Four appeared on deck in morning clothes with top hats. They were greeted by the owner of the steamship company and taken to his home for a luncheon. Japan had 270 Christian missionaries from

* He became, among other things, chief metallurgist of U.S. Steel's Homestead Works; assistant vice president of engineering, U.S. Steel; executive vice president, Tennessee Coal and Iron; and president of Firth Sterling Steel and Carbide Corporation.

various countries, 570 native pastors, 65,000 members of Christian churches, most of them of the educated class, and 120,000 Sabbath School pupils. Over the next twenty-four days the tour party was welcomed up and down Japan — in the home of Baron Shibusawa (a leading industrialist), by Baron Saketani (mayor of Tokyo), by presidents of Chambers of Commerce, at YMCAs, in Christian schools and churches, at massive Sunday School rallies, by missionaries in cities, towns, and villages. It was explained apologetically that the Emperor was in mourning for one year and could not receive them, but Count Shigenobu Okuma, soon to be Prime Minister for a second time, held a reception, and the mayor of Tokyo and members of the Chamber of Commerce gave a joint banquet. Chairman Heinz responded to the addresses: "We come to you with a message of good will and friendship. In our relations with you as a nation, our Republic had stood for peace . . . You have sent many commissions to our country. Why not send one charged with the important mission of discovering the best plans for the moral and religious foundation of your youth? The result would, I believe, enrich Japan's future beyond your highest thought." Some of the businessmen, to be sure, were confused; they asked Secretary Brown, "What is a Sunday School?" and they "were at a loss to comprehend why the business men of America should undertake such a tour for such an object." But the fact that the Americans did not drink their toasts in wine, Brown observed, asking instead for fruit juice or mineral water, "made a profound impression" on the Japanese. One prominent man sent up a note that he, too, did not drink wine, and another "was so impressed that he has readjusted his life and now regularly attends the church."

The hosts in each city insisted that the next World Sunday School Convention in 1916 should be held in Tokyo. In Hiroshima, scene of the first Sunday School visitation in Japan seven years earlier, three meetings were held. At a giant gathering for men there, James Kinnear spoke on "Purity as a Life and National Asset." Master Kinnear took pictures of everything and whenever accommodations were crowded shared a room with Valet Whatley and stayed in Japanese rather than "European" hotels. In Nagasaki, the sixty-second city visited by the entire party or its delegations, the port city from which the group left Japan, Heinz addressed a Sunday School rally at which the Methodist Girls' School sang "Shout the Glad Tidings, Messiah is King." When young Kinnear photographed women carrying baskets of coal to the ship's bunkers, a Japanese sailor seized his camera and exposed the film.

Korea had won its independence from China in 1895, but it was made a Japanese protectorate a few months later and in 1910 was taken over as a possession. There the party met "the most wonderful demonstration of Sunday School strength seen in the Orient." The place was Seoul, which turned out 60,000 adults and 40 missionaries in a great rally on the old palace grounds and 14,700 children a week later. "Such earnest devotion on the part of the children and adults we never before witnessed," Heinz wrote on the margin of his *Book of Psalms*.

China was emerging from a revolution when Chairman Heinz led his group into the country in May. The young Manchu Emperor had abdicated his throne the year before, and the revolutionaries had created a republic, its constitution based on that of the United States. The Chinese showed "very kindly feelings for all Americans," for Washington had recognized the new government a few days before the arrival of Commission Four. It was widely known, moreover, that the United States had been using its share of the $333 million indemnity imposed on China after the Boxer Rebellion to provide scholarships for Chinese students in American colleges.

Shanghai: A banquet tendered by the Chinese Chamber of Commerce. (Potage of birds' nest with pigeon eggs, broiled shark fins, fried tripes, fried livers of fowl, roast goose with pancakes.) A Sunday School gathering of 10,000 in Chang

Subo's Gardens, with the children searching for 1000 eggs hidden about the park. Missionary meetings at night.

Nanking: A Sunday School Field Day with an audience of 3000 Christians. Chairman Heinz presents certificates to one hundred young men and women who have passed an examination in the teacher training course, the first to be awarded in China. At a Chamber of Commerce banquet, Chinese officials protest the free distribution of cigarettes by British and American tobacco merchants; they say the companies are seeking to fix a habit on people that "ruins the health, wounds the brain, and causes disease."

En route to Hankow: a two-day trip by steamer up the Yangtze-Kiangsi River, very muddy and a mile wide. The river is infested by brigands, and during a stop at Nganking, a band of "rough-looking men" scramble aboard the vessel. They are driven off by the blows and the brandished pistol of the first officer. During a stop of several hours at Kiukiang, a delegation visits the Methodist Hospital managed by "Mary Stone," a famous Chinese woman surgeon trained at Ann Arbor, Michigan.

Hankow, center of the tea trade. A reception by General Li Yuen Hang, Vice President of the Chinese Republic, in his official residence. Luncheon at the homes of the missionaries assembled at the College Compound of the Protestant Episcopal Church Mission, with its fine school buildings, library, chapel, and dormitory. A visit to the large hospital and school for the blind maintained by the Wesleyan Methodist Church of England. A luncheon tendered by the Chamber of Commerce. At the close of his address, Heinz asks those present to raise one hand for China and one for America, and then to join hands as a figure of union, "which was heartily responded to."

Peking: A thirty-six-hour train ride from Hankow through parched, famine-striken country. A reception by Yüan Shih-K'ai, President of the Republic, held at the Winter Palace of the old Dowager Empress, where she had plotted to sweep

foreign influence and Christianity out of China through the
Boxer Movement. This is the first large group of Americans
ever admitted to the grounds. Each person, including Master
Kinnear, sits on the throne from which the Manchu conquerors
for generations had ruled China. A banquet is given by the
Chinese-American Society, with forty separate dishes. The
members visit, by special permission, the Chinese House
and Senate, the Summer Palace outside the city walls, the
Boxer Indemnity College built with part of the $11 million in-
demnity paid to the United States, and the British Legation,
where in 1900 the foreign community had been besieged for
two months until relieved by an army assembled from the
troops of a half-dozen nations. (Each foreign legation in Peking now holds a strong force of its own soldiers armed and
equipped to withstand another siege.) As a crowning event,
the commission visits the Temple and Altar of Heaven, China's
most sacred spot. A Sunday School Field Day is held there,
the first of its kind attempted in Peking, and the first time a
body of Chinese and Americans have joined in worship at the
sacred Altar.

Tientsin: On the way to a dinner held at the Provincial
Club, the liveried driver of a carriage holding Heinz and Kinnear snaps his whip at a coolie and is arrested. A crowd
gathers, becomes excited, and begins to utter threats. Heinz
feels something has to be done, though he is not sure what it
should be. He stands up in the carriage, waves his arms, and
shouts, "Hurrah for the United States of America!" The
crowd laughs. A lady missionary coming up at that moment
explains who the visitors are, and the people disperse. Heinz
leaves $200 for the YMCA in Tientsin and $100 at the hospital.
("We try to leave our stamp of approval at all centers.")

Shakaikwan: On an overnight stay near the Great Wall of
China, Heinz persuades Master Kinnear to gather up nine
bricks from the Wall on the promise that he will have one

for himself when he gets home. He mails four of them from Shakaikwan.

Mukden, Manchuria: In the Astor House hotel, Heinz writes, "Hardest day since leaving home. Temperature high, pulse 92. I wondered if the Lord was going to take me home, since our work is finished today. Have lost sixteen pounds since leaving home."

En route through Manchuria he writes, "A great country. Russia and China ambitious. No one but God knows." In Changchun, on the border of Russian territory, a crisis arises. Heinz has been doggedly paying freight for several months on the boxes of 57 Varieties so as to have provisions on the eight-day train ride across Siberia. The Russian baggagemaster refuses to allow them to be loaded on the train to Harbin. Heinz enters the station, followed by his son and his valet, and assails him in rapid-fire German, promising — it is not clear which — either bribes or trouble. He emerges carrying a box of spaghetti; Clarence follows with a box of baked beans and William Whatley with apple butter. The other men gather up the rest of the boxes. At that point the Russian porter, observing a trail of sawdust leaking from the box of spaghetti, refuses to allow them in his car. Heinz breaks open the boxes, distributes the bottles and cans among the twenty-nine members of Commission Four, and boards the train unmolested.

The Russian State Express, coming from Vladivostok and boarded at Harbin, has eleven cars, one for express, one a baggage car, one a diner (with a piano at one end), the others first- and second-class sleeping cars. It is not the beautifully outfitted and staffed de luxe express, for it had not been possible to reserve twenty-nine berths on that train. Master Kinnear, in fact, has to ride second class "in a compartment with four Russians and no fresh air." No one on the train speaks English, but the conductor fortunately speaks German.

The train, drawn by a wood-burning engine, averages thirty

miles an hour for eight days, stopping almost every hour for more fuel. Service in the dining car is interminably slow, but the meals, when they finally arrive, are excellent. A Russian attendant rents them some small oil stoves for use in their compartments. At almost every station the peasants flock around with butter, eggs, crackers, cheese, and wheat bread, and it is generally possible to buy sterilized milk in a station shed. They find the children selling bouquets — edelweiss, lilies of the valley, and other wildflowers — irresistible.

Though he is exhausted throughout the first week of the journey, Heinz is enchanted by the black soil of the prairie lands, by the thickness of the forests, and by the finest horses he has ever seen. "A beautiful country," he writes in the *Book of Psalms* on June 7. Then, "Delightful scenery and weather . . . A *wonderful country* . . . Wonderful soil. Emigrants at depot to Siberia. Big boots, heavy clothing, as though it were mid-winter." He sees uniformed soldiers at every station and concludes, with the other members, that Siberia is an armed camp. Near Irkutsk he sees a string of manacled convicts marching to a prison car, on their way to work communities in Siberia. The train passes the Monument of Tears on the seventh day — the marble column dividing Europe and Asia where exiles bid goodbye to their friends and family. Heinz tries to stop the train long enough for everyone to have his picture taken beside the monument, and he offers to pay the railroad the cost of the delay, but the train officials are not sympathetic to the suggestion.

The train arrives in Moscow on June 11. There are no welcoming delegations, no receptions by state officials, for no missionary of any foreign country is permitted in the country, and the 900-odd Protestant Sunday Schools in Russia are forbidden to proselytize children of members of the Orthodox Greek state church. "No meetings here," Heinz writes, "the only city since leaving San Francisco (but we are in Russia)

. . . All our party visit the art gallery, churches, etc. One church was celebrating its 300th anniversary. The simple kissed the tomb, kissed the priest's hand, had their foreheads pencilled with oil. Some tears."

At the Hotel Astoria in St. Petersburg, he gives a farewell dinner for those leaving for Zurich by way of Stockholm, Christiania (Oslo), and Copenhagen. He gives a luncheon the next day for those traveling by different routes. He goes by way of Warsaw, Berlin, Leipzig, and Nuremberg and arrives in Zurich on June 27, just short of four months after leaving the United States.

The convention lasted eight days. Commission Four made its report. A Japanese delegate delivered a speech in which he presented an invitation from the National Association in Japan for the Eighth World Sunday School Convention to meet in Tokyo in October 1916. "The Convention in Tokyo," he said, "may help the mutual understanding of the East and West, and thus promote the peaceful settlement of all difficult problems of different races and nations." Sir Francis Flint Belsey, speaking on behalf of the British delegation, moved the acceptance of the invitation. Heinz seconded the motion on behalf of the United States delegates. He was supported by Kinnear. It was passed "with unanimous voice and great enthusiasm." The convention then voted a resolution of special thanks to H. J. Heinz "for the constancy of his interest in the Association's welfare." The Americans elected him to their highest post — chairman of the Executive Committee of the American Association.

Heinz arrived back home in August 1913. He engaged a full-time "Sunday School secretary" to help him with his added duties, at an annual salary of $3000, and he added a room at Greenlawn to serve as a Sunday School office. The trip around the world had cost him $30,000.

CHAPTER 15

Adventures in Herr Professor Doktor C. von Dapper-Saalfels' Neues Kurhaus

The schoolboys sang this morning on their way to the country, where they assist the farmers to bring in the crops, which are very good this year. They are now cutting the rye and the second hay, and the oats next week. Fruit is also plentiful this year.

Henry J. Heinz, writing from
Bad Kissingen, Germany,
August 14, 1914

ONE DAY when Heinz got off the train in New York City after a stay of several weeks in California he found an affectionate and respectful letter from his son Howard. Among the reports on business and news of the family there was a plea: "Please, Father, do not change the prices of any of the products until you have discussed them with us in Pittsburgh." The plea was a portent of Henry Heinz's changing position in his company. He was still titular head of the House of Heinz. He addressed the sales and branch managers at the annual January convention, made his annual tour of inspection of the branch factories and salting stations during their harvesting seasons, and went on periodic visits with Sebastian Mueller to buy horses in Kentucky. On all important matters he was consulted, and where there were differences of opinion his decision was law. But with his new responsibilities, his range of other interests, his frequent trips abroad, and his advancing age, he had less and less to do with his company's daily transactions, and what he had to do with them was becoming intermittent and erratic. Company operations, run by competent men, were now less interesting and less of a problem to him than the operations of the World Sunday School movement. In the early years he had been doggedly persistent in detail and paperwork, spending his evenings on correspondence and accounts, but for decades he had not applied himself to office routine. His oldest associates could not remember "that he ever spent twenty consecutive minutes at detailed desk work. He could rarely be induced to listen to an elaborate financial statement; but he would spend hours in the plant with a group of workers over some seemingly trivial detail in the handling of a label." He was a man for action, not for reading and thought.

During his travels, Heinz bombarded his son Howard with commanding directives and affectionate reproaches. From San Francisco he wrote to urge a larger advertising appropriation:

> If things are not brisk, I am willing to borrow money in order to reach people who can afford to buy. My interest in the business is such as to justify my doing this rather than do without. If my methods of advertising have been a failure the world at large would have made the discovery e'er this. I now insist that we act. I urged this before I left home but cannot find a single advertisement in the magazines. Are you asleep? Read this to the advertising department.

On the subject of old age:

> You may think that at my age I am rusty. My friend John Wanamaker, when his son leaves for six months, runs both establishments as well as in his fifties. He is only seventy-seven years young this coming June. Some of you will be in my class in years some day and then you will think of these things.

Some advice on working methods:

> You must get outside away from the desk. Your health would be better, your services in the organization of the departments

would be increased, you would have the opportunity to travel and see for yourself, and get the cobwebs cleared away from your eyes. O, I am tired of the desk. Find someone to take your place at the desk.

The more I think of it the more I am pained. You know you enjoy better health not at the desk, you accomplish more, the results are greater away from the desk, and yet you are determined to stay at the desk. I appreciate you too much — you are working too hard at the desk.

On Howard's relationship to other company executives:

Be careful not to overdo it [at board meetings]. Give your partners a chance to say something, and let the majority decide. I would like to know what the members of the board think when I am absent and you try to dominate. You know that Wanamaker makes friends among the Board. When you are fifty years of age and younger men are coming on, it would sound better.

On his motives for writing:

I know you will think I am hard on you. I am the opposite. I am easy . . . I am preaching a little this morning because I feel deeply. If I love you I must speak the truth and say the things that will help you. Unless you feel pained this letter will not have served its purpose at all . . . If I am wrong in anything I will take it back voluntarily.

In sad fact, Heinz was experiencing an inevitable ailment: he was becoming a superannuated man. Times and techniques were changing. He had always been receptive to change — indeed, he had done more than most men to produce it. Now he frequently resisted new ideas, new attitudes, new technology. His resistance was marked by his distrust of a new breed of men — the chemist — coming into the industry and into positions of increasing power. He had disliked chemists ever since two of them had come over from Heidelberg, flourishing their diplomas and degrees, giving orders, and disrupting operations. But Howard Heinz had majored in chemistry at Yale, and he and Sebastian Mueller were running the company, with Cousin Frederick Heinz in charge of the farms, his son Charles in charge of the Pittsburgh plant, and they were quietly bringing in college-bred chemists to conduct research and to apply scientific methods to the process lines.

Herbert N. Riley was one of these, brought in from the University of Pittsburgh in 1912. For protective coloration he was entered and carried on the books as an accountant. "I found myself," Riley said, "a young bacteriologist just out of college, puzzled as to how I could make myself useful in such a business. I was supposed to come in just on trial. When I first got there it was terribly exciting, so much *work* to do.

"In those days the moon was considered as having much to do with the success of food processing. Every operation was secret, and the man who possessed the secret guarded it jealously. Everything was in code and was locked in the safe.*

"I was the Unwanted Man. I was suspect — but I was doing a lot of suspecting myself. I had to get a special permission or a special order even to let me in to certain places to see what was going on.

"For instance, pickles. It seemed that only men with certain God-given knowledge could successfully salt cucumbers into pickles. They were men of some standing of whom the management stood somewhat in awe. Our pickle salter was a fellow named 'Shady' Graves, and he was one hell of an important person. He had a little hard top hat on and a cutaway coat and a professional business air about him. He wouldn't let anyone come into the place while he was at work. His great thing was to put a finger into the pickle tanks, take it out with a great sweep, shove it into his mouth, suck it and say,

* Instructions were keyed to the code word ADONICUSEM — A standing for 1, D for 2, M for zero.

'Ah — yes — two bushels of salt in *there* . . . three bushels of salt in *here.*'

"But the biggest prima donna of the lot was the Italian operatic tenor in charge of spaghetti, specially brought over from Italy. It is a very simple job, really. The point is that if spaghetti dries unevenly you get a broken strand. This colorful Italian gentleman was always yelling around the place and being the 'big boss.' I had to get a pass to see him, too. They knew that when I came around there would be trouble coming. I used to watch him. He would flicker his hands around about as if he was fingering lace cuffs. He would stick his hand out of the window to 'feel' the air, rubbing the tips of his fingers together, to determine just how to adjust his drying process.

"I got a hygrometer for $400 and that was the end of him. Of course, when I put the hygrometer in at first all the stuff began to go wrong. It was sabotage. After all, you can't blame them. It was their jobs that were going.

"The young scientists demonstrated their ability and gradually gained the confidence of the men responsible for processing. As a result, within a few years the salting of pickles was being done by high-school students who worked for us during the summer months. They used a salimeter and simply followed instructions and got results that were uniformly better than those enjoyed by the experts who had preceded them. When control instruments were installed the drying of spaghetti quickly became a very simple operation thoroughly understood by all the employees of the department.

"In 1918 we began to apply new scientific controls to quality, and actually referred to the section doing that work as the quality control department. We think we may have been the first in American industry to use that phrase, but if we were not we at least created it for ourselves out of our own experience.

"Everything is on a process sheet now [1959]. Nowadays we tell everything we know to each other. We've got such a lot to learn we'd be finished if we didn't."

Shortly after his return from Zurich in 1913, Heinz started to build a very large, $500,000 brick-and-marble social service center for children, equipped with swimming pool, gymnasium, auditorium, workshops, club rooms, and roof court on grounds next to the plant. This was the Sarah Heinz House, an outgrowth of Howard Heinz's small Covode House started more than a decade earlier. Heinz dedicated the settlement house to "Youth, Recreation, Character, Service" and built it "as an expression of approval of his son's efforts and as a memorial to his deceased wife, in whose honor it was named." (The Sarah Heinz House is still very active in 1973.)

The social service center was part of a program to stop the deterioration of properties in what had been downtown Allegheny, especially in a dwelling district near the plant. Streets that had held good working-class residences were becoming crowded with houses of prostitution, with a flight of former owners to the hills north of the city. Against the advice of real estate consultants, Heinz approached the problem by the simplest and most direct route. He set up a real estate department, the Progress Realty Company, opening two offices staffed with clerks, repairmen, and trained investigators. Several hundred houses were quietly bought up, the deeds in the name of James W. Kinnear, and transferred to the company without record at $1 each. Some of these were demolished for the Sarah Heinz House construction, but most were repaired, improved, and rented. The district revived and the venture paid a net income of between 5 and 6 percent on the amount invested. The red-light houses moved some blocks away.

The summer following his return from the Zurich meeting, Heinz made his annual trip to Bad Kissingen for two weeks of "cure," rest, and weight-gaining in Professor von Dapper-Saal-fels' Sanitorium. He traveled with his valet and with W. N. Hartshorn of Boston, a friend and colleague in the Sunday School movement.*

Kissingen, one of the loveliest watering places in Germany, with about 6000 permanent inhabitants and attractive homes, grounds, hotels, shops, public buildings, and sanitoriums, lay among the hills of the Franconian Valley in northern Bavaria, sixty-five miles east of Frankfurt am Main. The medicinal properties of its warm springs, strongly impregnated with iron and salt, had been recognized since the sixteenth century. In 1911 the state had spent two million marks for improvements at the springs, and it built a railroad direct to Frankfurt, short-ening the travel time from four and a half hours to two hours. It was a cosmopolitan community with as many as 40,000 visi-tors in the season. An Austrian band of sixty pieces played three times a day beginning at 6:30 in the morning. The cure was serious business in Bad Kissingen.

There were 170 guests at Dapper's when Heinz and Hart-shorn arrived, most of them English, French, Russian, and American. Among the Americans were well-known lawyers, educators, merchants, bankers, and August Busch, son of the St. Louis beer manufacturer, who had arrived from a villa he owned in Germany in his own automobile with his wife, two daughters, and German chauffeur. Heinz had a room with a sun parlor, and there in his spare time he kept a record of a fa-mous treatment at a famous German spa:

> At 6:30 A.M. a rubdown with brandy and salt water. At 6:40 a
> glass of hot milk to be drunk slowly. 7:00 at the Springs drink-

---

* William Newton Hartshorn (1843–1920) was president and publisher of *Pris-cilla,* for decades one of the most popular women's magazines. He had been chairman of the executive committee (1902–1911) and president (1911–1914) of the International Sunday School Association. He was a vice president of the World Sunday School Association and had preceded Heinz as chairman of its executive committee. He was a Baptist.

ing the celebrated Rákoczy water. 9:15 a glass of Max Brunnen "Spring." I constantly walk while sipping the water, keeping time with the band.

At 8:30 a few crusts of dry bread, plenty of butter and chocolate. At 9:30 take either a needle bath for circulation or electric or douche and spray, either of the three. Everyday at 10:00 I am found in the vapor room where I inhale some medicated vapors for my throat, which is a little under normal.

At 10:30, second breakfast composed of fried eggs in butter, a glass of hot milk, a cup of rich creamy soup. During the day I am expected to consume not less than one-fourth pound of butter, which is made fresh daily. I then have a little time from 11:00 to 1 P.M. A little walk, not too much, so that you will hold fast till I am expected to take a Solar Bath in the city bath house.

Dinner is served at 1:15 P.M., composed of soup, fish, meat, vegetables, chicken, sometimes a smaller bird, stewed fruit or compote, and a rich pudding to close. You feel fully satisfied and are urged to eat all they serve you. Professor Dapper calls it exercizing the stomach.

At 2:15 P.M. you retire. By the side of your bed there is placed a chafing dish or frying tin. There is an arrangement with a false bottom which contains sufficient water to generate steam heated by alcohol lamp placed in a recess at the bottom. In the pierced tin are placed two moor (mud) pads. When hot, they are rolled up in oil paper, placed in a towel, and exercized for one-half hour over the stomach, at the end of which the alcohol is exhausted — like myself. I go to sleep until 4 P.M. I then resort to the dining room once more to consume a glass of hot milk with three or four crusts of dry bread in different colors and kinds, and am expected to consume twice as much butter as bread.

At 5:00 I can do a little walking. Shopping or reading until 7:00, when I dress for dinner, as is the custom at the Dapper Sanitarium, at 7:15, consisting of three or four kinds of sliced cold meats, mashed potatoes, hot chicken, stewed fruit or compote, winding up with a light pudding, but all puddings and vegetables contain plenty of butter. I manage to eat one-third of a pound of butter per day.

Heinz had promised his valet "a new London hat" if he took off as many pounds as Heinz added. The valet, "by exercizing and abstaining from starchy foods and butter and sugar," succeeded in taking off seven pounds the first week; Heinz added only three-and-a-half pounds to his weight in ten days.

> Professor Dapper has added another story and rather a handsome roof to the main building, extended his bath houses, and placed a new laundry in his basement. Already 65 patients from South America, Africa, England, Continental Europe, and America are represented. Lord Chesterfield is one of the latest arrivals. Professor Dapper informs me he will be full up next week. He'll then have to engage rooms in other buildings near his premises for the patients. It is becoming renowned. The only institution of its kind. There are many others similar but have not the use of the splendid Ràkoczy Water.

On Monday, July 27, Heinz and Hartshorn heard disturbing rumors, mutterings, of war between Germany and Russia. The next day, Austria declared war on Serbia; Russia mobilized; and on Saturday, August 1, Germany declared war on Russia.

Sunday morning a great crowd gathered around the music stand at Bad Kissingen. The orchestra played national and patriotic airs and the people joined in the singing. The next day, Germany — having refused a British request to join a four-power conference — declared war on France and invaded Belgium. Heinz wrote to Howard:

> I can only write a postcard in German today, since letters cannot be forwarded owing to the political mixup, and I cannot correspond on business matters. I will just say that the excitement among the people of this city of six thousand inhabitants is impressive . . . I am still in hopes of a change for the better and that the most terrible may yet be averted. Of the 140 guests at Dappers there are only 70 left, Russians, Frenchmen, and other foreigners having returned to their respective homes. Today I have written the American consul requesting that he furnish me a passport, which I must have to leave Germany.

And two days later, on August 5:

I have received no letters from America since last week, as no mail is given to any foreigners. This morning England declared war on Germany and we cannot say at this writing whether we leave from Germany or England. There are still very many Americans in Germany, but since the Germans as well as the English are the friends of the Americans, we have nothing to fear. We are not permitted to write any letters, all correspondence must be on post cards and in the German language. We hope that the nations will still arrive at some peaceful arrangement and that America will do all she can to aid them to establish peace.

Banks refused to make any payment whatsoever on traveler's checks or letters of credit. Heinz twice attempted to send a cablegram to the United States by way of friends in China or Japan but was refused. A few days later the commander of the city posted a notice: If visitors took photographs of themselves to his office he would identify and endorse them so that the postmaster might hand over their mail. When they went to the government building, officials singled out all Americans and took them to the head of the long line of foreigners. At the post office they learned that of the 135 clerks there, half had been called into military service and the remaining 65 were doing double duty. In a few days banks allowed a payment of $10 on checks, raised it for a brief time to £50 or $250, and then again reduced the amount. No foreigners were permitted to drive automobiles outside the city.

On August 7, some 2000 men in the ages twenty-one to thirty-two from an area within ten miles of Kissingen were gathered in the Kurgarten to be selected for service. They were marched past the sanitorium that afternoon on the way to a train of boxcars outfitted with improvised board seats. Among them was August Busch's chauffeur. They would be paid twelve cents a day; each needy wife would receive six marks per month and each child four marks. The Red Cross gave out coffee, rolls, and chocolate at the station.

Kissingen was a center for selection of horses. Heinz watched officials at improvised tables under the park trees inspect and test the horses brought in by the farmers, placing a tag with a fixed price and the name of the former owner around the neck of those chosen. These, too, were shipped away in boxcars.

Of the sanitorium's employees, thirty went immediately into the military, including the chief clerk with a wife, two children, and nineteen years' service. A number of the chambermaids left to help their family harvest the crops. From his sun parlor window Heinz could see a broad expanse of country burdened with ripening crops of grain, apples, and other farm products. Women, old men, and schoolboys were at work in the fields and orchards, the children working without pay as a gift to their country. The weather, he said, was unusually hot, even for August.

August Busch started a subscription paper for contributions to the Red Cross, setting a goal of 10,000 marks for the Americans remaining in the sanitorium and giving 2000 marks himself. Heinz gave 1000 marks.

For two weeks the Americans in Kissingen were without mail, without foreign newspapers or telegrams, without knowledge of what was going on outside the circle of the town. There was concern that America might have lost its head and joined the war. There were rumors that Congress had chartered all the passenger-carrying ocean vessels in American ports and was equipping them with American officers and stewards and would send them, under the protection of the flag and American warships, to some neutral port in Europe to rescue American citizens. "The days come and go," Hartshorn wrote, "and we know absolutely nothing. We are thinking about the condition of our business. We are trying to be patient and wait till our government can come to our relief." He wrote of "our present imprisonment" and of "this war-cursed country." The first official news came on August 10 from the American Embassy in Berlin: ocean liners were indeed being chartered in neutral European ports to take Americans home, women and children to be taken aboard first.

Americans in Kissingen were struck by the intense enthusiasm, even the feeling of liberated joy, with which the people greeted the war. Wives standing beside their husbands at the railroad station, some with babies in their arms, implored their men, "Go out and hit them hard." Others expressed gratitude that they were permitted to suffer, work, and sacrifice for their country. Heinz talked to a young flower woman from whom he had bought flowers for several years. Her brother, she said, had already gone to the front and was a member of a brigade that had captured 1100 Cossacks. Her face was radiant with smiles as she told it. Her fiancé, she said with tears in her eyes, would leave on August 21. "We were to have been married in a few months. I wish I could go, too. I would hit them hard."

Heinz and Hartshorn were much taken with a German Jewish family staying at the sanitorium. "Mrs. Stettenheim is a most interesting and unusual character," Hartshorn wrote.

She is a great bundle of sympathetic activities. She loves to go among the soldiers and the wives and friends of the men who are going to war and watch for opportunities to minister to their need. Her sympathy also extends to the people who, like ourselves, are stranded here.

When it was known that war had been declared between Russia and Germany, there was a great activity among the Russians to return home. A large crowd had gathered about Cook's Ticket Office. In this crowd was a young woman apparently in great distress. She was beautifully gowned and had a fine face, but her eyes were wet with tears. Mrs. Stettenheim approached her and learned that she was here with her father and desired above all things else to go to Russia. She could not go, for although she had 4,000 rubles, equal to about $2,000, she could not exchange this sum of money for an amount sufficient to pay her railroad ticket for her father and herself, to get to her husband and child. Mrs. Stettenheim immediately took from her well-filled purse sufficient gold-money for the weeping, frantic woman to purchase her tickets. No receipt was given, but there is no doubt that this generous lady will receive the full amount from the Russian woman she liberally advanced to her.

Mrs. Stettenheim also extended her sympathy to the two elderly gentlemen from America; she bought some red, white, and blue baby ribbons and fashioned for each an American flag for his lapel.

On August 12 Heinz got a message through to Van der Bok & Sons in Rotterdam: please wire his son Howard that he was well and hoped to be permitted to leave for Holland with all his baggage by the twentieth. On August 14, in his fifth and last German postcard:

> I hope to be home by the time the brickwork on the new warehouse is being started, and it is to be hoped that you will use for the walls all concrete material which has been accumulated. I should also prefer to make a new contract for the different stories . . . When this postal reaches you I hope to be in Rotterdam, and I will instruct Mr. Van der Bok where to reach me with any communications that may come from you. As soon as I am in Holland I will wire you . . .

Heinz and Hartshorn left Kissingen on an undivulged date to return home by an unknown route. One of the last persons they saw was G. J. Lehmann of Kassel, who called on them at the sanitorium. He was a member for Germany of the executive committee of the World Sunday School Association and editor of the Free Church Baptist Publications in Germany. Herr Lehmann was in high spirits. He proudly told of a father in Kassel who had gone off to the front with his seven sons, all together in one company. He promised to send them a photograph of this remarkable family. He deeply regretted that he was himself several years past the age at which he might volunteer to bear arms.

On the way home Hartshorn and Heinz composed "A Call to Prayer" for troubled times:

"Our Father, Thou Prince of Peace; may thy kingdom come in all lands; may thy will be done by all nations and may peace reign in all the world; may the spirit of the Golden Rule become the standard of our relations with one another."

CHAPTER 16

The Master Merchant
in His Seventies

Good golfing, good health, good friends, and fair appetite.

Henry J. Heinz,
Diary, March 1, 1916

IN 1915, in his seventieth year, Heinz seemed to have an extraordinary restlessness, a habitual, perhaps compulsive, desire to keep moving from place to place, to be ever busy and to mingle with people. His itinerary in 1915–1917 is exhausting to contemplate. And yet he was unfailingly cheerful in his travels, undisturbed by the inevitable indignities of train rides and hotel life, pleased with and interested in whatever and whomever he met.

Sisters Mary and Hettie were his housekeepers and hostesses on those infrequent occasions when he settled down at Greenlawn for an extended stay. For some reason that he could never understand, they complained that they never knew at what time Brother Henry would come home for lunch, or whether he would come at all — and if he did come, whether he would come alone or bring twelve people with him to be fed. There were other minor crises, like the time he found several rooms of the house decorated with beautiful hardy hydrangeas. He knew that he had no hardy hydrangeas in the greenhouses or elsewhere, and on inquiring, he found that two of the new maids had gone through the grounds of the neighbors after dark and cut them. And there was the time Sister Mary went to a sanitarium for her health and there felt that she had made such a miraculous recovery that she wrote Sister Hettie to throw away all her medicines at home; from now on she was going to trust God and wanted nothing left to hinder her cure. Miss Hettie threw away every last bottle. Back home, Miss Mary said in some agitation, "I had a bottle of brandy here when I went away, but someone has taken it."

He spent pleasant hours with Howard and Betty and Irene and John Given and his four grandchildren. A houseguest recalled that when the children were naughty on their visits to Greenlawn, they were sent to bed without their suppers or without dessert. The children always bore this punishment with such grace and fortitude that their parents sometimes told them, and anyone else present, what good children they were not to rebel. The guest later learned from little Sarah Given that the maids always smuggled the children down the back stairs to the kitchen and gave them all they could eat.

He started 1915 by journeying with Clifford to San Francisco, traveling in the S. S. *Great Northern* by way of the Panama Canal, which had opened the previous August. He was a delegate for the Commonwealth of Pennsylvania to the Panama-Pacific Exposition. The assignment was doubly pleasant, for his company had an exhibit there. He recorded his movements and brief impressions in the margins of a six-by-seven-inch *New Testament* he carried:

April 2, 1915: Arrived San Francisco. Stopping at a hotel in the Exposition Grounds while studying the wonderful Exposition. Do not register [at the hotel] by permission, which saves me from reporters. Will begin to study our exhibit. 9 people to conduct it.

April 3: Doing the Expo. Walk through Expo Palaces on way to our exhibit. Mr. N. G. Woodside with me and Mr. Foster, our Expo manager.

April 10: Fine to spend evenings [with the] throng at the Midway at the Expo.

April 28: Still hard to leave this fine Expo. I bid farewell to our people, 10 at the main exhibit. Use searchlights to help make it more effective.

To Howard he wrote of his enthusiasm for the future of the West Coast:

Our opportunity in California is now. We ought to advertise and refer to the Exposition and our exhibit. You ought to appropriate at least $25,000 for Oakland and San Francisco to work in harmony with our splendid display which we are daily improving. The demonstrations are great. We are taking many orders and it is only a beginning. You can see "57" in thirty foot letters flashing out across the Bay in San Francisco. It is the only sign of its kind in San Francisco. I would like to have the firm's consent to paint for a year some bulletins calling attention to our exhibit in the Food Products Building, but if you think it not wise I will forego the privilege. It is a question of opinion and sentiment as to whether we should be among those who break the skyline.

During the next month (April 16–May 20) he attended a state Sunday School convention in Stockton, where he delivered four addresses in two days and lectured to 600 boys and girls in the high school. Called on Luther Burbank, sixty-seven, "the wizard in changing flowers, fruits, etc." Looked over the company's olive groves at Corning. Took the Union Pacific for Omaha ("Fine equipment. Barber shop, manicurist, bathroom, reading room, library, observation car, diner"). Met with the staff and salesmen of the Omaha branch. Visited Lake Geneva, Wisconsin, where his son Clarence, an invalid, was being cared for in the home of Peter and Pauline Heinz. Spent one day at Greenlawn and went on to Philadelphia to visit John Wanamaker, meeting in his office with the board of the Pennsylvania Sunday School Association. Visited his daughter Irene the next day in New York, passed some time with his grandchildren in the Horace Mann School, and called at the World's Sunday School headquarters. Spent a few days at Greenlawn and left for Chicago to attend the board meeting of the International Sunday School Association.

A main interest, whether Heinz was at home or traveling, was his private museum, called by a curator of the National Museum in Washington, "the largest and best private collection of its character in America." He had some 5000 accessions now, and he had a full-time curator, Otto Gruber, who arranged the pieces for display and prepared several catalogues. The new fireproof museum adjoining the garage cleared the billiard room and the fourth floor at Greenlawn of a congestion of pieces. George Penniman, his Sunday School secretary (he had served W. N. Hartshorn for ten years in the same capacity), gave lectures on world geography and history in the museum, speaking to groups of schoolchildren two afternoons a week and to an open audience Saturday afternoons, using lantern slides and exhibits from the collection. The pieces were classified into these categories: miniatures, antique watches, miscellaneous jewelry, walking canes, Venetian and other glass, European pottery and porcelain, silver and plated ware, terra cotta and marble, furniture, oriental and Chinese rugs, Chinese pottery, Canton and cloisonné enamels, Chinese temple paintings, needle-painting, Chinese and European textiles, ivory netsukes (a small Japanese toggle, usually decorated with inlays or carvings, used to fasten a purse or other article to a kimono sash), Chinese chopsticks, lacquer inros (small oriental compartmented cases), Japanese and cinnabar lacquers, European ivories, Chinese soapstone carvings and other hard stone and jades and crystals, Japanese ivories, European and American paintings, and European bronzes, clocks, and copper. There were, in addition, a collection of old Bibles, manuscripts of the early Methodist Church, some 250 volumes on costumes, and such curiosities of time and place as bricks from the Great Wall of China and the Appian Way. Purists would say that Heinz collected in too many fields and without proper self-discipline, but he did what he enjoyed most, and in several fields he relied on the best authorities, bought with discrimination, and ended up with collections of the first ranks — notably in his ivories, jades, and timepieces. He had been made Honorary Curator of Ivory-Carvings, Timepieces, and Textiles at Carnegie Museum and spent hours with Dr. William J. Holland, the director, arranging, labeling, and discussing the pieces he had given the museum or placed there on extended loan. Dr. Holland, a world-famous entomologist and paleontologist, who caused replicas of the *Diplodocus carnegiee* to be given to a dozen national museums, was no man to suffer bores, even wealthy bores with valuable collections. He found Heinz "always filled with a certain spirit of gaiety and mirth, which made him a most attractive companion."

Heinz's purchases were now mainly directed at filling gaps in his collections, strengthening his oriental section, and upgrading the furnishings at Greenlawn. He spent long hours going over his treasures and his plans for them with Otto Gruber, with whom he had a close, often wordless rapport. When Gruber died unexpectedly, the ivories and jade, the watches and the curios lost much of their appeal; for several months Heinz could not bring himself to look at his collections.

On a buying visit to W. & J. Sloane Company on Fifth Avenue in New York an incident occurred that caused Heinz to write a pained and revealing letter. He sent it to William Sloane Coffin, a director of the company, Howard's roommate at Yale, and best man at his wedding.

> Your note of the 10th inst. deserved an earlier reply, but in my hurry to leave for Augusta, I laid it aside with other letters, intending to answer it after my arrival here.

I note you refer in your letter to a misunderstanding. There was no misunderstanding so far as I was concerned. I was desirous of finding a fine rug and it was not a question of price so much as of quality, otherwise I should not have told you to charge whatever was right. That in itself was sufficient to show my confidence.

I called upon your Mr. Tussell and expected to leave the order with him, as I had done on former occasions, as well as with other capable men in your well organized establishment. He remarked that Mr. Coffin wanted to see me. I assumed that you desired to say a word to me as the Father of your old time friend, but instead you acted the part of the salesman. In my long years of experience, the principals of our house always delegate these duties to men who are appointed for that purpose.

The following morning while passing your house, I concluded it would be well to see your Mr. Tussell and tell him that under the circumstances, I desired to cancel the order, in the hope that I might forget the incident.

Howard is now away, and I have decided that I will not speak to him about this matter.

Heinz was reluctant to cause pain or embarrassment in such a way, especially with others present; a number of incidents indicate that unwillingness to hurt a person's feelings was one of his strongest characteristics. His letter to an English agent was typical. The agent, an art dealer, was negotiating to buy nineteen ivories for him from a private British owner. His instructions to the man read, "Feel your way with the old gentleman. Let him understand that his price is away out of reach and that you hesitate to make him an offer unless he has some lower price to make you. Should he urge you to make an offer, you may then make him an offer of £500. You must use your judgment as to whether it would not be better to say that you will come back again and let him think it over. Do not hurt the old gentleman's feelings."

The Heinz conservatory was an interest second only to the museum. He had ten greenhouses in all, one of them with a dome that had to be raised at intervals to accommodate a rare

tropical tree that would not stop growing. He had, among
other plants, trees, and flowers, nine varieties of sweet peas,
250 orchids, hothouse peaches and English grapes hanging in
five-pound purple bunches, and 65 varieties of chrysanthe-
mums, including a Wells Late Pink twelve feet in diameter
with 693 single pink blooms. Ten thousand people visited the
chrysanthemum show in the first two weeks of its three-week
fall show.

Despite such attractions at Greenlawn, the traveling continued, though now confined to the United States. He spent
three days in July 1916 at Atlantic City ("Our Pier keeps me
busy. Has been my hobby for 16 years") and several weeks
with Irene and Howard and their families at Manchester-by-
the-Sea, near Boston. There he played nine to eighteen holes
of golf daily, celebrated Irene's forty-fifth birthday with a
party, and made a side trip to Boston as the guest of his friend
Hartshorn. "My daughter-in-law," he wrote, "is kind and affectionate to me, as are my lovely grandsons." One of the
grandsons, H. J. Heinz II, remembers, at age eight, being
taken on his grandfather's knee about this time and being told
with a twinkle, "When *you* are old enough to go into the business, I expect you to do better than your father will do."

He made another trip to Atlantic City in September, this
time traveling by "auto car" with Mary and Hettie and one of
their friends. They covered only thirty-five miles the first day,
spending the night at Greensburg.

September 27, 1916: Bedford overnight. Leave at 10 o'clock for
Gettysburg. All well, fine roads.

September 28: Remain at York, Pa., and attend a moving picture
show where most people go for a little amusement, the *modern*
amusement for all classes.

September 29: Our auto party are congenial, happy and contented. Fine roads, good fresh air. Arrive Philadelphia afternoon.

In October, at a convention held at Erie, Pennsylvania, he was elected to a tenth term as president of the State Sunday School Association. On the margin of Heinz's diary, Penniman, his secretary, wrote on October 11: "Mr. Heinz on the morning of his 71st birthday was asked how he felt. Instead of giving a verbal reply, he jumped over a chair. No further explanation was necessary." The next day Heinz gave a carefully planned banquet at New York's Hotel Astor on behalf of the World Sunday School Association "to reach one hundred well-known businessmen to increase our constituency."

November 13: Newark, New Jersey, to look over new warehouse for Branch.

November 16: W. N. Hartshorn joins me on trip to Hot Springs, Va. at 5 P.M. Due at 8 A.M. tomorrow morning.

November 17: Hot Springs. Fine fall, good golfing. Stop Hotel Olmstead.

November 18: 500 at this fine hotel. Good quiet people. Golfing, horseback riding, tennis and baths.

November 20: Mr. Hartshorn and I attend a colored meeting where addresses were made and a resolution passed in memory of Mr. Booker T. Washington, the Negro educator.

November 27: Atlantic City to rest a day or two. S.S. work too strenuous for my strength at three score and ten. God knows best.

December 3: New York. Last night attended a banquet of the Japan Friendly Society. The Honor Guests were Baron Shibusawa of Japan, the Ambassador to Washington, and eight Japanese who accompanied the Baron. We had entertained the party at our Home Thanksgiving a week ago.

In February 1916, their old differences long forgotten, he journeyed to Atlanta to visit Brother John, who, now sixty-seven, had been ill for months.

February 16: Atlanta. I call on Brother John and find some better. He can answer yes or no, shake or nod his head, and extend his left hand.

February 17: Mrs. Blanchard and family are very kind to him during the past year and good nurse at night and Brother Peter's daughter-in-law during the day. A good physician and today we counseled with a great specialist.

February 18: Left Brother in good care and came to Augusta today to join my friend John Bindley and family at Hotel Hampton Terrace.

February 27: Whites from north attend the Baptist Tabernacle to hear Dr. Walker, the Southern Black Orator. We were fed. $500 offering this morning. Howard much interested in this church. New Building.

March 1: Augusta. Good golfing, good health, good friends, and fair appetite.

March 13: St. Augustine. Am golfing here. Fine course, nine holes at the Country Club.

April 27: Philadelphia. Meeting of World S.S. Assoc. executive committee. Forty present from 15 states, Canada, Africa, India, and the Philippines. A remarkable meeting. My guests at lunch. In the evening Mr. Wanamaker entertained at dinner at his beautiful country home Lyndhurst. Fifty-four at a very fine occasion. A wonderful address by John R. Mott on the work of the Y.M.C.A. in the battle countries of Europe.

May 23: This evening met and heard W. J. Bryan at the General Conference in Saratoga Springs. Mr. Bryan gave a wonderful lecture on "Suffrage for Women, Peace, and Temperance," to 4000.

In July he spent several weeks traveling about western Canada by train.

July 16: Arrived Banff in the Canadian Rockies 6 A.M. A wonderful locality, snow-capped mountains, valley and waterfalls. A fine hotel with many guests. Met here the Duke of Connaught,

Uncle of King George of England, the retiring Governor-General of Canada.

July 19: Left Banff this A.M. Arrived wonderful Lake Louise, Alberta, at noon. Spent the day resting.

July 20: Lake Louise. Met today Burton Holmes, the travelogue lecturer, and had an interesting visit with him. Walked about Lake Louise.

July 25: Vancouver, B.C. Met the officers of the British Sunday School Association. Also was a guest of the Rotary Club at lunch. In the afternoon had a ride about the city and Stanley Park. Learned that 350,000 Canadians have gone to war. In some towns ten per cent of the population. Visited the Hudson's Bay Co. Store. This company is one of the largest business houses in the world.

He attended a conference of Heinz salesmen in Seattle and sailed down the coast to Los Angeles, where "Howard and Betty met me at the ship with their automobile and took me to their home (leased) at Pasadena."

August 7: Worked practically whole day with Howard making special plans for his work upon his return.

August 8: We drove by automobile to Los Angeles to study the method of motion pictures, etc. Betty very kind and thoughtful toward me.

August 16: Spent most of the day in San Francisco, about four hours in Gump's Antique Store.

August 17: Spent the day in the fields of Alameda visiting fruit, tomato and cucumber growers.

August 18: A quiet day incognito in Oakland keeping away from reporters.

August 20: Sunday at Lake Tahoe Tavern. A beautiful and restful place 6000 feet above sea level. Charming view of a lake 23 miles long. Snow-clad mountains, beautiful bays and a magnificent forest. Saw one giant fir tree 150 feet high and another 25 ft. circumference.

August 21: Spent the day, 9:30 to 6:30, on Lake Tahoe in the "Catalina" fishing. Mr. Penniman and I caught 26 trout from 3 to 6 P.M. Considered a remarkably good catch. Will send some to friends in California who are ill, also to Mrs. Howard Heinz.

August 23: Had lunch with the Denver Advertising Club and ten ministers and spoke on the S.S. and advertising. In the afternoon had a ride to the wonderful Lookout Mountain, 7,500 feet high.

August 25: Denver. Spent the day in a visit to the pickle fields. A ride of 150 miles. A very busy day.

August 26: Saturday. Met the HJH salesmen, Denver Branch. In the evening heard Charles E. Hughes, the Republican candidate for President. 14,000 people present. A remarkable address. Met him personally in his hotel room.

Less than a month later, in Pittsburgh, he served as chairman and introduced Hughes at a rally of Republicans that filled the Music Hall of the Exposition Building. He finished his introduction in time-honored orotund fashion: "I have the esteemed honor and privilege to present to you the next President of the United States of America, Charles Evans Hughes."

October 11: Arrived York, Pa., at 2 P.M. on my birthday and at the annual convention of the Pennsylvania State S.S. Association. 72 candles at my table, 72 roses by the ladies. A presentation of a silver tray with the names of all officers and 67 county presidents engraved on it, etc. Was overcome by the appreciation of all.

October 28: New York. Col. Foster assisted me in selecting 1800 umbrellas for employees of our Pittsburgh factories, our custom and a great pleasure for over forty years. I leave for home tonight, ten hours by train to Pittsburgh.

November 4: New York. Dined with Irene, then came to Cooper Union to hear Theodore Roosevelt (now the greatest force in America and the most loved, especially by the plain people, the masses). Address 70 minutes.

November 28: Leave for Battle Creek Sanitarium, Michigan, for rest, fit for Managers' Convention next week at our Pittsburgh Works.

January 23, 1917: New York. Purchased a number of screens, etc. that came from the Imperial Palace in Peking, as printed in the American Art Association catalogue.

February 8: Miami. At Hotel Royal Palm. Join Mr. Bindley and family on fishing trip. Returned same evening with 10 foot shovel nose shark. Weight 700 pounds. Great sport for the party.

February 10: Miami. Spent a quiet day with my daughter-in-law Betty in this thriving village. A real estate boom on.

February 14: Engaged a 65-foot yacht, invited Howard and Betty on a four-day cruise. Left at noon. Anchored within 100 yards from W. Mellon's houseboat and spent the evening with them.*

February 16: All feeling very well. Did some successful fishing today, very joyable and restful.

Friday 23: My friend John Bindley and family have been urging me to be their guest at their house, "The Pines." I consented to go as soon as Howard and Betty leave for the north. Therefore I go to their home this afternoon.

March 10: Had tea with the Mellons from Pittsburgh.

March 17: Joined the Bindley Family on cruise their chartered yacht Savannah. This noon through the Everglades.

March 22: Am the guest of my friend James R. Mellon and family at his winter home in Palatka, Florida. Drove out to see the salt petre factory, 40 miles. Many acres of trees, the leaves of which are used for the purpose. The first experiment in America. Make 400 lbs. per day.

March 26: Visit the saw mill of which my daughter-in-law Betty is part owner. They cut only cypress lumber, thousand feet per

---

* William Larimer Mellon, son of James Ross Mellon, banker. J. R. Mellon was brother to Andrew W. and Richard B. Mellon.

day. Only the Rust family are the owners of the timber and mills.

Early in April, Heinz started for Pittsburgh, where he would attend the wedding of his youngest son, Clifford, thirty-three, to Sara Moliere Young of Crafton (a suburb of Pittsburgh). In the course of the northward journey he stayed several days in Washington.

April 5: Listened to the debate in Congress on the question of declaring war with Germany.

President Wilson had called the new Congress, elected in November, into special session on April 2. The Senate had passed a war resolution on that day. Heinz witnessed the debate in the House on Thursday — a debate that lasted through the evening and into the early morning hours of Good Friday, April 6, when the members voted 373 to 50 to declare war. President Wilson signed the Declaration that afternoon.

Elizabeth Granger Rust before her marriage to Howard Heinz in 1906.

H. J. Heinz with sister Henrietta and son Howard in Bad Kissingen, Germany, around 1905.

The five-story open rotunda of the Administration Building, decorated for a dedication reception, April 1908.

Meeting of the Board of Directors of the H. J. Hei
Company in the President's office, May 26, 1909. Th
was the first meeting of the Board attended by all
members. From left around the partner's desk a
Howard Heinz, W. H. Robinson, Nevin G. Woodsid
J. N. Jeffares, Clarence N. Heinz, Sebastian Muell
and H. J. Heinz.

A parlor at Greenlawn

Greenlawn around 1919, after Heinz had made many external changes. The museum for oriental art is at the left. The largest of nine greenhouses is at the rear left.

Howard Heinz with his father in the first of the Panhard-Levassors he brought from Paris, standing before Greenlawn in 1900. The car had the power of six horses, a double chain drive, and manufactured its own acetylene for the headlights.

H. J. Heinz astride his blood bay saddle horse in 1907, before the stables at Greenlawn.

Heinz made unexpected visits from time to time to the farms during the harvest season. Here, in 1908, he encourages the workers to greater efforts in gathering cucumbers.

A pleasant spring day at Greenlawn in 1910, marked by a visit from the grand-children. Nearest to Heinz are John, Jr., and Sara Given, children of his daughter Irene. Right, Elizabeth Rust Heinz holds H. J. Heinz II, present chairman of the board of the company.

H. J. Heinz with his grandchildren in 1916 before the conservatory at Green-lawn.

CHAPTER 17

As Seen Through Other Eyes

He was a good man.

Roy Fair,
H. J. Heinz's chauffeur,
March 29, 1972

WHILE THIS BIOGRAPHY was being researched and written, a number of persons who had known and worked with H. J. Heinz were interviewed. Most, of course, were of advanced age — several in their nineties — and they had known him only in the last years of his life. In addition to Lillian Weizmann and James W. Kinnear, Jr., those interviewed included employees who became company executives, a stable boy turned wagon driver, and Heinz's personal chauffeur in 1917–1918.

George Penny, born in 1882, was the son of a Heinz employee. While on summer vacation from grade school, he got $3 a week working around the stables. He became a driver for Heinz salesmen when he was sixteen years old and was given the assignment of delivering the goods donated by the company to various good and useful causes. When he was seventeen he left the company to become a plumber, with a sideline of trimming and preparing bulldogs for the pit fights held on Herr's Island.

"My father worked as an engineer at Heinz on boilers, machines, and furnaces. I would use the company swimming pool on Sundays while my father was working in the machine room, where they made the plant's electric power. My dog always swam in the pool with me.

"My father got a Waltham watch for twenty years service, 1889–1909, but two years later when all the mechanical employees got a raise and he didn't, he quit. Mr. Heinz several times told him there was always a job waiting for him at the company if he wanted it.

"All the Heinz horses were black except one white horse named Leander in the middle of a three-horse show team. Every day when this team would go out the gate, a man in the shipping department would step out and give Leander a toby — a stogy. Well, the horse became addicted to tobacco and whenever he saw that man he would go after him, pulling the wagon and the other two horses with him, wherever he was, up over the sidewalk, until he got his stogy.

"When the horses were replaced by gasoline trucks, Mr. Heinz gave Leander to the city fire department, where he was put as the middle horse in a three-horse steam pumper. Somebody explained to the firemen that Leander had to have a stogy each day."

Ralph J. Pfeiffer, born in 1892, went to work at the Heinz Company in August 1909, salary $3.50 a week. He progressed to an executive position in the planning and scheduling department and retired in 1957.

"I began as Mr. Heinz's office boy. I would carry mail and run errands for him. One time he handed me six volumes of a set called *Crowned Masterpieces of World Literature.* Oh, it was dull stuff in there. He said, 'Young man, I'm giving you these six books. As soon as you can demonstrate to Mr. McCafferty * that you know what's in these books, I'll give you the other six volumes.' Well, I never got the other six volumes and the first ones have long since disappeared.

"He was great for mottoes. He had them all around the wall in his office. He called me in there one day and he said,

* E. D. McCafferty, secretary and legal officer of the company.

'Young man, I want you to memorize these mottoes. Some day I'm going to ask you to repeat them.' He never got around to that. There are only two I remember. One was 'The fellow who doesn't do any more than he gets paid for doesn't get paid for any more than he does.' The other was:

> 'O mortal man
> Of every act beware,
> For one false step
> May bring an age of care.
> Ever thy credit keep,
> 'Tis quickly gone,
> Raised by a thousand acts,
> But lost by one.'

I always pass that one on.

"Once I asked Mr. Mueller what the Christmas presents were going to be. It was an umbrella again, but he said, 'I can't tell you what it is, but I can tell you; it will go up the chimney down, but it won't go down the chimney up.'

"Mr. Heinz had to inspect and approve all the brick before it went into any of the buildings. I remember different times the superintendent of building and the architect would bring up the samples of brick and lay them out on that big railing, about this wide, that went around the light well in the Administration Building. Mr. Heinz would come out and he'd grab a couple of bricks and hold them over the light well and clap them together. I used to think, if ever one of those bricks broke it would go down into the fish pond and fountain five stories down."

John D. Bolton, born in 1890, was a graduate of Muskingum College who in 1914 went to work in the laboratory of the Manufacturing Department. At the time of his retirement in 1955, he was in charge of the company's process engineering.
"He had a habit — he would meet somebody he knew and

he would give them something. He would return from a walk without his watch, his stickpin, cuff links, anything that he had. I was so amused, I remember my superior Mr. G. F. Mason telling me, he met him on the street and Mr. Heinz said, 'Well, hello, Glenn,' and later, 'I want to give you something.' Well, he had given everything away except a souvenir postal card he had in his pocket, so he gave that to Glenn. The spirit was there.

"He was out on one of his walks one day when a fellow down by Heinz Street stopped him and asked for money to buy a meal. He said, 'No, sir, I'll give you no money, but if you go up to that white building I'll see that they give you something to eat.' That was where we had our restaurant. So that was on his mind, and he met one of the employees he knew quite well, Oscar Smith. He says, 'Oscar, a man down here asked me for money and I told him no. And I told him to go up to the building and get a lunch. Now, you see that he gets a good lunch.' Then he looked up toward the building. 'There he is right now in front of the door, Oscar.'

"Well, the panhandler had blown, of course, as soon as he saw he wasn't getting any money. The man he pointed out was A. W. Ginn, the sales manager. Oscar and Ginn were good friends. Oscar goes up to Ginn and he says, 'Ginn, come on, you're going to get a free lunch.' He says, 'You're crazy, I just had my lunch.' 'Don't make any difference. Mr. Heinz told me to see that you got a good lunch and he's watching. Now come on up to the restaurant and don't argue.' He managed to get Ginn into the building and out of sight.

"Later, Mr. Heinz got rather erratic, but he never lost his dignity, he always retained his poise. His peculiarities always leaned toward him having his own way. Toward the last, he was so insistent on doing what he wanted to do, he would just disappear without telling anyone where he was going.

"I was down at our Princeton, Indiana, plant, and Mr. Mueller called me. Mr. Heinz had disappeared, and from all the checking they did in Pittsburgh they believed he was on his way to Princeton. I said, 'There's only one way he can get here and that's by the seven o'clock train in the morning.' Mr. Mueller said, 'You check the train. If he's on it Mr. McCafferty will be right down.'

"So I go down at seven o'clock in the morning with a Ford car. And off steps Mr. Heinz. He was bright and cheerful, freshly shaven, immaculate. I spoke to him. I didn't embarrass him at all. I said, 'I have a car, Mr. Heinz, I'll take you to the factory.' 'That's fine.' I took him out to the factory. The hotels were so poor in Princeton there was no question of going to a hotel. While he was going around the factory with the manager I called Pittsburgh and told Mueller he was there. He said, 'Drive him over to Evansville to a hotel and see that he's properly taken care of, and McCafferty will be down in the morning.'

"He would argue with a person, but he never wanted to embarrass anyone. I was out in Bowling Green, Ohio, one week. Mr. Mason was there, and George Becker, an agricultural man. Mr. Heinz came out. We saw that his rooms were O.K. at the hotel, the old Millikan Hotel. We were available to him any time he needed us. We ate together in the second-floor dining room, where they had round tables. We couldn't find him for dinner. We waited, we rapped on his door, we looked all over the hotel. Finally we decided we would go to the dining room and he would show up. There he was, sitting by himself at a table for six over in the corner. He motioned to us. He said, 'You know, boys, I'm leaving in the morning and I wanted to do a little something for the waitress and I didn't want to embarrass her by having you fellows around. So I came early.' In those days a dime tip was something. After he went out I asked the waitress, 'How much did he give you?' She said, 'Five dollars.' He wouldn't give her five dollars in front of us.

"It was on this same occasion that he was to address a Sun-

day School class on Sunday morning. Mason and I decided
that we had work to do at the factory, we were sorry but we
couldn't go. Mr. Heinz said, 'That's all right, George here will
go.' So George Becker had to go to Sunday School. Heinz
told them when he started, he said, 'Now ladies and gentlemen, when I begin to talk about Sunday School, you don't
know when I'm going to finish. I don't know myself how long
I'm going to talk.' And Becker said he talked about an hour
and a half."

*William K. Wilson, born in 1882, went with the company in
1904. He worked in the manufacturing department until his
retirement in 1945.*

"Every sales convention they had E. D. McCafferty to talk.
He was a very quaint fellow. He was a great reader, a great
student of the past ages. He'd talk about everything they
didn't know about. I tell you, he would talk about the damned-
est things that you would ever expect a man to talk about. I
often used to say, 'Boy, those fellows coming in from the sales
department, they certainly go out with their skulls cracking.'

"Mr. Heinz was a good speaker. You could always hear him.
But he wasn't to be compared to his son Howard. Howard
was a very brilliant talker.

"Mr. Heinz would come to the annual sales convention on
one occasion only, at the opening night. He never talked more
than ten or fifteen minutes. What the audience wanted to do,
they wanted to find out, how did you sell ketchup in your district? Now, Mr. Heinz, he would talk about their souls, about
odd things that had happened in the business. He would
begin, 'Now, gentlemen, you are at the beginning of the convention. Are you all comfortably placed in the hotels? Do you
like your rooms? Is everything satisfactory? Now, are you a
good neighbor in your community?'

"He would have his salesman out to his house that week.

There were a hundred salesmen out there, and I was out there. At his home. He showed us through his museum and then in a certain room he said, 'Boys, I want you each to pick out anything you want, and I'll tell you about it after you've picked it out.'

"I picked out a cane. Good Lord, there were canes there from all over the world. He said, 'Young man, you have taken the choice of my collection.' It was a cane made from a tree he had admired in the Vatican Garden when he was received by Pope Leo the Thirteenth. I still have it today."

Hugh N. Woodside, of Portage, Wisconsin, was the older son of Nevin G. Woodside, who was fifty-seven years with the Heinz Company, for several decades as general sales manager and a director. Hugh worked for the company in the Midwest until his retirement in 1959. He grew up next door to the Sebastian Mueller house in Pittsburgh's East End.

"Mr. Mueller was one of the most immaculate men I ever saw. He wore a Vandyke beard and never had one hair out of place. He was always just so. He could do almost anything. He knew the factory, he knew what he was doing.

"One year, I think it was 1914, I went over to the factory to see Mr. Mueller, and I said I'd like to have a summer job again. He said, 'OK, Hughie. Come on over with me.' We were in the office building. We went across the company street to the factory. And he said, 'Hughie, can you roll a barrel?' He meant, not on the side, but on the rim. I said, 'Yes, sir, I think so.' 'Well,' he said, 'let me see.' I hadn't rolled a barrel since the summer before, but I took a five-hundred-pound barrel and managed to roll it. He said, 'That's pretty good. Here, let me show you.' And he rolls the barrel down the street fifty feet at full speed. He was a disciplinarian. When you learned something from him you learned it.

"There was the time Heinz had to buy some vinegar from

the Fleischmann Company to fill a rush order. He made a pretty hard bargain and got it at a low price. Now, vinegar has what are called 'eels' in it, tiny organisms that wiggle. They don't hurt anything or anyone, but Heinz always took extreme care and advertised that it strained out all the eels. The salesman would hold up two bottles to the light and you could see that the Heinz vinegar was clear.

"When the vinegar arrived, Heinz called up Fleischmann and said, 'Max, this vinegar you sent me, it has eels in it.' There was a pause and then, 'Henry, at the price you're paying, what do you expect? Goldfish?' "

Roy Fair was twenty-four in 1917 when he went to work as H. J. Heinz's chauffeur. He came from employment at the Presbyterian Hospital, where he had driven the city's first motor ambulance.

"Mr. Heinz had five families living in the apartments over the garage — two gardeners, the butler, and two chauffeurs. All had their own apartments. The other chauffeur drove Miss Hettie. The gardener, named Lynch, later worked for seventeen years for Mr. Lehmann in New York. None of the wives worked in the house. I got one hundred dollars a month and the free apartment, which I learned was later rented out for one hundred twenty-five dollars a month.

"We had two daughters, five and seven, and one born there. The gardener also had small children. Mr. Heinz was a great man for children. He loved children. He would come over and nurse my youngsters — I mean, set them on his knee and talk to them. We tried to keep them off the grass but he said, 'That's what the grass is for. The Lord put it there, let them play on it.' The children around the neighborhood used to call him 'Foxy Grandpa,' after the funny-paper character with that name.

"He had seventeen people altogether. The cook, the housekeeper, and three or four maids lived in the house. The others, mainly workmen around the place and assistant gardeners, went home at night.

"There were five automobiles. First, a 1912 Pierce Arrow. It was the most awful thing to drive you ever saw. It had metal to metal brakes, if you know what that means, that got hot and would stick. No self-starter and a tough baby to crank. A twenty-five-gallon tank, gravity feed, and four miles to the gallon. It took practically half a day to change a tire. It had two bodies, one for summer and a winter body, called a Berlin body, with a rack on the top. You changed these every spring and fall. Mr. Heinz had the winter body, the top, raised six inches so he would have more window to look out, for a better view.

"Then a 1914 Cadillac coupe. A 1914 National. A 1918 Twin-Six Packard, Miss Hettie's car, the only good one. And a 1914 Buick truck, one-half ton. Mr. Heinz was not interested in any of them.

"I drove the truck once to Harrisburg to get some machinery for the plant, because of a railroad freight embargo. A two-day trip. The following morning the back end of the truck fell out when we went to use it. The parts cost seventy dollars. I did all the work on the cars — it was part of my duty. I was putting it together when he came out. I said, 'Mr. Heinz, we had a big load on that truck. I think a little heavier than the truck was supposed to haul.' 'Well,' he said, 'it did what we wanted it to do, didn't it?' 'Yes, it did.' He said, 'I've always got a little money to give away but none to throw away.' With that he gave me a ten-dollar bill.

"Time meant nothing to him. One day I had the car at the side entrance and Miss Hettie or the housekeeper said, 'Roy is waiting for you.' He said, 'That's what I'm paying him for. Let him wait.' Which was true. I wasn't kicking.

"All the time I was there he was adding on to the house.

Stone masons, plumber, carpenters. He stopped one of the carpenters one day as he was going by with his saw and started to talk to him. The carpenter kept inching away to get back to work. Mr. Heinz said, 'Young man, if I'm willing to pay you to talk to me, stand still until I'm finished.'

"He was a man who was always measuring things. We were out one day and he wanted to measure something at one of the houses. He would stop a half-dozen times, and each time I'd have to crank the Pierce Arrow again. He said to Mr. Penniman, who was with him, 'Do you have a tape measure, Mr. Penniman?' 'No, I haven't.' 'Roy, do you have a tape measure?' 'No, I haven't.' He said, 'Every man should carry a tape measure with him.' Mr. Penniman said, 'Do you have a tape measure, Mr. Heinz?' They both laughed.

"He'd get me out at noon and I'd have to buy my own lunch. So I kept buying my lunch, and a few little items that he'd send you for, and at the end of the month I'd turn in a bill. Which was no trouble, of course. One day he said, 'Roy, why don't you eat up at the office building. We have a restaurant there where you can get just as good food as you can get anywhere in the country.' 'Well,' I said, 'I didn't know about it, but I'll be glad to do it.' So I went up there and ate after that and signed my name, and that's all there was to it.

"One day a fellow was trying to peddle him some stock. He came out to the house to sell him. Mr. Heinz said, 'Well now,' he said, 'I'm a very busy man, but I'm on my way to town. I'm going down to the barber shop. If you like you can ride with me.' So the man got in and started talking stock to him. The old gentleman listened all the way downtown. When we got down to the hotel he said, 'Well, young man, very nice talking to you, but I never speculate.'

"He always had his hair trimmed at the Anderson Hotel, where the Heinz Hall is now.°

° The Heinz Hall for the Performing Arts, dedicated September 10, 1971.

"He used to like to play golf. I caddied for him. He was so slow, though. He'd stop and talk and the people in back of him would get a little put out, you know. He wasn't really much of a golfer. He seldom played a full game when I knew him, only a few holes. He loved a high hill, loved to see around. He'd look off somewhere and he'd say, 'What is that settlement over there?' If I told him I didn't know, he'd say, 'Well, now, you must try and remember those places, because it's very important.' It wasn't important at all. It was only Brushton or Hazelwood.

"He had all the energy in the world. You couldn't keep up with him. He didn't do it on me, but he did it on the chauffeur before me. The chauffeur stopped downtown to let a street car pass or something, and when he got to where he was going, Mr. Heinz wasn't there. He had hopped out and kept on going when the car was stopped. He found him later at the factory.

"I left when I had a quarrel with the housekeeper. She told me to take her somewhere, so I changed my clothes. She changed her mind and I changed my clothes back again. Then she changed her mind still another time a half-hour later, and I said, 'You go out and jump on a streetcar, it's good enough for you. I quit.' I hated to quit, but when you're young you don't think too much about it. Mr. Heinz never held it against me. He said to my wife, 'When Roy's mad, I know he's mad.' He was a good man.

"I went to work for Mrs. L. A. Brenneman and I stayed there twenty-four years and nine months."

CHAPTER 18

The Death of the Founder

They will come no more,
The old men with beautiful manners.

Ezra Pound,
I Vecchii

ON AUGUST 18, 1917, five months after the declaration of war on Germany, one week before his fortieth birthday, Howard Heinz became United States Food Administrator of Pennsylvania (at $1 a year). For the next twenty months he was at home only intermittently and was rarely in the company office. He spent most of his time in Philadelphia, where he was also a member of the War Industries Board. Compelled by his father's stern injunction and the sense that he was involved in history, he kept a diary throughout most of these months.

Henry Heinz was immensely proud of his son's success and service. He was unreservedly against Germany — partly as a result of remembered resentment against German brutality in China during the Boxer Rebellion, chiefly, he said in a number of speeches, because of the arrant militarism he had seen in Germany in his yearly visits there. He may have been at least a little impressed, though he never showed it, at the caliber of his son's new associates — Herbert Hoover, Edward T. Stotesbury, Jay Cooke, Joseph Widener, Samuel Rea, President of the Pennsylvania Railroad, and, as Howard noted in his diary, "the very biggest men in Philadelphia." Cooke, the grandson of the "Financier of the Civil War," was Howard's administrator for Philadelphia County and put him up as a wartime member at the Union League Club, Huntington Valley Golf

Club, the Racquet Club, and the Rittenhouse Club. Howard reported all such events to the family, sometimes in a circular letter, identifying each of his associates by the college he had attended.

With his travels curtailed during the war, Henry Heinz spent more time at home and at the Pittsburgh plant. He supervised conversion of a part of the grounds at Greenlawn to a War Garden, with good crops of tomatoes, potatoes, beans, and cabbage. Labor was hard to get, with steelworkers making as much as $5.25 for a ten-hour day, and coal was scarce, but he kept the museum and the conservatory open to the public every afternoon. The annual chrysanthemum exhibit was held, with more than a thousand people admitted to the greenhouses on the opening Sunday. The flowers were all given away at the end of the show. Flowers were sent regularly to the nearby Kinnears, whose son James was with an American infantry outfit in France.

Heinz spent many pleasant hours with Howard's wife Betty, who was lonely, and his two grandchildren, Jack, his namesake, nine, and Rust, four. He was close to Jack (H. J. Heinz II), who recalls today, "We used to play golf together when I was ten. I beat him once, and he was a little miffed about that." Irene made long visits to Greenlawn with her Sarah and John Given. He laid many plans for what he intended to do when the war was over and won. He would retire on October 11, 1919, on his seventy-fifth birthday. He would organize a mammoth celebration for the company's fiftieth anniversary, also in 1919. He would have a good, honest professional man write up his life story; he had already discussed it with the Reverend John F. Cowan, who was doing Y.M.C.A. work in uniform in California army camps. Dr. Cowan had been editor for fourteen years of the Sunday School periodicals issued by the Methodist Protestant Church, and he had dedicated one of his books for juveniles, *The Jo-Boat Boys*, to H. J. Heinz.

Dr. Cowan had agreed to begin writing the biography, as well
as a booklet on the fiftieth anniversary, as soon as he was discharged.

He would also build an addition to his main museum at-
tached to the garage and a gallery to hold all his oriental art in
one place — his jade, ivories, teakwood screens, black lacquer
armchairs, paintings on silk, Japanese dolls, and the rest. The
plans for the oriental gallery were ready and waiting: one
room twenty by thirty feet, like the Time Office at the factory,
with a balcony running around it inside, lighted by a glass
dome, with no windows except a single art window in front.
The glass cases would be covered by sliding wooden panels
when the room was not on exhibition.

He had come to believe that the furnishings at Greenlawn
were not of the quality and taste they should be. Changing
them would be expensive but he would do it gradually, buying
the best antiques on the market. Meanwhile he continued to
buy for his collections; in January 1918, at the American Art
Association Galleries in New York, he paid $1690 for twenty-
one oriental pieces.

In the summer of 1918, Howard Heinz made several stirring
speeches before trade groups in which he explained why the
war would last five years longer. On September 15, 1918, he
took his son Jack through the Pittsburgh factory for the first
time. In October he and Betty spent a week at Hot Springs,
Virginia — the first full week they had been together in almost
a year. He spent the first ten days of November at the Food
Office in Philadelphia, returning home on Sunday, the tenth,
the day Kaiser Wilhelm Hohenzollern fled to Holland.

He was awakened at 7:00 A.M. by ringing bells and blowing
whistles. He read the morning papers aloud to Jack and Rusty
"so that they would remember what had happened."

I started to town where I never have witnessed such a sight.
Every business house had given their people a holiday and the
crowds were so dense that it took me an hour to go from Fifth

Avenue and Grant to Liberty and over the Federal Street
Bridge, a distance of only seven blocks. Everybody was yelling,
some singing, some crying with joy. Most people were carrying
flags. They tried to march, some with a banner from their business. Many motor trucks were loaded with office girls. Paper in
bits was thrown from office windows so that the air looked like
in a snow storm.

He went to his office and found the plant shut down, the employees in a mad celebration, the company's trucks out in pa-
rades, loaded with cheering girls.

> Then went to lunch at the Duquesne Club with Mr. Wood-
> side, where I found father and Clifford, Mr. Robinson and Mr.
> Mueller. I took a ride about town with Mr. Robinson and re-
> turned home.

The following day H. J. Heinz had as his guests at the plant
Mr. and Mrs. O. A. Burroughs. Mr. Burroughs was marking
his fortieth anniversary with the company, having started on
November 12, 1878; he had the longest record of continuous
service of any employee. Howard Heinz spent that day in
Washington attending a meeting of the state food commissioners, during which he accompanied Mr. Hoover with the other
administrators to call on President Wilson ("I was not much
impressed"), contributed $8000 to the Belgium Relief Fund in
an auction of a $50 War Bond ("a very large donation in pro-
portion to my means"), and, on behalf of all the administrators,
presented an engraved silver loving cup to Mr. Hoover. He
spent Saturday, November 16, in Atlantic City with his father.

> I told him of Mr. Whitmarsh's suggestion in Washington *
> that a large company be organized under our name to make a
> complete line of groceries and have a chain of jobbers over the
> country to handle same. That sales could amount to a billion.
> He said it sounded like a dream, that he himself was too old to
> contemplate such a scheme.

* Theodore Francis Whitmarsh of New York, President of Francis H. Leggett
& Company, general merchandise, soon to become the acting food administrator.

Herbert Hoover cabled from Paris on December 22 to ask Howard to serve as Director-General of American Relief Administration for Southeast Europe and Asia Minor, with a staff of fifteen, headquarters to be in Constantinople. He accepted for an eight-month tour of duty, his fixed responsibility being "to organize the operation" of feeding some millions of hungry or starving people. He had William Watson Smith draw up his will. He thanked his father for the gift of another substantial block of company stock, the same as that given to Irene and Clifford. He traveled to Washington to absorb an eight-part message he was to deliver verbally to Hoover, went with Betty to a farewell banquet in his honor in Philadelphia given by "the Food Army," and spent a last few days with Betty in New York. On December 28 he sailed on the battered U.S. Army transport *George Washington*. He ate at a table that included Charles Schwab, Bernard Baruch, and Vance McCormick. There were seventy-seven passengers, most of them on their way to the Peace Conference, including Assistant Secretary of the Navy Franklin D. Roosevelt, cousin of Theodore. Walter Camp gave them lectures on the importance of regular exercise.

Elizabeth Heinz wrote her husband two long and affectionate letters each week.

> Your father seems [illegible] and goes East on January 11 and in another week to Miami. I am trying to be as sweet to him as I know how for I realize he is old and feeble. I think he misses you awfully . . .
>
> I took the boys to your father's for dinner. He is fine and leaves tonight for New York . . .
>
> Hettie has been sweet to me and I love her for her kindness and interest . . .

From the Hotel Bon Air, Augusta, Georgia, in February 1919:

> Can't you close your eyes and see it all? The bilious green wood work — the eminent respectability of the place — the

awful ventilation and that eternal four-piece orchestra which still holds forth every Sunday evening with Handel's Largo and The Eternal City. It's unchanged and awful . . .

HJH comes to Partridge Inn tomorrow [March 5, in Augusta] and I expect will be very happy to see the boys. I shall do everything I can to make him have a good time . . .

Your father has made Jack think he is remarkable and it will take some time and effort to get him back to normal . . .

Personally I do not care where I go as long as you are at the end of the journey. Wherever you are, and if I can get there, I will come.

She goes to a Negro church with Heinz and her sons and is ushered to a front-row seat:

Dr. Walker spoke about your father, about your work, and mentioned Jack. He also asked your father to lead in prayer. I am afraid I was amused, as it was a direct appeal for funds (cleverly done). Your father too saw it and we laughed over it together . . .

Your father came on Thursday with Bishop Hartzell, a dear old man.* They evidently had a wonderful five weeks in Florida, and both seemed so well . . . Your father looks so well and does not seem nervous at all, which makes it much easier for me. He came for dinner last night and I introduced him to everyone about him. He seemed to enjoy it . . . I have been with your father all afternoon. To Sunday School downtown, then to tea at the Denny's and now here to you. Your father and I had a long talk about you on the way home. He is tremendously fond of you and what you are doing and agrees with me that you might eventually take a diplomatic post for a few years. By that time I'll probably be dead, so you won't be embarrassed by a too-honest wife . . .

John [Given] is in Asheville with your father, from whom I

---

* Joseph Crane Hartzell (1842–1928), of Cincinnati, Methodist clergyman, was known as "The Diplomat of the Church" for his tact. A southerner, he was a leader in Negro causes and the problems of race adjustment after the Civil War. In 1896 he was consecrated missionary bishop for Africa, where over the next twenty years he made an outstanding record, completing twenty tours and traveling 1,300,000 miles throughout the continent. He was one of the most admired orators on the Chautauqua circuit.

had a lovely long letter today . . . The Bolshevik situation in Hungary is very disquieting. Are you quite safe? . . .

Sunday. This morning Jack, your father and I went to hear Dr. Walker, your colored friend. He preached a wonderful sermon and finally called on your father for the prayer, which he did beautifully. I play golf or ride with him every day . . . We go home on April 4 . . . Rust is getting big and naughty, for everyone notices him and of course is quite spoiled. Jack is doing fine in his lessons and looks splendid. He is a good boy and tries to do right — mostly. They are great fun . . .

She makes arrangements through the company to sail for Europe in May. She hopes to sail on the *Aquitania* on May 3 but cannot get her passport in time. Her maid declines to accompany her to Europe and she has difficulty finding another. She wishes her sister Helen in Saginaw would go with her and writes, "I feel so entirely alone and inadequate." She says on April 21, "Your father is in splendid health."

Long, detailed letters have been coming from Howard during these months, many of them to his father, and they are copied and circulated among the family, friends, and officers of the company. He writes from Brest, Paris, Rome, Constantinople, Trieste, Constanţa, Bucharest, Batoum, Tiflis, Eğridir, Erivan, Alexandropol, Trebizond, and Sofia. He learns that he was the first person Hoover requisitioned for the Food Mission. His fluent French and German are useful to him. His title is Director-General of South Eastern Europe Relief, Manager of the Grain Corporation, and Chief of the U.S. Food Mission. His office is in the abandoned U.S. Embassy — the largest headquarters outside of Hoover's in Paris. He gets 20,000 tons of flour a month — 800,000 sacks — for Rumania ("Pay when you are able"). In every city he enters he immediately breaks down the market price of wheat by selling American supplies to merchants for resale at fixed retail prices. This disgorges the supplies being hoarded in the warehouses by

that city's profiteers. He is honored everywhere he goes, as
though he were a minister plenipotentiary. Young King Boris
of Bulgaria addresses him as "Your Excellency." He meets
Queen Marie of Rumania and has lunch with King Ferdinand
and Crown Prince Carol. The French are grasping and cranky
about everything. He meets a Miss Jones, who was on the
round-the-world tour with father. In Tiflis he witnesses the
lowest depths of human misery. ("I saw women and children
lying in the streets, some dead, some dying, and no food anywhere.") Flour shipments to starving people are being crimi-
nally delayed by the harbor strike in New York. In Erivan he
is among the first foreigners received by the newly formed
(and short-lived) republic of Armenia; he reviews a march-past
of 500 troops and makes an open-air speech in French.

Henry Heinz returned to Pittsburgh early in April. He put
art works in place in the newly completed addition to the
main museum and inspected the work on the oriental gallery,
now nearing completion. He sat down with Mr. McCafferty
and went over his income tax return for 1918. He had an income of $433,054.51, of which $16,500 was from salary, $29,332
net from rents on 273 houses, $60,012 from interest, and
$325,795 from dividends on Heinz stock. His personal payroll
was $15,860, his charitable contributions $35,715, almost half
of which went to the three Sunday School associations of
which he was an officer. As shown on the copy of his filed return, he paid an income tax of $201,024.97, which was 51.6
percent of his net income.

He wrote or dictated six letters to his son in March, April,
and May. Those he composed in his own hand were so nearly
illegible that Penniman apparently accompanied them with a
typed version. He had no fear of the long-term outcome of the
disturbances in Europe:

I have not forgotten what an English policeman said to me twenty years ago when a speaker abused the Royal family, and finally abused the Mother Queen, Queen Victoria. I got partly on the side and partly behind the policeman, who said not to be alarmed, that the speaker was voicing the sentiments of his audience (which were 500 or more), and that they would all feel better, that some of the people would explode if they did not have an opportunity to have it out, each class in its own way. The middle class who, after all, rules the nation, will have balanced things at the proper time and the rabble element will realize that they themselves cannot accomplish anything by themselves and will go along with the people who, after all, are more sane in their plans for the future. Not that but many lives may be sacrificed through their nefarious methods of procedure . . .

I hunger for your return home. The responsibility has been rather a heavy one during my vacation in many ways, especially the important matters that come up with my younger partners, and I must decide questions that you would largely handle were you in a position to do so.

He wrote on April 30:

I started to write a few lines to you yesterday in lead pencil, but with so many things pending after my return home, I knew you would understand how trying it is for me and how it tires my wrist when I attempt to write, and I knew you would prefer to have me dictate to Miss Blair.

Sebastian and I drove up to your home [on Morewood Heights] the other evening. Sister Elizabeth is away with Hettie and Mary, visiting Harry Praeger in Baltimore. I said to Sebastian: "Betty will ask you to stay for dinner." He said he wouldn't stay, but I said, "You will when those two young ladies, Betty and her sister-in-law, Mrs. Rust, get after you." I said to Rust, "You go over and tell Uncle Sebastian you want him to stay for dinner," and then I walked away. Inside of a few minutes Rust came to me and said, "Grandfather, I told Uncle Sebastian I want him to stay for dinner."

On Sunday, May 4, he attended Sunday School in his old church, the Grace Methodist in Sharpsburg. Monday evening

he went to the Pittsburgh Press Club and listened attentively
to Ole Hanson, liberal mayor of Seattle (later the founder of
San Clemente, California), talk on the part labor intended to
take in the postwar reconstruction of the country. It was the
last time Henry Heinz appeared in public.

George Penniman wrote on Friday, May 9:

> Your father has asked me to write you, and give you a run-
> ning account of some of his recent movements, which I beg to
> say have been of the usual active, aggressive variety.
>
> Last week he spent three days in Cleveland, attending a meet-
> ing of the Inter-Church Movement of North America . . . The
> trip was a very restful one for your father. He had opportunity
> of meeting many friends; of social pleasures at meals and other-
> wise, and he slept fine the two nights he was in the city. He did
> not attempt to do any work, but simply gave himself up to a
> quiet enjoyment of the meeting and association with friends.
>
> Your father is planning to go to New York Sunday night to
> take up World's Sunday School matters for the following four
> days, which will bring him to Friday. I do not know what his
> plans will be after that, but he may of course remain in the city
> until Saturday to bid "Bon Voyage" to Mrs. Heinz, who sails, as
> you know, on the Mauretania on the 17th.
>
> Your father suggests that you get all the good pictures you
> can, so that you can visualize your trip on your return, for the
> inspiration and information of those who have followed you with
> great interest.
>
> Another matter: your father would be happy to have you, if
> you can find the time and opportunity, to look up the matter of
> purchasing some outstanding souvenirs of the Great War in the
> countries through which you passed. He especially referred to
> one or two cannon which might be found and which would have
> great historic value. He authorized me to say that you are at
> liberty to spend $1,000 for him in this direction and for this pur-
> pose, using your own judgment as to the purchase.

Henry Heinz did not go to the World's Sunday School meeting on Sunday; he became ill on that day. He had spent Friday at the office. The story goes that on that day he walked

down the company street and passed some workmen on a scaffold before an addition to one of the buildings. They were pitching bricks to each other, one brick at a time. He felt they would no doubt appreciate a demonstration on how it should be done. He climbed the ladder to the scaffolding. "Here, let me show you. We used to pitch them four at a time, like this." He could not quite manage four, but he did move them quite neatly in twos. Employees were watching him from the windows. It was hard going and he worked up a sweat despite the chill wind. He made a half-dozen more passes and came down off the scaffold.

He had a slight cold the next day, and when he woke on Sunday he felt so bad he decided not to go to church. He called Dr. Stewart N. Pool, his long-time friend and neighbor on Penn Avenue, who came over at once, ordered him to bed, and called in three specialists. A telegram was dispatched to Howard in Paris, care of Herbert Hoover. Prayers were said for his recovery in the Sunday evening services of all Methodist churches in the city. The Monday morning *Post* reported that H. J. Heinz was critically ill with double lobar pneumonia.

On Monday in Constantinople Howard Heinz called on the Grand Vizier and discussed with him what he and his officers had found in Armenia, where the Turks had massacred the population with unprecedented brutality. At 6:30 that evening he received a cablegram from Betty that his father was ill. Everything but age, she said, was in his favor; he had a wonderful heart and a fine constitution; unless his condition worsened she would sail on the seventeenth. Howard sent a Signal Corps cable that he would return home as quickly as he possibly could. He reached Bucharest on Wednesday after driving the last 170 miles from Constanţa in a Dodge truck, crossing the half-mile-wide Danube at Tutokainja on a raft made of canoes. There he found another cable from Betty; his father's condition was very serious; please advise her on whether to sail Saturday for Europe. In Trieste he hurried to the American Food Office and found a forwarded cable from Betty in Pittsburgh: his father had died on Wednesday, May 14, at 3:50 P.M.

Services were held Saturday afternoon in the East Liberty Presbyterian Church, with a "viewing" from 2:00 to 3:50. Bishop Hartzell read a prayer. James Kinnear, Dr. Holland, Frank Brown, Dr. Hartshorn, and John Wanamaker were among those present. The coffin was carried by ten employees of long continuous service, one of them Joseph Hite. Burial was in the family mausoleum in the Homewood Cemetery. Company plants and offices all over the world were shut on that day.

Sebastian Mueller said, "He was a father to us all. He reared us into manhood, and he guided us with a kind and gentle spirit." From Tokyo came a telegram signed by Okuma, Shibusawa, and Saketani, the three Japanese leaders who had welcomed Heinz in 1913. It read: "Your loss, world's loss."

Afterword

H. J. HEINZ had written his will on January 11, 1919; it was probated on May 26. He left an estate valued at $3,500,000 in personal property and $500,000 in real estate.

To his immediate family he bequeathed "some of my belongings which I value chiefly on account of their personal associations" — twenty-eight antique miniatures to his daughter Irene, his personal jewelry to Howard and Clifford, his collection of 103 meerschaum, Indian, and oriental pipes to John Given, his swords and guns to John Given, Jr., his antique fans to Sarah Given, a collection of autographed letters of the five queens of England to Elizabeth Heinz, "my watch, also the chain and locket . . . which I have carried since 1892" to H. J. Heinz II.

To his son Clarence, an invalid, he left $25,000 a year in trust during his lifetime. To Sister Henrietta he left the income from $100,000 in par value capital stock of the H. J. Heinz Company in "high appreciation of my said sister, who has graced my home for so many years and . . . in recognition of her fine Christian character and her genial companionship in travel both at home and abroad." He left bequests to Sister Mary ($5000 a year for life), Brother John and his four children, Brother Peter and Pauline, various nieces and nephews, the daughter of his old friend Dr. E. M. Wood, the widow of the curator of his art collections, and his servants according to their length of service.

He gave a collection of 100 watches, 100 ivories, and 35 Heidelberg canes, already on permanent loan, to the Carnegie Museum. He left $250,000 to the University of Pittsburgh in memory of his mother, $55,000 to three Pittsburgh hospitals, $30,000 to five social service agencies, $10,000 to the Grace Methodist Protestant Church of Sharpsburg "in memory of the pleasant and profitable associations of myself and my family with said church and Sunday School," and $300,000 to the Allegheny County, Pennsylvania, World, and International Sunday School associations. To the city of Pittsburgh he offered the Heinz Conservatory and the acre of ground on which it stood for use by the people. The residue of his estate went in equal portions to Irene, Howard, and Clifford.

For some months events continued on at Greenlawn almost as though Henry Heinz were alive and away on a journey. The Chrysanthemum Exhibit was held in the fall. Work on the Oriental Gallery was completed, and Dr. Walter Hough, head curator of anthropology of the U.S. National Museum in Washington, undertook to arrange ninety-eight choice pieces in the new display cases. J. F. Cowan appeared in Pittsburgh to write the Founder's biography. He met with Howard Heinz, who retained him also to prepare a book on his experiences as food administrator in Pennsylvania and southeastern Europe. Dr. Cowan lived and worked for some months at Greenlawn, writing an account during that time on "my experience of being butlered and of the establishment of a millionaire." He dined each evening in a black tie dinner jacket with Miss Henrietta and her guests. Miss Heinz, he wrote "dearly loved her brother, and could never speak of him and his passing away without tears. Once she had to leave the room, on account of weeping. She felt that his taking off was premature, and that if he had taken better care of himself and conserved his energies more, and if some of his friends had not encouraged him to go into so many new things, that he might still be living. She seemed to feel that ill-advised friends encouraged him to sacrifice himself, when it meant so much to him to live."

Dr. Cowan felt that Mr. Heinz, if he were alive, would have worn him out by getting him involved in a dozen other things and "would probably want to change the writing and edit it to the last comma . . . However that may be, I miss him. I want his sunny smile and his genial friendliness; for he was one of the most sincerely friendly men I ever knew." He had a number of meetings on his projected book with Howard Heinz, who "told me enough exceedingly spicy and gripping incidents to show that he had, stored away in his memory, material, with what was in his diaries and files, to make an interesting book. His idea was to preserve it chiefly for his children and friends, issuing a small edition of, say, 200." Neither the biography of H. J. Heinz nor Howard's account of his experiences was ever published.

On November 8, 1919, the Oriental Gallery was opened and dedicated, about 300 invitations having been sent to a select list of Pittsburghers. On Thursday evening, December 18, some 200 branch managers and their head salesmen were entertained at Greenlawn, and the next evening, employees with twenty years' service, in accord with the custom established years earlier. On Saturday, in the company auditorium, a banquet organized by a committee of employees was held to celebrate the company's fiftieth anniversary, with 3000 guests present, including the governor of the Commonwealth. Since no caterer would undertake such an order, the guests were fed on 1500 chickens baked quite successfully in the company's bean bakers.

The city of Pittsburgh, having studied the offer of the conservatory as a gift, declined to accept, there being no accompanying endowment with which to maintain it. The heirs offered to add a considerable portion of ground to be known as Heinz Park. The city again declined. "I think," Dr. Cowan wrote, "the heirs are a little discouraged about disposing of the place . . . What is to become of all these collections, no one seems to know . . . Dr. Hough hoped the heirs would decide to keep it as a museum, showing how a millionaire lived." But a few years later, Greenlawn, the conservatory, and the new Oriental Gallery were razed and the area turned into thirty-three lots for houses. The garage was converted into apartments. Two large stone Chinese garden lanterns that stood before the house were removed to the Atlantic City Ocean Pier.

During the week of December 13, 1920, the American Art Association Galleries in New York held a five-day unrestricted public sale of "The Very Extensive Collection of the Late Henry J. Heinz of Pittsburgh." In all, 1077 lots were sold for $51,134. The heirs had bought a number of pieces at the appraised values before the sale; they bought more in open bidding at the auction, and gave most of these to the Carnegie Museum. The paintings, appraised at $8218, were sold at separate auction.

Howard Heinz assumed the presidency of the company. On his death in 1941, at age sixty-four, his son, H. J. Heinz II, became president; he is now chairman of the board. (His son, H. J. Heinz III, thirty-five, great-grandson of the Founder, is a member of Congress from western Pennsylvania.)

The company became a publicly owned corporation in 1946 with sale of stock listed on the New York Stock Exchange. In 1954 it changed its distribution system and began to service independent retailers, hotels, and restaurants through wholesale food distributers; the army of "travelers" disappeared and the sales conventions ended. The company limited the use of its 57 Varieties symbol in 1969, because it was making some 1250 different "varieties," had acquired companies with other brand names, and needed a broader corporate identity. The company discontinued its plant tours in January 1972, ending a custom seventy-five years old, on the ground that the automated processing lines were of limited interest to the general public.

In 1954, The House Where We Began, in which Heinz started his business eighty-five years earlier, and which he had moved down the river in 1904 to the plant site, was disassembled, taken to Henry Ford's Greenfield Village in Dearborn, Michigan, and faithfully reconstructed, with use even of some of the mortar from the old house. There it stands amid the homes or workshops of (among others), Noah Webster, Thomas Edison, and the Wright Brothers.

The house is not inappropriately placed. H. J. Heinz was a pioneer organizer of large-scale production, one of the founders of a new industry, and one of those who developed the public corporation into an effective instrument for producing goods and services. He was among the remarkable men who in scarcely more than a single generation made the United States into a great industrial power. He threw his substantial weight behind two of the most progressive ideas of his time: that factory hands deserved a clean and pleasant working environment with opportunities for self-improvement and that the federal government should pass and enforce legislation to outlaw the production, labeling, and sale of unclean, adulterated foods. In both crusades he and his company were over and over cited as the positive example of what industry could achieve.

Heinz's ideas for running a business were elemental and uncomplicated, but in their time they were bold and new, and they helped to work revolutionary changes in an activity close to the center of human interest: the growing, processing, and marketing of food. In recent years the original concepts of that industry have led to developments of extreme sophistication: analysis of soil conditions by electronic computer, mechanical harvesting of improved strains of fruits and vegetables, computer-controlled continuous processing lines, flash sterilization, aseptic filling under vacuum conditions, and that American marketing phenomenon, the massive self-service supermarket.

William James held that the great purpose of life is to leave something behind that outlasts us. Heinz has done that. His living monument is the company he founded, nurtured, and brought to major estate. It is an industrial giant now, with seventeen worldwide companies and 35,000 employees. It had sales in 1972 of $1.1 billion and it earned $42 million. Fortnum & Mason is still a customer.

The history of the past century has not been so kind to Henry Heinz's social philosophy. It is now considered naive and simplistic to believe that the possibilities for improving the moral and intellectual condition of mankind by education are unlimited, or that virtue and happiness are sure to follow an advance in material well-being, or that (in Heinz's words) "there is an increasing brotherhood and a nobler manhood among the peoples of the earth," or that teaching the Golden Rule may bring universal peace among nations. But given the opportunity, Henry Heinz might observe gently that the road of upward progress has always been painful and beset with reversals, that the world is young, and that the last word is not yet in on man's struggle against ignorance, stupidity, and evil.

Notes and Sources
Bibliography
Index

Notes and Sources

CHAPTER THREE (*Pages 27–39*)

27   Young Hettie remembered. Cowan, p. 13. Hettie told Cowan that their father "was so touched by the devotion of Mary, the eldest daughter, to the object for which they were all striving that he declared that when the debit was paid, Mary should have the first thousand dollars they saved. She invested it in some stocks that she bought very cheap, and they turned out so well and yielded her an income for the next twenty years."

CHAPTER FOUR (*Pages 40–50*)

40   For the material on early diet, agriculture, and marketing in this chapter I am chiefly indebted, among others, to Gerald Carson, Richard O. Cummings, Stevenson W. Fletcher, Earl C. May, William H. Sebrell, Jr., and James Haggerty, and Edwin C. Hampe, Jr., and Merle Wittenberg.

41   Poor physical appearance of Americans. See Cummings, p. 10. American diet was deficient because of too great a dependence on meat: the European diet was fortified by the vitamins in wine, home-brewed beer, potatoes, and cabbage. It is still a common sight in U.S. Army mess halls to see soldiers eat their meat and scrape their vegetables into the garbage pail.

43   Against the tomato. In 1820, Robert Gibbon Johnson stood on the courthouse steps of Salem, Massachusetts, and ate a raw tomato, while an assembled crowd waited expectantly to see if he would drop dead. Tomatoes were commonly found in the diet of many Americans by 1869, but the prejudice against them still persisted in some social and economic levels to the end of the century. An English publication, *The Licensed Victualler & Catering Trades Journal,* said in June 1899, "A taste for fresh tomatoes has to be acquired, and there are many people who miss the healthful properties of this vegetable through not being possessed of a liking for it."

46   The farmer and rancher could feed. He now feeds thirty-nine others.

49   Crocks, wooden tubs, and glass jars and bottles. For collectors of Heinz containers: crocks were used up to 1915. Use of the word "Heinz's" on the label was replaced by "Heinz" between 1895 and 1900. Use of "F. & J. Heinz Co." continued in catalogues to 1892, four years after the change of the firm name. Products were sold in three grades in 1892: Keystone Brand Extra Fancy, Standard Brand, and Duquesne Brand. Around 1886 the company introduced a "Howard's Brand" of tomato catsup (sic), apple butter, mincemeat, mustard, preserves, and jellies.

CHAPTER FIVE *(Pages 51–71)*

60   fn. "Speaking telephone." Lorant, p. 184.

CHAPTER SIX *(Pages 72–85)*

74   Madame Lillian Nordica. Her name appears on the printed pas-
      senger list filed with the Heinz papers.
75   Alfred Edward Newton London. *The Greatest Book in the World
      and Other Papers,* 1925, p. 218.

CHAPTER SEVEN *(Pages 86–100)*

88   Sister Mary, who never married. Cowan, p. 10, says that Mary
      Heinz adopted the children and cared for them until they were
      grown, to protect them from an incompetent stepmother.
94   Pittsburgh Exposition buildings. The original Exposition Hall was
      situated in Allegheny on the north shoreline of the Ohio River.
      This was later the site of Exposition Park, the Pittsburgh Pirate's
      baseball field, and is now the site of Three Rivers Stadium.

CHAPTER EIGHT *(Pages 101–117)*

101   Terra cotta Pompeian brick. John Brendan Kelly, Philadelphia
      building contractor, Olympic sculling champion, father of Prin-
      cess Grace of Monaco, one-time bricklayer's apprentice (1907–
      10), used to visit his friend Gerard Ryan, brick contractor, in
      Pittsburgh. On every visit they would go to the Heinz plant,
      stand there shoulder to shoulder, and admire the superlative brick-
      work in the buildings. (Source of information is Dr. James S.
      Tipping of Pittsburgh, who knew Ryan.)
103   Penn Avenue. I am indebted to Hartley G. Fleming of La Jolla,
      California, for correspondence on these families and his hand-
      drawn map of the area showing the location and ownership of the
      principal houses. Mr. Fleming lived as a boy on Meade Street, a
      block east of H. J. Heinz's Greenlawn; his father was vice presi-
      dent and cashier of the Farmers Bank. He writes: "I met Mr.
      Heinz for the first and only time about 1909. My mother and I
      were walking along Penn Avenue past his house one aay when a
      small, neat man walking in the opposite direction spoke to us
      pleasantly and introduced himself as Mr. Heinz. When we parted
      a few minutes later, he presented me with one of the small, green
      plaster pickles. Of course, I was overwhelmed, not knowing that
      he habitually carried a pocket full of them for this purpose.
          "Later my best girl lived on the other side of the Heinz resi-
      dence, so I frequently took short cuts through the Heinz property
      to visit her. My route passed between the back of the house and

the stable, but nobody ever stopped me, although there were often gardeners working in the grounds."

104   Dreiser. *Newspaper Days,* 1922, pp. 387, 388, 392.

105   Dr. E. M. Wood. The Reverend Dr. Wood, "my genial companion," accompanied Heinz on a number of trips to Europe. Their birthdays fell on the same day, though Wood was six years older. On one of the trips to Europe, they promised each other that the survivor would speak at the funeral of the other. Heinz performed that duty on May 27, 1912. Forty ministers attended the funeral.

109   The trip to Thebes. Heinz visited Thebes in 1894 and again in 1911. I have taken the liberty of quoting this single passage from the 1911 diary.

113   Saw Henry Irving and Ellen Terry in *Faust. Faust* was Henry Irving's greatest financial success, running 600 nights and earning a million dollars. It used elaborate electrical effects and colored lighting for the first time in a theater, as when the swords in the duel between Faust and Valentin flashed sparks.

CHAPTER NINE (*Pages 118–133*)

122   A baggage check. The statement has been printed a number of times that Heinz distributed brass checks. No checks are known to exist, but William W. Woodside, whose father, Nevin G. Woodside, was responsible for the Heinz exhibit, saw one and clearly remembers that they were white pasteboard. It seems obvious that brass checks would have been prohibitively expensive in the numbers distributed.

123   Arthur Baum. Baum.

130   "57 Varieties." A later date for its development is commonly given, but I have found the slogan used in Heinz advertisements as early as 1892.

130   Prague . . . Heinz ketchup bottle. The sign stayed up until November 1972, when it was dismantled for repairs and rehabilitation.

CHAPTER TEN (*Pages 134–148*)

138   Russell H. Conwell. Victoria Case and Robert Ormond Case, *We Called It Culture—The Story of Chautauqua,* 1948, p. 10.

139   Heinz Auditorium. According to Lillian Weizmann, Heinz got the idea of building an auditorium for employee use on a trip to the National Cash Register plant in Ohio, which had a small auditorium available for employees.

144   The information on Heinz's philosophy on paternalism is from *Human Life,* August 1910.

145 Harry W. Sherman. Rochester (New York) *Times,* October 30, 1899.

CHAPTER ELEVEN (*Pages 149–165*)

149 Largest producer of pickles. From "The Pickling Industry," an undated article in an unidentifiable but obviously authoritative trade magazine, filed in the Heinz Company scrapbook, 1901 or 1902.

150 Heinz's statement to the eastern financiers is from McCafferty, p. 107.

150 English parties. Letter dated November 29, 1898, in Heinz archives.

151 A $15 million limit. Letter from George Watson, retired general sales manager of Heinz-Canada, to Adolph Siegmann, January 18, 1970.

152 The story of Heinz, Hite, and the gasoline trucks is from the author's interview with Ralph J. Pfeiffer, April 3, 1972.

153 The story of the Heinz salesman astride the pickle atop the wagon is from the author's interview with George Penney, May 6, 1972.

156 Sister Hettie's complaints can be found in Cowan, pp. 19, 93.

160 "The Sociological Work Connected with the Factory." Heinz also talked on "Industrial Betterment, or, Movements for Improving the Condition of the Employed" at the Get Together Club dinner in the concert hall of Madison Square Garden, New York, on March 26, 1901.

161 Panhard-Levassor. William Penn Snyder III of Sewickley, Pennsylvania, collector of antique cars, discovered the Panhard in the early 1960s behind a sealed-up wall in the former stables at Greenlawn. H. J. Heinz II gave it to him. Mr. Snyder spent several years restoring the car, entered it in a spring meeting of the Antique Automobile Club at Hershey, Pennsylvania, and won first prize.

161 The news story on the automobile club is from an undated clipping from an unidentified Pittsburgh daily paper, 1901, in Heinz Company scrapbook.

163 Ogontz School for Young Ladies. See "A Schoolgirl's Album," *American Heritage,* December 1971.

164 Howard Heinz had decided in France to make a round-the-world tour, returning by way of Japan. He canceled his plans in Marseilles on January 1, 1907, and started directly home on receiving a cable that R. G. Evans, general sales manager, had died of pneumonia. He wrote in his diary, "I received the greatest shock I have had since I lost my mother in 1894. The personal loss is more to me than I can describe, for he was sort of a second father to me."

CHAPTER TWELVE *(Pages 166–180)*

166   Dr. Wiley's tribute to Heinz is from *A Golden Day*, p. 58.
167   The new machines. Earl Chapin May, *The Canning Clan*, 1938.
168   fn. It has been suggested. Baum.
170   For the story on the pure food battle I have drawn chiefly on Dr.
       Wiley's works, Mark Sullivan, James S. Turner, and Gerald Carson.
172   Howard Heinz gave a forthright statement. "President Roosevelt
       asked me quite frankly in a conference at the White House why
       any food manufacturer should ask for a law designed to restrict all
       food manufacturers. The opinion prevailed in government circles
       that the people were the ones to demand such a law for their own
       protection, rather than the manufacturer. I replied . . . that I
       hoped to see a law passed that would require the use of sound,
       wholesome raw materials, put up in clean factories by sanitary
       methods, under proper government regulation. For this last, I told
       the President, would inspire a confidence in commercially pre-
       pared foods, and my company would get its full share of the larger
       business; in helping the industry we should be helping ourselves."
       "The Industry of Food," 1932.
176   The story of President Roosevelt and bad whiskey is told in Mark
       Sullivan's *Our Times*. Roosevelt's statement to Wiley is the one re-
       counted to and remembered by Herbert N. Riley, Heinz Executive
       Vice President, and told to the author in 1956. Sullivan points out
       that Roosevelt, in his autobiographical account of the pure food
       battle, takes full credit for himself and does not mention Dr.
       Wiley.
176   fn. Anne Lewis Pierce. Miss Pierce, as director of the Tribune In-
       stitute conducted by the New York *Tribune,* made the statement
       in a page-long *Tribune* story of her visit to the Heinz plant in
       1922. Part of the article was reprinted in the Heinz 57 *News* for
       July 11, 1922.
180   Clarence Francis. *Historic Meeting*, p. 104.

CHAPTER THIRTEEN *(Pages 181–196)*

182   The gift to the Anti-Saloon League. One letter was written by the
       National Retail Liquor Dealers Association, March 5, 1905; an-
       other by the National Liquor League of the United States, March
       11, 1908; a third by the United States Brewers Association, July 2,
       1908. Heinz declared that the rumor originated "from an individ-
       ual connected with the Anti-Saloon League" who was "menda-
       cious, unreliable and entirely unworthy of confidence" and who
       acted "in an effort to receive for himself some political recogni-
       tion."

187 "The most remarkable study ever made . . ." The statement appeared in "What's the Matter with Pittsburgh?" in the Boston *Evening Transcript* in an undated four-column article, probably January 1909. Jacob A. Riis said that he had never known the results of an investigation to have such widespread and practical currency. (*Pittsburgh Survey*, Vol. 6, p. 493.)

188 The other Pittsburgh donors to the survey were Wallace H. Rowe, founder of Pittsburgh Steel Company, Benjamin Thaw, and Mrs. William R. Thompson.

189 "The most splendid ceremonial hall in America." James D. Van Trump, *An American Palace of Culture*, 1970.

CHAPTER FOURTEEN (*Pages 197–211*)

199 The William Merritt Chase portrait is part of the collection of H. J. Heinz II.

202 The information on the trip around the world is from Frank L. Brown, the Heinz diary, and the author's interview with James W. Kinnear, Jr.

211 The trip around the world had cost him $30,000. Los Angeles *Times*, March 8, 1915.

CHAPTER FIFTEEN (*Pages 212–225*)

213 "twenty consecutive minutes . . ." Potter, p. 77.

215 Herbert N. Riley's comments are from Potter, pp. 70–72; H. J. Heinz II's "The H. J. Heinz Company Story," and the author's interview with Riley in 1956.

217 Sarah Heinz House. John L. Elliott of the Hudson Guild in New York called it "one of the best-built and most efficiently equipped buildings for social work" he had ever seen.

219 Heinz's weight-gaining regimen is taken from a diary he had kept at Dapper's in 1911.

222 Hartshorn's comments on conditions in Germany are from "Memorandum of Events at Kissingen."

CHAPTER SIXTEEN (*Pages 226–238*)

226 The information on life at Greenlawn is from Cowan, p. 23, and the author's interview with Roy Fair, H. J. Heinz's chauffeur.

230 Dr. William J. Holland. *Annals of the Carnegie Museum,* December 15, 1919.

CHAPTER SEVENTEEN (*Pages 239–249*)

246 Heinz and Max Fleischmann. A somewhat similar story to that of Heinz and Fleischmann is told in Bennett Cerf's *Laughing Stock,*

1945, p. 213. Mr. Woodside attests to the veracity of the Heinz incident.

CHAPTER EIGHTEEN *(Pages 250–261)*

251   He would retire. Cowan, p. 20.
252   A gallery to hold all his oriental art. Cowan, p. 51.
252   The furnishings at Greenlawn. Cowan, p. 54.
261   Elizabeth Heinz attended the funeral and returned to New York to sail alone on the *Caronia* on May 29. She risked the chance that she would pass her husband in midocean, for she had received no acknowledgement of her intention to sail. The *Caronia* arrived at Liverpool at 7:30 A.M. on June 12, and Elizabeth Heinz looked down from the railing to see her husband waiting for her on the dock.

AFTERWORD (Pages 262–267)

264   The unpublished manuscript of Howard Heinz's experiences is in the Heinz archives.

Bibliography

ORIGINAL SOURCES

THIS BOOK is based on previously unexamined and unpublished material in the Heinz family and company archives. At the time the work was researched and written, the papers were stored in two "attic" rooms in the Heinz plant in Pittsburgh. (They are now to be professionally catalogued and stored.) In this company, family-owned until 1946, identities of family and firm were so closely intertwined that there could be no separation between private and business affairs; the two are found in the same repository and frequently in the same document.

The primary manuscript sources are:

1. The personal diaries of Henry J. Heinz. These comprise eight pocket-size volumes for the years 1875–1882, seven such volumes for the years 1884–1889, one volume for the years 1891–1893, and three volumes for the year 1894. Heinz kept a diary for the years 1870 or 1871 through 1874 and for the year 1883, but these volumes are missing and cannot be found.

In addition, Heinz kept a daily journal of a trip he took to Egypt and Europe in 1911. He made marginal jottings of his activities and whereabouts from August 24, 1904, to November 21, 1905; from May 19, 1912, to December 4, 1913; and from March 31, 1915, to April 23, 1917.

Heinz was careless and inconsistent in his orthography; I have corrected it in most of the diary entries quoted.

2. The personal diaries of Howard Heinz, his son, as follows: on a trip to Europe with a friend in 1895, on a trip to Bermuda in 1899, on his first months working for the company in 1900–1901, on a short visit to the Yale bicentennial in 1902, on a four-month trip to Japan with his father in 1902, on his wedding, honeymoon, and trip to Europe in 1906,

and on his experiences as food administrator in Pennsylvania and relief administrator in southeastern Europe in 1918–1919.

3. A diary kept by Elizabeth Rust Heinz on her trip to and first weeks in Europe, from May 30 to June 24, 1919.

4. A body of family letters over the years 1873–1919. These include letters from Anna Schmitt Heinz, Henry J. Heinz, Howard Heinz, Peter Heinz, Clarence Heinz, Sebastian Mueller, Elizabeth Rust Heinz, and correspondence between Howard Heinz and Herbert Hoover.

5. An unpublished book-length manuscript of Howard Heinz's experiences as food administrator in Pennsylvania and relief administrator in southeastern Europe in 1918–1919.

6. "Memorandum of Events at Kissingen," at the outbreak of war in 1914, by W. N. Hartshorn, publisher of *Priscilla* magazine. This, a thirteen-page typewritten manuscript, seemingly was not published.

7. Early handwritten recipe books compiled by Heinz and his staff, also containing other miscellaneous information of a personal and business nature.

8. A mass of other loose personal papers saved by Henry J. Heinz and his heirs, too varied to itemize, ranging from the report cards of his children in the Sharpsburg public schools, to the date, place, and cost of many of his art accessions, to the lectures given by the tour guides at the plant and the Atlantic City Ocean Pier.

9. An unpublished ninety-four-page typescript "Diary of My Life at Greenlawn, Pittsburgh," by the Reverend John F. Cowan, who worked there for a time on a biography of H. J. Heinz (not extant) and a book for Howard Heinz. This typescript is in the Pennsylvania Room of the Carnegie Library in Pittsburgh.

Heinz Company material in the archives includes:

1. Five large scrapbooks containing newspaper and magazine articles on the company and its owners through the years 1873–1919. The value of such clipping books is simply beyond reckoning in a work of this kind, since no amount of time, money, and labor combined could uncover and collect such articles, many of them from obscure and long-dead publications. Unfortunately, some of the clippings are unidentified as to source and exact date.

2. A very large scrapbook containing all Heinz Company print advertisements from the 1880s into the 1920s.

3. The Heinz Company employee publication, started as *Pickles* in 1897 and continued after 1903 as *The 57 News* into the 1930s. The publication is valuable both for its record of daily events and its obituaries and for its interviews with retiring employees.

In the course of carrying out another assignment in 1956, I interviewed the late Herbert N. Riley, then Heinz Executive Vice President, on the history of the company and the story of the Pure Food Law controversy. In 1972 and 1973 I interviewed twelve other persons: Messrs. John D. Bolton, Roy Fair, George Penney, Ralph J. Pfeiffer, Adolf Siegmann, William K. Wilson, William W. Woodside, and Miss Lillian Weizmann, all retired or former Heinz employees now living in Pittsburgh; Hugh N. Woodside, retired employee living in Portage, Wisconsin; James W. Kinnear of Birmingham, Alabama, son of Heinz's personal lawyer and one of those who accompanied Heinz on the round-the-world trip in 1913; Mrs. Clifford S. Heinz, widow of Heinz's youngest son; and H. J. Heinz II, grandson of the founder of the company.

PRINTED SOURCES

One life of Henry J. Heinz had been written before the present work: E. D. McCafferty's *Henry J. Heinz, A Biography*, 233 pp., privately printed in Pittsburgh in 1923. Mr. McCafferty was private secretary to Mr. Heinz and corporate secretary of the company. The work is an original and valuable contribution by one who knew the subject well, but the tone is worshipful and some of the information is palpably false, e.g., "The [1875] crash came; but his manner of meeting his creditors was such that almost all felt good-will and confidence, and those who had been his personal friends became still warmer and closer."

The Magic Number: The Story of "57" by Stephen Potter, London, 182 pages, 1959, is a history of the Heinz Company of England, but the first five of twelve chapters are given to H. J. Heinz and the American beginnings. The late Stephen Potter (author of *Gamesmanship, Lifemanship,* and *One-Upmanship*) produced a spirited and witty work, but many of the facts on the American section are inaccurate and the research is uneven. Potter visited the Heinz plant in Pittsburgh but did not find or was not admitted to the Heinz archives and therefore did not use the diaries, letters, and other papers.

Nicolas Appert. *The Art of Preserving All Kinds of Animal and Vegetable Substances for Several Years.* London, 1812.
Arthur W. Baum, "In Grandpa's Shoes — Young Mr. Heinz of Pittsburgh," *Saturday Evening Post,* June 25, 1959.
Frank L. Brown, *A Sunday School Tour of the Orient.* New York: Doubleday, Page, 1914.
Gerald H. Carson. *The Old Country Store.* New York: Oxford University Press, 1954.
——. "Who Put the Borax in Dr. Wiley's Butter?" *American Heritage,* August 1956.

[Catalogue.] *Catalogue of Antique and Modern Art Objects Consisting of Porcelains, Bronzes, Embroideries, Ivory and Wood Carvings and Antique Curios Collected by H. J. Heinz While Traveling through the Countries from Which they Came and Now in the Billiard Room of his Residence at Greenlawn, Pittsburgh.* Pittsburgh: Privately printed, 1909.

——. *Catalogue of Art Objects and Antiquities on Free Exhibition at Heinz Ocean City Pier.* Pittsburgh: Privately printed, no date.

—— . *Catalogue of the Collection of Watches Belonging to Mr. H. J. Heinz of Pittsburgh, Deposited by Him in the Carnegie Museum,* Pittsburgh, William J. Holland, ed. Pittsburgh: Carnegie Institute, 1917. 33 plates.

—— . *Catalogue of Curios in the Private Museum of H. J. Heinz Comprising Music, Art, Literature, Natural History, Ornithology, Mineralogy, Conchology, Archeology, Ethnology, etc.* Pittsburgh: Privately printed, 1898.

—— . *The Very Extensive Collection of the Late Henry J. Heinz of Pittsburgh, Penna.* New York: American Art Galleries, 5 vols., Dec. 14, 15, 16, 17, 18, 1920.

John F. Cowan. "Diary of My Life at Greenlawn." See page 280.

Richard Osborn Cummings. *The American and His Food: A History of Food Habits in the United States.* Chicago: University of Chicago, 1940.

Stevenson Whitcomb Fletcher. *Pennsylvania Agriculture and Country Life, 1840–1940.* Harrisburg: Pennsylvania Historical and Museum Commission, 1955.

A Golden Day—A Memorial and a Celebration—Pittsburgh: Privately printed, 1924.

"The Good Steward," *Forbes* magazine, March 1, 1971.

Edwin C. Hampe, Jr., and Merle Wittenberg, *The Lifeline of America — Development of the Food Industry.* New York: McGraw-Hill, 1964.

H. J. Heinz II. "The H. J. Heinz Company Story," *Christian Science Monitor,* March 26, 27, 28, 1956.

Howard C. Heinz. "The Industry of Food," in *A Basis for Stability,* Samuel Crowther, ed. Boston: Little, Brown, 1932.

"Heinz 57 Varieties," *Modern Packaging* magazine, February 1950.

Historic Meeting to Commemorate Fortieth Anniversary of Original Food and Drug Act. New York: Commerce Clearing House, 1946.

Lawrence A. Johnson. *Over the Counter and on the Shelf — Country Storekeeping in America, 1620–1920.* New York: Bonanza Books, 1961.

Stefan Lorant. *Pittsburgh — The Story of an American City.* Garden City: Doubleday, 1964. Articles by J. Cutler Andrews and Sylvester K. Stevens.

Earl Chapin May. *The Canning Clan — A Pageant of Pioneering Americans*. New York: Macmillan, 1938.

E. D. McCafferty. *Henry J. Heinz, a Biography*. Pittsburgh: Privately printed, 1923.

Garrett Chatfield Pier. *Catalogue of Antique Chinese Jade Belonging to the Collection of the late Mr. H. J. Heinz*. Pittsburgh: Privately printed, no date, probably 1919.

The Pittsburgh Survey, Paul Underwood Kellogg, ed. New York: Survey Associates, Inc., 1908–1914, 6 vols.:

  Women and the Trades. Elizabeth Beardsley Butler.

  Work-Accidents and the Law. Crystal Eastman.

  The Steel Workers. John A. Fitch.

  Homestead: The Households of a Mill Town. Margaret F. Byington.

  The Pittsburgh District. Symposium by John R. Commons, Robert A. Woods, Florence Kelley, Charles Mulford Robinson, and others.

  Pittsburgh: The Gist of the Survey. Paul Underwood Kellogg.

Stephen Potter. *The Magic Number: The Story of "57."* London: Max Reinhardt, 1959.

Charles Robson, ed. *The Manufactories and Manufacturers of Pennsylvania of the Nineteenth Century*. Philadelphia: Galaxy, 1875.

William H. Sebrell, Jr., James J. Haggerty, and the editors of *Life*. *Food and Nutrition*. New York: Time, 1967.

Mark Sullivan. *Our Times: The United States, 1900–1925*. Vol. II: *America Finding Herself*. New York: Scribners, 1927.

Edith Elliott Swank. *The Story of Food Preservation*. Pittsburgh: H. J. Heinz Company, 1942.

James S. Turner. *The Chemical Feast*. The Ralph Nader Study Group Report on Food Protection and the Food and Drug Administration. New York: Grossman, 1970.

Harvey W. Wiley. *An Autobiography*. Indianapolis: Bobbs-Merrill, 1930.

——. *The History of a Crime Against the Food Law. The Amazing Story of the National Food and Drugs Law Intended to Protect the Health of the People Perverted to Protect Adulteration of Foods and Drugs*. Washington: Printed by Harvey W. Wiley, 1929.

—— and Anne Lewis Pierce. *1001 Tests of Foods, Beverages and Toilet Accessories, Good and Otherwise*. New York: Hearst's International Library, 1916.

Mitchell Wilson. *American Science and Invention*. New York: Simon and Schuster, 1954.

Index

Lehmann, G. J., of Kassel, Germany, 224

Leslie's Weekly, 171

Levering, R. M., Heinz employee, 65, 67, 70, 95

Lewis, Helen, 100

Lewis, Henry Heinz, 58

"Little Egypt," dancer, 121

Loeb, William, Theodore Roosevelt's secretary, 177

Lovejoy, Francis T. F., Carnegie partner, 103

Lutz, Julian, HJH's shorthand writer, 62

McCafferty, William E. D., Heinz employee, 199, 240, 243, 244, 257

McClelland, Dr. Robert W., 115

McCormick, Vance, 254

McCrum, George, 30, 36

McCrum, Robert, 25, 36

McCrum, Mrs. Robert, Sarah Heinz's mother, 30, 35, 73

McKay, Miss Edna, 162, 163

McKim, Mead & White, 120

McKinley, William, 159, 162

McMaster, Alderman Samuel, 21

McNally, George, Heinz employee, 33

Mapleson, Col. J. H., 74

Marie, Queen of Rumania, 257

Marshall, Thomas, Heinz & Noble attorney, 23

"Mary Stone," Chinese surgeon, 207

Mason, Glenn F., Heinz employee, 242, 243, 244

Mathews, John L., quoted, 181

Mellon, Andrew William, ix, 237

Mellon, James Ross, 237

Mellon, Richard Beatty, 103, 237

Mellon, William Larimer, 237

Mertz, Herr, of Wiesbaden, Germany, 85

Mesta, George, Pittsburgh manufacturer, 103

Mesta, Perle, 103

Meyers, Moses, Heinz employee, 73

Miller, William, HJH's cousin, 59

Monongahela House, 42

Moore, Alexander P., Pittsburgh publisher, 103

Morgan, Dr., 37

Morgan, J. Pierpont, 188

Mott, John R., YMCA official, 234

Moyle, Mrs. William, grocer, 14, 16, 25

Mueller, Sebastian (1860-1938), HJH partner and brother-in-law, 83, 86; marries Elizabeth Heinz, 98-99; 126, 140, 143, endows Eden Hall Farm for Heinz employees, 148; 150; becomes a partner in firm, 151; 163; in charge of company crusade for a pure food law, 172, 176, 178; 212, 215, 241, 242, 243; described, 245; 253, 258; on HJH, 261

Mueller, Mrs. Sebastian. *See* Heinz, Elizabeth

Mulvany, John, painter of "Custer's Last Rally," 124, 125, 129, 132, 139

Munholland, William, Heinz employee, 15

Murray, Rev. J. J., 53

Nesbit, Evelyn (Mrs. Harry K. Thaw), 189

Newton, Alfred Edward, quoted, 76

Noble, E. J., becomes HJH partner,